Design, History and Time

Design, History and Time

New Temporalities in a Digital Age

Edited by
Zoë Hendon and Anne Massey

BLOOMSBURY VISUAL ARTS
LONDON • NEW YORK • OXFORD • NEW DELHI • SYDNEY

BLOOMSBURY VISUAL ARTS
Bloomsbury Publishing Plc
50 Bedford Square, London, WC1B 3DP, UK
1385 Broadway, New York, NY 10018, USA
29 Earlsfort Terrace, Dublin 2, Ireland

BLOOMSBURY, BLOOMSBURY VISUAL ARTS and the Diana logo
are trademarks of Bloomsbury Publishing Plc

First published in Great Britain 2019
Paperback edition published 2023

Cover design: Avni Patel
Cover image © David De Lossy/Getty Images

A catalogue record for this book is available from the British Library.

A catalog record for this book is available from the Library of Congress.

ISBN: HB: 978-1-3500-6065-4
PB: 978-1-3503-5991-8
ePDF: 978-1-3500-6067-8
ePub: 978-1-3500-6066-1

Typeset by Newgen KnowledgeWorks Pvt. Ltd., Chennai, India

To find out more about our authors and books visit
www.bloomsbury.com and sign up for our newsletters.

Contents

Section 3 Days, Hours, Seconds

Figures

Contributors

Carlos Bártolo is a Graphic Design graduate [ESBAP, 1990] with a master's degree in Equipment Design [FAUP, 1998] and a PhD in Design [FAA-ULL, 2021]. He has taught project-related (Design) and theoretical (Art, Cinema and Design History) subjects at Lusíada University, Lisbon, Portugal, since 1995. His studies focus on the field of Portuguese Design History, researching the Design object as an ideological communication support, especially in extreme political spheres. His PhD research considered how the Portuguese dictatorship (1926-1974) tried to evoke its social and moral values through the design of 'modern' ideal home interiors by appropriating national archetypes. The chapter in this volume was written in the context of the project 'Iberian modernisms and the primitivist imaginary' (PTDC/ART-HIS/29837/2017) – co-financed by COMPETE 2020, Portugal 2020 and European Union (European Fund for Regional Development)

Dr Anne Burke is Senior Lecturer in Photography at Middlesex University. With an interest in ideas of place, mobility and belonging, her research has encompassed practices of slow travel, whether on foot, making long rowed journeys by sea in an Irish curach or cycling the Irish border. Her background in Latin American studies and as a human rights lobbyist has informed a focus on the role of visual culture in the construction and contestation of identities, including through exploring historical ethnographic archive collections and contemporary practices of protest

Dr Emily Candela is a historian of design and science, whose practice spans writing, curating and broadcasting. She produced the experimental radio show Atomic Radio, is a former curator at the Victoria & Albert Museum, and was awarded the Design History Society's 2021 Design Writing Prize. Emily is a Senior Tutor at the Royal College of Art, where she leads the Communication Design MRes Pathway.

Barry Curtis initially taught at Hornsey College of Art and then at Middlesex Polytechnic where he was a founder and editor of *BLOCK* magazine and related publications and events (1979-1986). He was Head of the School of History of Art, Design and Film, Director of Research and Professor of Visual Culture at Middlesex University, before moving to the Royal College of Art. His ongoing research practice and areas of interest include media, environment and popular cultures.

Toke Riis Ebbesen is Associate Professor in the Department for Design and Communication at the University of Southern Denmark, Kolding. His focus is broadly on design communication, digital design and digital publishing, based somewhere in the cross-section between design history, material culture studies and design semiotics. He is the former owner of a digital book consultancy and has been employed as programmer, book editor and project manager, hence his interest in the temporal intricacies of digital reading devices. Currently, Toke is studying how design is mediated on social network media and the design of social network media.

Seher Erdoğan Ford, RA (she/her) is an Assistant Professor in Architecture at Tyler School of Art and Architecture, Temple University in Philadelphia, PA. Seher received her BA in Architecture and MArch degrees at Yale University where she was selected as the co-editor of *Perspecta 43*, entitled 'Taboo.' Her current research and creative projects engage in sensory inquiry through the lenses of multisensory representation, architectural heritage and pedagogy, while experimenting with diverse media. Seher's work has most recently been published in *Modelwork: The Material Culture of Making and Knowing*, and *Journal of Architectural Education* and supported by the AIA New York Center for Architecture's Arnold W. Brunner Grant. Seher previously taught at Kadir Has University in Istanbul and practiced as a licensed architect in New York.

Michael Findlay lectures in architectural history in the Bachelor of Architectural Studies programme at Otago Polytechnic in Dunedin, New Zealand. His research focuses on New Zealand's contribution to international modernism, particularly the infl uential group of architects that established themselves in England between the wars. He has been fascinated with the modernist house High and Over for over thirty years after seeing it by chance in an unbound 1931 copy of *Architect and Building News* at the Auckland School of Architecture library. Unless you like concrete- and steel-framed windows, do not sit next to him at conference dinners.

Dr Stephen Hayward teaches MA in Industrial Design and MA in Material Futures courses at Central St Martins, University of London. His main task is to foster critical thinking via projects, workshops and dissertation support. Over the past fifteen years, his research has tracked the concerns of contemporary designers. This agenda currently includes design for trust, play, superstition and the status of the post-digital object.

Dr Zoë Hendon is Head of Collections and Associate Professor (Practice) at the Museum of Domestic Design and Architecture (MoDA), Middlesex University. Her research interests include the history of the museum's collections and the uses of these and other collections in teaching in a higher education context. She has published in *Art, Design & Communication in Higher Education*, the *Journal of Design History*, *Architecture and Culture* and *Museum and Society*.

Dr Sally-Anne Huxtable is Head Curator of the National Trust, and the Chair of the Board of Trustees of the Design History Society. She is also an Honorary Research Fellow in History of Art at the University of York, and a General Editor of the Manchester University Press series *Studies in Design and Material Culture*. Sally was previously the Principal Curator of Modern and Contemporary Design at National Museums Scotland and has worked for Dallas Museum of Art, Tate Britain and the De Morgan

Foundation, as well as being the former Editor of the *Review of the Pre-Raphaelite Society*. She has published widely on nineteenth and early twentieth century art and design, as well as contemporary receptions of Victorian and Edwardian visual and material culture. She is currently working on a Special Issue of *Journal of Design History* on Design and the Occult.

Dr J. R. Jenkins is a design historian with a focus on socialist material and architectural culture, in particular the public art and design of the former East Germany. Her book *Picturing Socialism: Public Art and Design in East Germany* (Bloomsbury, 2021) looks at how art and design in public space developed in its function and visual and material forms as it intersected with internal discourses in the GDR and the broader influences of socialist realism, modernism and postmodernism. Other published research topics include the representation of the female figure in East German public art, colour in East German architecture, and the reception of East German public art in reunified Germany. She has taught graphic design history and theory and practiced as a designer in London, Berlin, Paris, Cairo and Cornwall.

Dr David Lawrence is an architectural historian, teacher, illustrator and writer. He is currently associate professor at Kingston University London. David teaches architectural and interior design, historic building conservation, museum studies and design history and theory, and has held honorary research fellowships with the London Transport Museum and Network Rail.

Professor Anne Massey is Professorial Fellow in Design and Culture at the University for the Creative Arts (UCA). She is best known for her work on the Independent Group and post-war British culture, including *The Independent Group: Modernism and Mass Culture in Britain, 1945–59* (MUP, 1995), based on her PhD thesis. She wrote the definitive chronicle of the Institute of Contemporary Arts, *ICA 1946–68* (ICA, 2014) and a biography of its first and only female Director, *Dorothy Morland: Making ICA History* (LUP, 2020). She has published on design, including *Interior Design Since 1900* (Thames & Hudson, 4th edition 2020) and *Women in Design* for the same publisher (2022).

Dr Claire McAndrew is a social scientist working within architectures and practices of care. She focuses on new frameworks for participation — drawing upon contemporary theory, research and debate around architecture, technology, community and public engagement in the production of the built environment. Her writing and practice consider the use of co-creation methodologies to shift social practices and enact more care-full capacities. Claire is a Senior Research Fellow in Public Engagement and Co-Director of Automated Architecture (AUAR) Labs at The Bartlett School of Architecture, UCL. She is also Co-Founder / Chief Communities Officer at AUAR Ltd.

Dr John Potvin is Professor in and Chair of the Department of Art History at Concordia University, Montreal, where he teaches on the intersections of art, design and fashion. He is the author of *Material and Visual Cultures Beyond Male Bonding* (2008), *Giorgio Armani: Empire of the Senses* (2013), *Bachelors of a Different Sort: Queer Aesthetics,*

Material Culture and the Modern Interior in Britain (2014), winner of the Historians of British Art Book Prize, and most recently *Deco Dandy: Designing Masculinity in 1920s Paris* (Manchester UP, 2020). He serves on the editorial and advisory boards of several international peer-reviewed journals, was book review editor for *Interiors: Interiors, Design and Architecture* (2011–13) and is Associate Editor of the *Journal of Design History*.

Dr Niels Peter Skou is Associate Professor at the Department of Design and Communication, University of Southern Denmark (SDU). He has a background in intellectual history and a PhD on the Danish designer, architect and cultural critic Poul Henningsen and his views on design and democracy. Niels Peter is part of the Design Culture research group at SDU and co-editor of *Design Culture: Objects and Approaches* (Bloomsbury, 2016). His research interests include conceptions of time, use of history and changing concepts of nature and the common in Scandinavian Design Culture.

Foreword

Barry Curtis

At the 1976 Middlesex Design History Conference on 'Leisure', 'the future' was characterized by technological optimism. The focus was primarily a retrospective interest in popular culture, but there was an anticipation of the technologizing of work, and a future society of 'enforced leisure', combined with the emancipatory potential of education. It would have been hard to foresee the technological abundance in the possession of every conference delegate in 2016 and equally hard to account for the failure of work to dwindle away.

In spite of attempts to 'leave the past' by exorcizing the ghosts of historical association, or exploring the 'timeless' potential of classicism/primitivism, designed objects remain attached to their time of production, use and provenance and also to the futures that they engage with and predicate. Svetlana Boym[1] reminds us that the past is composed of lost futures that can exert their influence on nostalgia. Design is always 'more of its time', when conjuring with revived ideas and appearances. The activity of rehearsing the past is stimulated by the drive to disrupt a continuum in order to produce revisionary futures; design is always an exercise in rearticulating history and exploring 'probable worlds'.

Temporal revisions and paradoxes played an important part in theories of 'post modernism' that were beginning to impact British academic culture at about the same time that Design History was shaping up as a plausible course of study. More pragmatically, design historians were needed to teach studio practitioners who were sceptical regarding the capacity of traditional Art History to extend their range of reference and help them to assess the social significance and impact of their work

Aspects of what was to become Design History always played a marginal role in the disciplines of Art and Architectural History. Sociology, Psychoanalytic Theory, Connoisseurship and Histories of Technology provided some of the founding texts for the limited bibliographies of early Design History programmes of study.[2] The intellectual mood of the 1970s was a particularly rich one for exploring 'material culture'. An anthropological vein was present in the teachings of Richard Hoggart and other social critics,[3] Mass Observation[4] and Raymond Williams,[5] whose formula of 'Dominant, Residual and Emergent' was particularly applicable to understanding the coexistence of different temporalities.

The idea of 'style' already had a long history – particularly in the work of German art historians, and in the influential and much-xeroxed essay by Meyer Shapiro,[6] which considered 'style' as a 'symptomatic trait' for the 'synthesizing historian'. 'Cultural Studies',[7] which was coeval, was also interested in objects and their uses, with a particular emphasis on how they could be mobilized ideologically. The idea of style as a polemical device drew attention to the compressed timescale of dress and its particular uses of historical association and revival. 'Fashion' was relatively low on the hierarchy of design studies, but the ways in which it drew from the periphery and created meaning by recycling, juxtapositioning, fetishizing and deconstructing provided significant insights into the slower moving realms of product design and architecture.

The most conventional way of conceiving time in relation to the history of art is through 'period style' – the study of how styles matured, became mannered, hybridized and entered into 'undead' forms that could be reclaimed and reactivated. Insights were derived from contemporary Film Studies and the extraordinary project of *Screen* magazine and New Left Books in the 1970s, making the work of Russian, French, Italian and German theorists available in English. Walter Benjamin, whose work first appeared in English in the early years of formulating courses in Design History, made it possible to think of history as a fluid, opportunistic medium that can be reanimated to illuminate the present.[8]

Charles Jencks played a significant role in demonstrating how different ideological imperatives competitively ebbed and flowed over time – his famous diagram, which he went on elaborating in successive publications, first appeared in 1971.[9] Reyner Banham was influential in a number of ways – his columns for *New Society* demonstrated how close readings of everyday objects could yield complex meanings.[10] Banham saw 'history' as his academic discipline, but criticism was what he did for a living. Banham's 'timeliness' was one of the vital ingredients of the Design History syllabus. A willingness to deal with what Adrian Forty called 'Objects of Desire' projected the syllabus out of the durees of 'History' and into the realm of 'everyday life', where the focus became directed, particularly by feminist design historians, to comprehend users and their 'habitus' in a personal, political realm.[11] Before 'actor network theory', design historians routinely considered objects as imbricated in a material-semiotic interaction of use and identity.

In the 1970s, the first stirrings of postmodernism revalidated 'the presence of the past' and projected it into hybrid futures.[12] The 'parody' and 'pastiche' that were characteristic of that mood were evident in a shift into a new realm of imaginative engagement with futures, explored in the fictions of William Gibson and other 'punk-hyphenated' writers and designers who celebrated the arrival of a new cybernetic culture but situated it in hauntingly archaic forms.[13] Other challenges to Design History as a simple historical continuum were mounted in its early years by Buckminster Fuller,[14] Victor Papaneck,[15] Bernard Rudofsky[16] and the *Whole Earth Catalog*[17] who extended the scope of enquiry outside the contexts of the 'developed' world and professional designers into the realms of 'ad-hocism' and ecology.

The forty years between the conferences have seen radical changes and a massively expanded field of studies. Banham, as early as 1960, provided an important modus operandi for studying design. In his influential *Theory and Design in the Second Machine Age*, he warned that 'technological culture' is 'fast company' and that keeping up with it is an obligation for historians.[18] In a time of Virtuality, Connectivity, Creolization and the 'Internet of Everything', the essays in this book suggest new ways of understanding the complex temporal relations inherent in design, and the futures they address.

Notes

1. Svetlana Boym, *The Future of Nostalgia* (New York: Basic Books, 2002).
2. See Antony J. Coulson, *A Bibliography of Design in Britain 1851–70* (London: Design Council, 1970).
3. Richard Hoggart: *The Uses of Literacy* (London: Chatto & Windus, 1957).
4. Mass Observation, whose work from the 1930s was expertly summarized in Tom Jeffrey, Stencilled Occasional Papers, Birmingham Centre for Contemporary Cultural Studies 1978.
5. Raymond Williams, *The Long Revolution* (London: Chatto & Windus, 1961), later developed at length in Raymond Williams, 'Dominant, Residual and Emergent', in *Marxism and Literature* (Oxford: Oxford University Press, 1977), 121–7.
6. Meyer Shapiro, 'Style' in Alfred L. Kroeber (ed.), *Anthropology Today*, (Chicago: University of Chicago Press, 1953), 287–312.
7. The Centre for Contemporary Cultural Studies, founded at the University of Birmingham in 1964.
8. Walter Benjamin, *Illuminations* (London: Harper Collins, 1973).
9. Charles Jencks, *Architecture 2000: Predictions and Methods* (London: Studio Vista, 1971).
10. See Reyner Banham, who contributed to *New Society* from 1965 onwards. Also see *A Critic Writes* (essays selected by Mary Banham, Paul Barker, Sutherland Lyall, Peter Hall) (Oakland: University of California Press, 1999).
11. Adrian Forty, *Objects of Desire* (London: Thames and Hudson, 1986).
12. Paolo Portoghesi, *The Presence of the Past* (London: Academy Editions, 1980).
13. First novel 'Nuromancer' in 1982, short stories in 'OMNI' from 1981.
14. Robert W. Marks, *The Dymaxion World of Buckminster Fuller* (Garden City, NY: Anchor Books, 1973).
15. Victor Papanek, *Design for the Real World: Human Ecology and Social Change* (New York: Pantheon Books, 1971).
16. Bernard Rudofsky, *Architecture without Architects* (New York: MoMA, 1964) and *The Unfashionable Human Body* (London: Ruper Hart Davis, 1972).
17. *The Whole Earth Catalog*, 1968.
18. Reyner Banham, *Theory and Design in the First Machine Age* (London: Architectural Press, 1960).

Acknowledgements

This volume developed out of a Design History Society conference held at Middlesex University from 8 to 10 September 2016. As editors, we would like to express our thanks to all the participants in that conference: speakers and delegates, peer reviewers and panel chairs. Thanks also to the Design History Society and to Middlesex University for hosting the event.

Our primary thanks are due to all the contributors to this volume: we are aware of the huge irony of asking people to write about 'time' when they are frequently already overcommitted, and we are grateful for the enthusiasm and professionalism shown by everyone involved.

We acknowledge the Design History Society's continuing support in the form of a research grant for image reproduction costs associated with this book, and we are also deeply grateful for the help and support of our editors at Bloomsbury, Rebecca Barden and Claire Constable.

Introduction

If you believed that there's a bond between our future
And our past
Then try to hold on to what we had,
We build them strong, we built to last
'cause this is a mighty town,
It's built upon solid ground
And everything they tried so hard to kill,
We will rebuild.
>   (Excerpt from 'Big River', Jimmy Nail, 1997 © Warner/Chappell Music, Inc.,
>   BMG RIGHTS MANAGEMENT US)

This lyric from the Jimmy Nail song 'Big River' speaks of the importance of the past, of history, for moving into the future. Reminiscing about growing up by the River Tyne in the north-east of England, Jimmy Nail recalls the days, still in living memory, when the region was a major producer and exporter of coal as well as an international centre for shipbuilding. This is all gone now, and Newcastle upon Tyne's major industries include game design and call centres. This shift in the economy and in design has prompted the assembly of this volume, while not forgetting the importance of history in framing the present and the future.

Investigating the interplay between history and the contemporary, between future predictions and the present, this book presents new ways of investigating the subject of design history. The book offers different ways of thinking about changing attitudes to the temporal in the writing of histories of design. Design History as a discipline overlaps with several related fields, and contributors to this volume consider the subject from the point of view of design history, architecture, archaeology, archival studies, curating and queer studies. The edited collection asks how designers, design historians and design theorists might respond to the global challenges of time, the rhythms of work, the increasing speed of life and communication between different communities. How does the past inform the present and the future in terms of design? In the current era of rapid prototyping and slow design, this book reflects on the changing nature of time in relation to design history.

This introduction establishes time as a useful lens through which to view many of the issues of interest to the designers and design historians of today. In establishing this background, we also suggest some reasons why the question of time is particularly relevant to design historians now, in the early twenty-first century. The concept of time has recently been the subject of investigation in the fields of architecture, contemporary art, cultural theory, sociology, anthropology, philosophy and geography as well as within popular novels. From Christine Ross's *The Past is the Present: It's the Future Too: The Temporal Turn in Contemporary Art*[1] to Paula Hawkins's popular thriller *The Girl on the Train*,[2] the theme of the folding and interleaving of time has become an everyday part of contemporary culture. Yet it seems that this temporal turn has received comparatively less attention from the perspective of design history. An exception is Judy Attfield, who opened up some important debates relating to design and time in *Wild Things: The Material Culture of Everyday Life*. In her chapter 'Time: Bringing Things to Life', she worked through the importance of everyday life and the subjective in the consideration of material culture, design and its history. She argues that each of us has a highly personal and subjective relationship to material culture and to our own bodies experienced through time:

> Time implies a beginning and an end – birth and death, eternity and mortality. It is experienced through duration, frequency, longevity, change and finitude, through the relation of the body to the material world of things – as inexorably rushing towards the future or gradually evolving from the past but rarely, if ever, still.[3]

Design, History and Time: New Temporalities in a Digital Age takes forward her arguments and traces the temporal from the point of view of design. Here we provide a brief overview of some of the arguments, outlining the ways in which they are relevant to the practice of design history, as well as the ways in which design history might extend and develop the arguments for other disciplines.

As humans, we are all aware of the phenomenon that we call 'time', and we have devised numerous methods to measure and regulate the passing of time. The design of sundials, clocks, astrolabes, calendars and other temporal devices were central to the development of modern society. The accurate measurement of longitude, for example, made possible exploration by sea and hence colonial expansion by Western powers. This book is not about clocks or other time-measuring devices per se, but it is worth briefly noting their importance as designed objects. As David Landes argues, ancient Chinese and Islamic horology was considerably more sophisticated than European. However, the invention of the mechanical clock was, he suggests, 'one of a number of major advances that turned Europe from a weak, peripheral, highly vulnerable outpost of Mediterranean civilization into a hegemonic aggressor'.[4] Clocks were central to the rise of European power from the late Middle Ages because they facilitated commerce and navigation, and because accurate timekeeping was important for both scientific discovery and the mechanization of industrial processes.

But while Attfield notes the subjective or 'existential' nature of time, she also draws attention to 'historical time'. How then might we deal with 'historical time' in the digital age? The post-industrial landscape of the north-east of England is an appropriate place to begin a discussion of the historiography of time. In his seminal essay, E. P. Thompson drew attention to the ways in which the experience of time was altered by industrialization in the period between the middle ages and the nineteenth century. 'Clock time', he argued, replaced the older patterns of work and rest, as industrialization meant that more people worked for a wage rather than for themselves.[5] According to Thompson, time became a commodity to be 'spent' rather than 'passed'. Clock time became associated with thrift and with discipline, and with the related ideas of a separation between work and leisure, and between the spaces of work and the spaces of home. As Barbara Adam notes, the notion of clock time is linked to Max Weber's Protestant work ethic. While not explicitly mentioning time, Weber's ideas established an association between rationalization and a particular attitude to work:

> The asceticism associated with the Protestant ethic is one not of contemplation and absence of activity but of rationally calculable action. Such action implies an expectation of predictable and controllable regularity within a universally applicable time, an empty time which measures the same abstract units anywhere and everywhere, a time that is applicable equally to work, leisure and caring activities.[6]

The regularization and control of time was thus central to industrialization, and implied a particular relationship to capital, as will be discussed in several chapters in this volume.

E. P. Thompson's argument rested on the emergence of clock time as a replacement for older, premodern conceptions of time, based on the religious calendar and on the seasons. Benedict Anderson argued that the rise of nationalism in the nineteenth century was predicated on what he called 'homogenous empty time', developed as a secular alternative to previous religious or dynastic rule.[7] This was made possible in part by the development of print capitalism (i.e. newspapers and novels) in the nineteenth century, which enabled people to imagine themselves part of a new entity called a nation. Anderson's 'homogenous empty time' is the idea of days, weeks and years proceeding as predetermined, equally spaced and infinite units, in contrast to the simultaneity implicit within religious notions of time, in which cosmology and history were inextricably linked. 'Homogenous empty time' thus implied both progress and secularism, and was the basis on which ideas of 'nationhood' could be built and shared between millions of people who had never met.

More recent scholars have questioned the universality of Thompson's and Anderson's conceptions of time, pointing to the 'polytemporal' nature of lived experience. Historians have challenged the universality of Thompson's notion of clock time, or have drawn attention to the ways in which an overemphasis on commodified time risks the exclusion of those whose lives are not governed by the temporal constraints of hourly paid labour: women looking after young children, retired people, unemployed people and so on.[8] Partha Chatterjee notes that the idea of 'homogenous empty time' is not adequate for a discussion of postcolonial temporalities.[9] Both clock time and homogenous empty time describe a utopian ideal rather than a lived reality: we all arguably experience what Kevin Birth calls 'polyrhythmic temporalities' throughout each day, and indeed each lifetime.[10] Nevertheless, Thompson and

Anderson are a useful starting point for a discussion of time not as a 'given' but as a socially constructed idea which is thus capable of historical analysis.

Design history as a discipline is perhaps uniquely concerned with questions around the future because of its roots within design education and studio-based teaching. The subject grew out of the need to offer undergraduates studying vocational design subjects the opportunity to develop a critical understanding of their chosen field, in terms of both its history and its contemporary practice. From the beginning, design history therefore had a complex relationship with time: it was simultaneously situated in the present, looking back to the past and educating designers to design for a future. As Ton Otto argues, 'All processes of design include a vision not only of the future but also of a past that makes the desired future possible.'[11] Perhaps as a result, design historians have long been interested in the new, the modern, underpinned by a future-focused concern expressed as a belief in the possibility of social improvement through better standards of design. Yet this future focus is not unproblematic: Dennis Doordan drew attention to the need for design historians to challenge the potentially exaggerated claims of designers for the futurity of their work:

> One of the persistent arguments advanced by the cultural avant-garde in the early twentieth century involved the claim that the present was irrevocably separated from the past. 'We stand on the last promontory of the centuries!' wrote FT Marinetti, the founder of Italian Futurism, 'Why should we look back?'[12]

In Doordan's view, designers have often promised a better future based on the erasure of the past, but design historians need not accept such claims uncritically; they may apply a more nuanced approach to their considerations of utopian promises.

If a concern with time is partly therefore about the way in which designed objects embody notions of the future, it is also about how time is implicit within the design of objects that structure our lives. This book is an edited collection of papers presented at the Design History Society Annual Conference *Design and Time*, held at Middlesex University in 2016. Middlesex University (formerly Middlesex Polytechnic) also hosted the second conference of Twentieth Century Design History forty years ago in 1976, just at the time when design history was beginning. The theme of that conference was leisure and design in the twentieth Century, and it is interesting to reflect on just how the subject has changed and how much the intellectual and technical environment has altered in the intervening forty years. At the 1976 conference, Stanley Parker discussed the historical trajectory of time in relation to leisure within a sociological framework, relating the increase in leisure time over the twentieth century in the Western world and the increased pace of leisure due to the greater choice and accessibility of leisure pursuits: 'The harried leisure class is growing as more people, despite inflation, are able to buy cars, colour television sets, music centres, boats, second holiday homes, and so on.'[13] The connection between designed objects, design history and temporality was thus implicit from the very beginning of the discipline.

Parker's arguments rested on a shared cultural understanding of the nature of time since, as Adam notes, it is possible to think of leisure time only once we have fully internalized the idea of work time: '"Free time" and its correlated leisure time are *derived* from commodified work time. They are produced time, time that has been wrested from employer's time, a *not-work time* that exists only in relation to the time of markets and employment.'[14] Design historians have addressed this tension between unpaid/leisure time and paid/productive activity more recently – for example, Stephen Knott in his discussion of amateur craft.[15]

According to Jonathan Woodham, design history was initially expressed as an 'embrace of such concerns as popular culture and ephemeral styling and consumption, and the study of the anonymous and every day'.[16] To express an interest in the ephemeral is to be concerned with time and its passing; and to be interested in consumption is to acknowledge the significance of the life cycle of objects, through time, beyond their initial conception by the designer, through patterns of promotion, sale, exchange, use and reuse. The recent focus within design history on the consumption and mediation aspects of our engagement with design is an indication of this greater awareness of the temporal nature of design histories.[17] An interest in the 'everyday' suggests temporality in an additional sense: Michel de Certeau's *Practice of Everyday Life* drew attention to the repetitive and routine aspects of our temporal experience. This is of interest to design historians because it raises questions about how we might write histories that use memory and personal experience to acknowledge what Moran calls the 'validity of nonlinear historical explanation'.[18]

It is clear that time and temporality have been a useful tool of analysis for design historians in various ways, but how might we need to adapt within the digital age? The notion of 'clock time' has arguably been superseded by the 'network time', in which digital technologies offer simultaneity, speed, the always 'on' and the always instantaneous.[19] The twenty-four-hour digital clock is a permanent feature on personal electronic devices, which network with the digital displays in bus stops, railway stations and airports; as Christine Ross has outlined, 'the flow of time has now been reduced to the instant, leading to quasi-instantaneous modes of connection between users. Digital media accelerates our experience of time and concomitantly reduces our sense of duration and distance.' Digital media has revolutionized the ways in which designers design, and how design historians access and record their material. These technologies increasingly dominate our lives, blurring the distinction between 'work' time and 'leisure' time, and appearing to be both a natural and an inevitable part of our world. Yet it is useful to be reminded of the designed and intentional nature of this time, as Judy Wacjman notes:

Consider, for example, the fiber-optic cable between Chicago and New York. While previous cables between the two cities had been laid along railway lines, the new cable takes the shortest route possible, even drilling through the Allegheny Mountains. It shaves 1.3 milliseconds off the transmission time of the earlier cables. 'Speed' is thus built directly into the design: the cable was laid where it was to make transmission faster. But what compels its use by financial trading firms isn't anything directly technical; rather it is the structure of competition among such firms. Temporal demands are not inherent to technology. They are built into our devices by all-too-human schemes and desires.[20]

This tension between designers and design history has dogged the field over the intervening forty plus years. Design practitioners and theorists have developed the areas of design research and design thinking to emphasize the contemporary and future-facing nature of the design process. This approach is not without its problems,[21] as Tony Fry, Clive Dilnot and Susan C. Stewart argue: 'In the vast majority of design research the capabilities of design are understood *essentially* ahistorically.'[22] This 'end of history' in the study of design has been paralleled by the development of design history as a subset of history itself.

This has led design historians to develop in-depth research which privileges the chronicling of the past and is linked with the ongoing concerns of history more broadly. With the dawn of the digital age, it would seem that another approach is to consider both within the same remit. As Penny Sparke has argued in the 'Introduction' to *The Routledge Companion to Design Studies*:

> This book has side-stepped (or perhaps superseded) the heated debate that has gone on for over two decades about the relative strengths and weaknesses of design studies and design history. Rather than trying to defend, or attack, either of these areas the *Companion* is employing the term design studies in a new, uncomplicated, baggage-free way as, that is, an umbrella term that embraces, in a non-hierarchical way, the side range of scholarship relating to design – theoretical, practice-based and historical – that have emerged over the past four decades or so.[23]

This volume takes a similarly inclusive view and comprises work from a broad range of disciplines including that of architectural historians, curators, designers, design historians, design theorists and photography. We are now in an age of the digital future, and design history has moved from the analogue into the digital age and includes both linear and more complex, variegated models for the conceptualization of time, a fact which this book hopefully represents. With the death of the avant-garde and with the 'death of the author', we are now in a moment when past, present and future fold into one another. How does design reflect this trend? What effect does it have on design and its histories?

As will become clear to readers, chapters in this book did not divide themselves into a neat order, chronological or otherwise. Themes recur and overlap across and between chapters, sometimes in unanticipated ways, suggesting syncopation and polyrythmia rather than linear progression. The division of this book into sections is therefore somewhat arbitrary, but broadly speaking represents a telescoping of time. Beginning with *Millennia, Centuries*, the focus is as broad as possible, with a look across hundreds of thousands of years. The idea of timelessness and eternity is touched upon before we zoom into millennia as the plural of millennium. The section then considers the time span of the century that then morphs into Section 2, *Centuries, Decades, Years.* This is perhaps more obvious for the study of design, which has been most concerned with the design of the nineteenth, twentieth and twenty-first centuries. Belying its roots in the teaching of design practice, the focus has necessarily been on the history of the recent past, what is now termed contemporary history.[24] The final section is devoted to *Days, Hours, Seconds* and considers the speeding up of the minutiae of everyday life, from the tube train to the process of designing digitized reading matter. As we hurtle into the microseconds that cannot hope to measure the speed of a contemporary computer, we arrive at a moment when all matter dissolves into atoms, back into the endless eternity of the universe, back to where we started from.

Notes

1. Christine Ross, *The Past Is the Present; It's the Future Too : The Temporal Turn in Contemporary Art* (Bloomsbury Academic, 2014).
2. Hawkins, Paula, *The Girl on the Train* (Doubleday, 2015).
3. Judy Attfield, *Wild Things: The Material Culture of Everyday Life* (Oxford: Berg, 2000), 213.
4. David S. Landes, *Revolution in Time: Clocks and the Making of the Modern World* (Cambridge, MA, and London: Belknap Press of Harvard University Press, 1983), 12.
5. E. P. Thompson, 'Time, Work-Discipline and Industrial Capitalism', *Past & Present* 38 (1967): 56–97.
6. Barbara Adam, *Timewatch: The Social Analysis of Time* (Cambridge: Polity Press, 1995), 88.
7. Benedict Anderson, *Imagined Communities: Reflections on the Origin and Spread of Nationalism* (London: Verso, 2016).
8. Adam, *Timewatch: The Social Analysis of Time*, 92–4.
9. Partha Chatterjee, 'The Nation in Heterogeneous Time', *Futures* 37, no. 9, special issue (2005): 925–42, doi:10.1016/j.futures.2005.01.011.
10. Kevin K Birth, *Objects of Time : How Things Shape Temporality* (New York: Palgrave Macmillan, 2012), 118.
11. Ton Otto, 'History in and for Design,' *Journal of Design History*, 29, no. 1 (2016): 59, doi:10.1093/jdh/epv044.
12. Dennis P. Doordan, *Design History: An Anthology* (Cambridge, MA, and London: MIT Press, 1995), xiii.
13. Stanley Parker, 'Leisure in the Twentieth Century', *Leisure in the Twentieth Century* (London: Design Council Publications, 1977), 8.
14. Adam, *Timewatch: The Social Analysis of Time*, 96.
15. Stephen Knott, *Amateur Craft: History and Theory* (London: Bloomsbury Academic, 2015).

16. Jonathan M. Woodham, 'Designing Design History: From Pevsner to Postmodernism', *Working Papers in Communication Research Archive, Vol 1(1): Digitisation and Knowledge*, 2001. ISSN 1177-3707.

17. Grace Lees-Maffei, 'The Production-Consumption-Mediation Paradigm', *Journal of Design History* 22, no. 4 (2009): 351–76.

18. Joe Moran, 'History, Memory and the Everyday', *Rethinking History* 8, no. 1 (2004): 60, doi:10.1080/13642520410001649723.

19. Robert Hassan, 'Network Time and the New Knowledge Epoch', *Time & Society* 12, no. 2–3 (2003): 226–41, doi:10.1177/0961463X030122004.

20. Judy Wajcman, *Pressed for Time: The Acceleration of Life in Digital Capitalism* (Chicago and London: University of Chicago Press, 2015), 2–3.

21. Kimbell, Lucy, 'Rethinking Design Thinking: Part 1', *Design and Culture*, 3 (2011): 285–306.

22. Tony Fry, Clive Dilnot and Susan C Stewart, *Design and the Question of History* (London and New York: Bloomsbury Academic, 2015), 151.

23. Penny Sparke, 'Introduction', in Penny Sparke and Fiona Fisher (eds), *The Routledge Companion to Design Studies* (London and New York: Routledge, 2016), 2.

24. See special issue: 'At the Crossroads of Past and Present – "Contemporary" History and the Historical Discipline', *Journal of Contemporary History*, 46, no. 3 (July 2011).

Section 1
Millennia, Centuries

In this section, we consider the broad sweep of time across centuries and into millennia. The three chapters deal with time in the sense of 'thick time', events which echo down through hundreds of years and impinge on the understanding, making and history of design. As Jeremy Till has argued, 'Everyday time is thus thick time, a temporal space that critically gathers the past and also projects the future.'[1] For Till, modern architecture has endeavoured to achieve the negation of time through its whitewashing of dirt as the ultimate trace of the rootedness of building in space and the passing of time.

The argument also relates to the history of design. As Barbara Penner and Charles Rice have argued in the case of the interior history of buildings, 'Interiors exist physically as environments that can be lived in and visited; they also exist in images and objects that travel through space and across time and seed new ideas about decorations, style and inhabitation as they go.'[2] Judy Attfield devoted an entire chapter to the subject of time in *Wild Things: The Material Culture of Everyday Life* published in 2000.[3] Attfield argues for a material culture approach to the history of design, which needs to encompass the everyday and well as grand designs. She notes the compression of time and space, elucidated by postmodern scholar David Harvey, and makes a plea for a more subjective understanding of time:

> At the conceptual level individuals consciously negotiate their relationship to time through life-choice decisions. But the material world of coffee spoons, clothes, and household goods also keep individuals in touch with life as a sense of time-passing in a day-to-day manner that is not necessarily articulated but just as, if not more, telling.[4]

It is this trans-temporal, non-linear sense of time, beyond analogue clock time that this section attends to.

In Chapter 1, Seher Erdoğan Ford takes the case study of the representation of stone over millennia as the temporal lens. Ford refers to Till in her analysis of the changing ways in which this material has been represented through time. She takes her discussion from early flint arrow-heads up to the latest in virtual reality technology. The apparent timelessness of stone is therefore challenged, and the time-based nature of its visual depiction for a range of specialisms, including archaeology, attests to the importance of thick time for understanding the history of design. How might our physical and tactile perceptions of the 'age' and 'timelessness' of the material world be challenged by our experience of Virtual Environments (VEs)?

Sally Anne Huxtable takes the work of designer Phoebe Anna Traquair as her subject. This overlooked artist and designer worked during the Victorian era, when Deep Time was controversially introduced in contention with the biblical understanding of time. Huxtable discusses Traquair's drawings of ancient fossils and links this with the artist's understanding of evolution within a Christian context. Her Arts and Crafts work is thus examined by way of a unique creative theoretical framework rather than simply as a follower of William Morris. Here a nuanced reading of a designer's understanding of 'time' (meaning more than simply 'nostalgia' or 'longing for the past') can lead us to a better understanding of that designer's work.

In Chapter 3, Anne Burke takes us on a train journey across Australia, with a detailed description in a style reminiscent of Nicholson Baker[5] or Iain Sinclair,[6] but this is a journey through unfamiliar territory. She skilfully incorporates a discussion of class separation, colonialism and different perceptions of time. Her glimpses of Aboriginal life and Dreamtime are contrasted with those of the colonizers, brought into stark relief by her occupation of the third class – 'red' class – of the train carriage. This different approach to considering the history of design succeeds in layering everyday experience with a broad history, with different perspectives on design and its history. Burke explores the negotiation of historical memory, with reference to landmarks of the aboriginal Dreamtime, in the design and laying of the Ghan's route. The use of photography in Burke's essay provides a further layer of meaning: photographs capture a fleeting moment of ephemeral time and 'preserve' it forever. These contrasting time perceptions bring together the broad sweep of this section, which consider time from a range of unexpected perspectives and, together, form a reminder that time itself is a cultural construction, which changes over time.

Notes

1. Jeremy Till, *Architecture Depends* (Cambridge, MA: MIT Press, 2009).
2. Barbara Penner and Charles Rice, 'The Many Lives of Red House', in Anne Massey and Penny Sparke (eds), *Biography, Identity and the Interior* (Aldershot: Ashgate, 2013), 23.
3. Attfield, *Wild Things: The Material Culture of Everyday Life* (London and New York: Berg, 2000).
4. Ibid., 235.
5. Nicholson Baker, *The Mezzanine*, (London: Granta Books, 1989).
6. Iain Sinclair, *London Orbital: A Walk Around the M25* (London: Penguin, 2003).

1 Designing Stone: Temporal Representation of a Timeless Material

SEHER ERDOĞAN FORD

The philosopher Karsten Harries notes that architects build against the 'terror of time'.[1] Jeremy Till, the educator and architect, confirms time as the common enemy for those who want total control over their design, and observes architects to be compelled in two directions: those who deny time and those who aim for timelessness.[2] One way of dealing with time entails considering and representing the temporal scale during the design process. While typical modes of architectural representation yield 'frozen' imagery – either by capturing a specific moment or by creating a veneer of 'newness' – new media technologies offer possibilities for built work to appear on a temporal continuum and to be understood in flux, by situating them in their historical and physical context. Time no longer poses a threat for architectural production if the tools and methodologies for representing it are implemented. Going even further, the representation of historical artefacts as projects that are no longer can offer insights into projects that are yet to be. With that, the critical question arises: How do we draw time? What form(s) and media does the temporal representation of architecture take?

In response to this question, I focus on stone and masonry construction, which are typically considered timeless in material culture. Based on ideas dealing with the close relationship between drawing and making, I propose a method of analysis that can span the extended history of an artefact. To understand the possibilities of drawing stone along the temporal scale, I look at historical, analogue examples – and their manipulation of media – to propose how digital environments may deliver a tangible and dynamic sense of time. Emerging virtual environments (VEs), particularly those dealing with architectural heritage sites, can help us reimagine what drawings are: not only a mode of representation but also an act of analysis and interpretation. Considering drawing in VE or VE as drawings or even the act of drawing VE offers new insights into the transformation of how we understand what drawings look like, what they deal with and how they function. These projects, considered as a new type of drawing that yields complex VEs, represent stone as applied in its changing historical context and revealing its own making.

Drawing decay, growth and regeneration

In *Architecture Depends*, Jeremy Till critiques the modernist architect's unwillingness to accept the mutability of their design over time.[3] In an attempt to freeze the idea, architects disseminate perfectly crafted, calibrated and curated images of their work. How their buildings may change over time in their appearance, use, feel and overall ethos is difficult for architects to grasp. As a result, Till argues that the dichotomy between the intent of the architect and the materiality of architecture grows to the point of dissociation.

Two accounts of stone, one from architectural history and another from cultural anthropology, diminish this conceptual gap between the idea and its execution by relating the material to the traditions and understandings of making. Architect and historian Robin Evans, in the chapter entitled 'Drawn Stone' from his seminal book *The Projective Cast*, discusses the history of stereotomy – referring to the techniques related to cutting stone using geometry and to achieve a three-dimensional configuration – as a direct extension of drawing. Going back to seventh-century France, stereotomic construction implemented drawing templates, called *traits*, which as a craft practice culminated during Renaissance architecture.[4] The traits are essential for the geometric understanding of the complex three-dimensional assembly, but also facilitate the off-site fabrication of components prior to construction. While Evans mentions the possibility that the traits did not document a finality but instead helped solve formal problems and resulted in design revisions, his focus is primarily directed towards the act of translation and interpretation. Traits, in masonry construction, functioned as the medium in which design registered during the collaborative process of fabrication.

Anthropologist Tim Ingold, in *Making*, extends the purview on the fabrication process to include the sourcing of the natural substance, its tooling and its continued transformation throughout the life of the building.[5] From his perspective, no built work is fixed in place or form. Unlike the traditional preoccupation with permanence in architecture, when considered as a material assembly in constant change, the narrative around a building also includes 'growth, decay, and regeneration'.[6] As such, the building is never 'finished' except perhaps in a legal sense. Therefore, with Ingold's broader framing of the idea of 'building-in-the-making', the function of drawing also expands to become a dynamic medium communicating an ad hoc and continuous process of change.

When discussing stone and its durability and transformation over time, the discipline of archaeology also offers insights. Chantal Conneller argues in *An Archeology of Materials* that the study of human activity from a material culture perspective is not only concerned with the functional significance of surviving artefacts but rather encompasses the entire *chaîne opératoire* – the sequence of social acts around the production, use and disposal of artefacts.[7] For example, with regard to a specific specimen of flint stone, the marks found on its surface create a visually interesting texture that are in fact residual from the act of removing fragments to use during various rites. Therefore, the texture represents something about the ritual of sourcing the substance from the earth, the act of manipulating it and its continued use as well. Could we, then, imagine *chaîne opératoire* as a methodology of studying an architectural artefact? This shift in our focus would suggest a kind of historiography that views materiality as understood through the amalgamation of textures. In turn, the built artefact can be situated not only in its physical context but also its cultural and historical milieu that resulted in the textural marks. The drawing would be not only of the project, but also would be an active process of reimagining the tactile presence of the building relative to its intangible past – an act of drawing forth the permeable and dynamic nature of any cultural invention.

Experiments with media

To answer the question of how we draw time through this emphasis on the tactility of stone, first I take a closer look at several canonical examples of analogue drawing techniques, which manipulate the tactility of their physical medium to construct a historical context for the stone. In examples from the early twentieth century, the specific technique of 'piquage' was used primarily to layer textures in localized ways. For example, in a piquage-style depiction of a stone wall, a non-uniform texture is achieved by multiple passes of tone over individual stones and by carefully preserving the sharp white background on one side of each stone through pricking the paper, and implying the depth of the cut. The ink wash can mimic the fluidity of sunlight, but the sharp highlights on the stone help locate each piece in their specific positions against the sun at a particular time of the day and in their specific positions relative to the neighbouring components.

The American architect H. H. Richardson, in his pursuit of the Romanesque style, also represents the stone wall as a masonry assembly with particular texture, but instead of evoking the daily cycles of time, he overlays a sense of historic time. For example, in his drawings of the Glessner house, Richardson employs texture as an affectation of weathered stone, to eliminate the temporal distance from Roman architecture and to situate his work in close proximity to its classical precedents.[8] The will to see rusticated stone is not merely a graphic exercise, but one that hews closely to the structural logic of the building. The legibility of the three-dimensional components are not once compromised in service of the 'aged effect'.

Further along the spectrum of imbuing age upon the drawing and therefore fixing it at a singular moment in history, we find Giovanni Battista Piranesi (1720–1778). The etchings of the eighteenth-century Italian artist reconstructed ruins and recast well-known architectural artefacts in archaeological scenes, in a scenario where the built environment is in return to a natural state, almost to a prehistoric moment. While the narrative of the image is one of regrowth and decay, the visual message connotes a singular moment in a very distant past. This reading of 'ancient' owes much to content but perhaps even more to Piranesi's particular choice of medium, where the etchings, through the use of incisions and repeated build-up of ink, display a unique texture that contributes to the reading of 'fuzziness' of the line and therefore of weathering and perhaps uncertainty. While Piranesi's work transposes the viewer in time, it does so by narrative devices and only peripherally deals with actual material history.

The historical practice of architectural depiction offers a wide variety of experiments with medium to generate tactile qualities creating specific yet still singular temporal readings. Taken collectively, the drawings suggest the elasticity of the temporal scale in architectural representation; individually, they fail to convey the dynamic nature of materials in flux. What possibilities does the digital space offer? The same risk of 'frozen imagery' persists with computerized production, but in a different way. In contemporary, digital documentation of architecture, the distance from the physical medium in the making of the drawing often translates to a loss of touch with the physical properties of the represented artefact. It is common practice to employ abstract patterns or 'hatches' that designate various types of stone, where the scale of building blocks may be adjusted to some level of accuracy and visual detail, but the finalized rendition is strictly *a-material*. The hatch pattern operates as a notational device rather than a signifier of physical properties, communicating the architect's specification of commodity as opposed to quality. (Interestingly, architects resort to exhaustive texts to achieve accuracy in product and material specifications.) This is partially because the graphic pattern, however specific in its geometry and dominating in its replicability, lacks medium specificity and therefore tactility. The resultant rendition connotes a drawing void of medium, an idea without mass, and exists in no particular moment in history but perhaps to fulfil the picture of the 'legal completion' Ingold refers to.

Another way in which images appear frozen or static results from the opposite strategy of abstraction and the striving for hyper-realistic renderings. Digital tools allow texture mapping to such great detail and 'fidelity' that the image asserts itself as exhaustive and true. As Baudrillard cautions in *Simulacra and Simulation*, the problem with virtuality is not that it is false but that is understood as singular manifestation of falsehood.[9] We understand the image to be a simulation – we do not mistake it for reality – but it oppresses any other image of possibility. In its brilliant appearance, the image functions as a black hole of possibilities, ambiguity or change. Propagated on the surface, textures with amazing level of detail function as visual patterns removed from their physical or historical context, that can be 'wallpapered' anywhere and everywhere since they impart such forceful convincing in their real-ness. Medieval-era stone exists without any connection to its traditions of making or cultural significance, and can be placed anywhere but cannot be further explored or known. Visually it mimics layers, but it has no depth to allow for discovery or imagination. Perceptually, the completeness of the visualization invites quick reads and material coding – polished concrete, buffed stone, weathered brick – shunning the slower tactile understanding of how the material feels to the touch as one is making it or living with it or experiencing it for the first time.

Virtual environments as drawings

But the virtual realm promises more. The technology that contains and connects vast expanses of physical and temporal space is VE – some of its applications being Virtual Reality (VR), Mixed Reality (MR) and Augmented Reality (AR). Returning to the notion of drawing and making being intertwined aspects of architectural design, instead of static images or even navigable renditions of digital models, considering VE as a new medium and a new type of space might unlock ways of reconsidering drawings as well.

Virtual worlds can be described as digitally constructed models which users can navigate in an immersive fashion and in which they can find varying degrees of reciprocity with the physical world. While terminology is still evolving, VE can be described as a gradient of a newer technologies – VR, MR and AR. In all cases, the access to VE is mediated by a device such as a smartphone or a head-mounted set or a room-sized installation. These technologies facilitate various forms of virtuality by juxtaposing physical and digital space (MR), or extending the digital into the physical (AR), or containing the physical within the digital (VR). If earlier modes of representation stretched the boundaries of their physical medium to claim a multisensory and dynamic space of representation – a more-than-visual rendition of an artefact over time – they did this by triggering virtuality. A genre of digital projects that are conceived as such dynamic and spatial platforms are digital reconstructions of historic sites created by multidisciplinary initiatives within the digital humanities field. Designed as information-rich environments for digital scholarship on architectural heritage, these platforms are primarily web-based and facilitate three-dimensional navigation within VEs in varying degrees of immersion.

How can VEs further the depiction of change over time in architectural representation? How can VEs employ the methodology of *chaîne opératoire* – life cycle of material transformation? In other words, how do we design the extended history of an architectural artefact with a focus on materiality in the VE? To answer this line of questioning, first we need to consider the unique qualities of the medium achieved by rapidly developing VE technologies. Where VE differs as a medium from digital visualization is that it incorporates the subject formerly referred to as the user or viewer as 'the interactor'. Of course, when we imagine occupying virtual space and examining the material properties of the surrounding architecture, the sense of scale demands attention. Unlike the critique of digital renderings that yield scaleless patterns, VE can actually create a full-scale understanding by re-placing the human body (the interactor) relative to the artefact. But more importantly, VE is capable of not only 1:1 representation, but also of leveraging the analytical function of scaled drawings to support the study of architectural materials represented in multiple scales to convey materiality. Lastly, VE can preserve, or generate, ambiguity. By incorporating external sources – such as digital archives and other scholarly projects – and heterogeneous content of different media, the virtual is a porous environment that is not exhaustive but collective. A dynamic repository of scholarship, VE facilitates authors to connect to information hosted outside of the model while allowing interactors to access a network from within the model. As a result, the interactor does not experience a 'finished product' but engages with the active production of knowledge.

While digital tools are thoroughly embedded within every aspect of architectural representation, 'immersive' interaction, as a unique quality of the digital medium, has been underutilized. Interactive representations of architecture are not limited to animated scenes but suggest dynamic platforms responsive to interactor's input and goals. From features that allow for temporal navigation to customized filters, built-in functions that enable the VE to 'filter' or 're-sort' change the way we conceive of the interactor's relationship to the content represented – the drawing – from a passive intake to an act of drawing forth an idea. The viewer as interactor is in fact also the maker, the writer and the reader.

This transformed outlook on the subject's involvement in VE and the multiple 'roles' they may play also harken back to the traditional fabrication process of stereotomic construction discussed earlier. The *traits*, as discussed in Evans's account of 'Drawn Stone', belonged in a pivotal moment in architectural production where the architect assumed a position off-site as the thinker and visionary, and the craftspeople, as an anonymous crew, implemented in stone the vision on paper. This separation (or the professionalization of the architect), propelled by the Renaissance dichotomy of thinkers versus makers, put more focus on the individual act of designing through drawing and in some ways abandoned the collaborative nature of craft in the field. Although the contemporary construction industry has grown into a robust network of collaboration, *traits* – as documents passed on from one trade to another through many rounds of translation and interpretation – exist in various forms, whether as drawings on paper or as digital three-dimensional models. As interactive platforms engaging multiple authors, VE may in fact transform our relationship to the notion of *traits* and recapture the spirit of the collective and simultaneous act of drawing and making practice. Projects like Digital Athens conducted by Duke's Digital Art History and Visual Culture Center and American School of Classical Studies in Athens, and Hypercities presented by UCLA and Harvard pursue this kind of a practice where authorship is dispersed across disciplines and geographies, via wikis and open-source access to code. As a result, VE becomes a representation of the collective knowledge.

In 'Drawn to Scale' from the collection of essays titled *From Models to Drawings*, Paul Emmons critiques the common perception of digital space as being 'scaleless' and therefore dissociated from the human body.[10] This poses a productive problem for VE to address. In fully immersive environments, the interactor can self-navigate and gain a haptic sense of the space occupied – a feedback system of the body's perception relative to the surrounding objects, an extended sense of touch that goes beyond the finger and skin. In parallel with the advancements in incorporating more robust and nuanced texture mapping onto digital models, accessing tactile perception within immersive VEs have come into the foreground. This is supported by scientific studies that show the combination of visual, auditory and tactile information constructs a much more immersive experience for the user than a higher level of visual fidelity alone could deliver.[11] The computer science behind this possibility is haptics, a term that is already familiar to architects but needs recontextualizing. As Mark Paterson discusses in his essay 'More-Than Visual Approaches to Architecture', haptic perception in VR goes beyond the isolated feeling of touch.[12] As a system, it helps living beings understand their bodies relative to their environment and other masses within this environment. Within VE, 'the edge', that spatial-temporal distance between the viewer and the work, collapses. In a perceptual sense, the viewer is located in spatial proximity to something that exists elsewhere through visual and haptic input. What this implies for architectural representation is that the subject can occupy a building at various incarnations of its architectural existence, but also understand its physical properties and scale relative to his/her own physical body.

But drawing to scale, as an act, is not only a practical tool of documentation but also a form of analysis, and digital space can integrate the multivalent nature of scaled representations within the full-scale environment. As an example, the Zamani Project by a team of researchers at the University of Cape Town, conceived as an African cultural heritage and landscape database, embeds measured drawings to specific scale within the digital model such that the interactor can find different technical views of an architectural element constructed of stone juxtaposed against the textured rendition of the stone.[13] In recreations of the ancient ruins of Petra in Jordan, for example, the nuanced rendition is achieved by laser-scanned surfaces scaffolded by digital modelling, but further developed by layers of orthographic projection drawings (Figure 1.1).

An argument can be made that the true potential of VE in relating a dynamic understanding of time through tactility lies beyond its visual capacity. Even

Figure 1.1 Site of Petra, Jordan, on the Zamani Project. Heniz Ruther, University of Cape Town.

sophisticated VEs that achieve a reading of 'age' through highly refined textures, nuanced interaction of forms and light, and the delicacy of atmospheric qualities, lack a level of credibility. Perhaps the reason is not lack of refinement but the contrary. Under the heading 'Here and Now', Till references the artist Laurie Anderson who expresses her mistrust of VR environments until 'they learn how to put in dirt'.[14] This comment is not only an explicit critique of the blinders on the contemporary charge towards photorealism (a black hole of possibilities), but also an implicit prompt to pursue 'dirt' – or the *undesigned* layers of architectural skin – as an intellectual device to conjure other possibilities by the interactor. The undesigned also suggests the unknown and uncertain aspects of the object of study, therefore it opens up the possibility for imbuing ambiguity into various kinds of inquiry.

Particularly when dealing with historical sites, documentation and archival information is often uncertain, leading to multiple or ambiguous readings. Although digital tools are designed for definitive input, aspects of visual and spatial language as employed in VE can create legible ambiguity – almost an oxymoron – essential for humanities-oriented inquiry. An ongoing collaboration between interaction designers and archaeologists at Monash University, the SahulTime Project has been developing an interactive visualization of Earth's history starting with Australia and, given the vast temporal and spatial scale, the team deals with a great deal of uncertainty.[15] As a strategy, the interface implements a designation of 'fuzziness' of data by graphic markers that literally exhibit gradients of visually fuzzy, red lines. The line is not merely a graphic marker but also a functional, interactive bar that the viewer can use to navigate the depths of archaeological bores. How crisp the definition of the line is, or how pixelated its edges might appear, suggest to the viewer the level of certainty the researches have on the accurateness of the data displayed. Simple and intuitive, the marker allows the content to remain 'open-ended' in nature and not conflated and confounded for the purposes of accuracy.

Faced with similar issues at the architectural scale, the Virtual St Paul's Cathedral Project constructed by an interdisciplinary team of researchers at North Carolina State University outlines their methodology of reconstruction in detail on the project website.[16] In a verbal narrative intertwined with historical drawings that informed the construction of the three-dimensional model, the authors describe their approximations and suppositions. Conceived as zones of certainty radiating out of the cathedral, which has the narrowest margin of approximation, the surrounding context buildings exhibit a gradient in terms of the certainty on material definition. The narrative also touches upon the fact that the exact hue of the yellow stone used in the cathedral is inconclusive due to its changing qualities in different atmospheric conditions. While the verbal narrative accompanied by the archival and new visual content makes the methodology clear, it also raises the question of whether the gradient could be visually conveyed within the VE. One such attempt is the 'uncertainty map' of digitally reconstructed Palladio's villa by architectural heritage researchers at University of Bologna.[17] Another experiment incorporating abstract drawings to convey process is the 'interpretation diagram' of the Swedish Pompeii Project by a team of researchers from Italy and Sweden.[18] While still in the early phases of refinement at the time of publication, both of these outcomes begin to suggest a visual language for spatial representation of knowledge in interactive, three-dimensional space for architectural heritage (Figure 1.2).

Another way to approach the visual and spatial representation of ambiguity warrants a reminder that for these types of digital cultural heritage projects the model represents what scholars know about the historical artefact, not necessarily what it was. The distinction, as thoroughly discussed in the article describing the process behind the Digital Karnak Project by Elaine A. Sullivan and Lisa M. Snyder, is crucial in establishing the essential function of virtual models relative to their referent.[19] VE does not aim to 'recover' the site, but provides a platform for scholarly discovery on the site. As a mode of drawing, it is not a documentation to be consulted for answers but a space to be cultivated for questions. Digital Hadrian's Villa Project constructed by the Virtual World Heritage Lab at Indiana University employs multimedia annotation features to create such a layered VE, where the interactor is actively making connections between the model that is clearly a representation to some level of

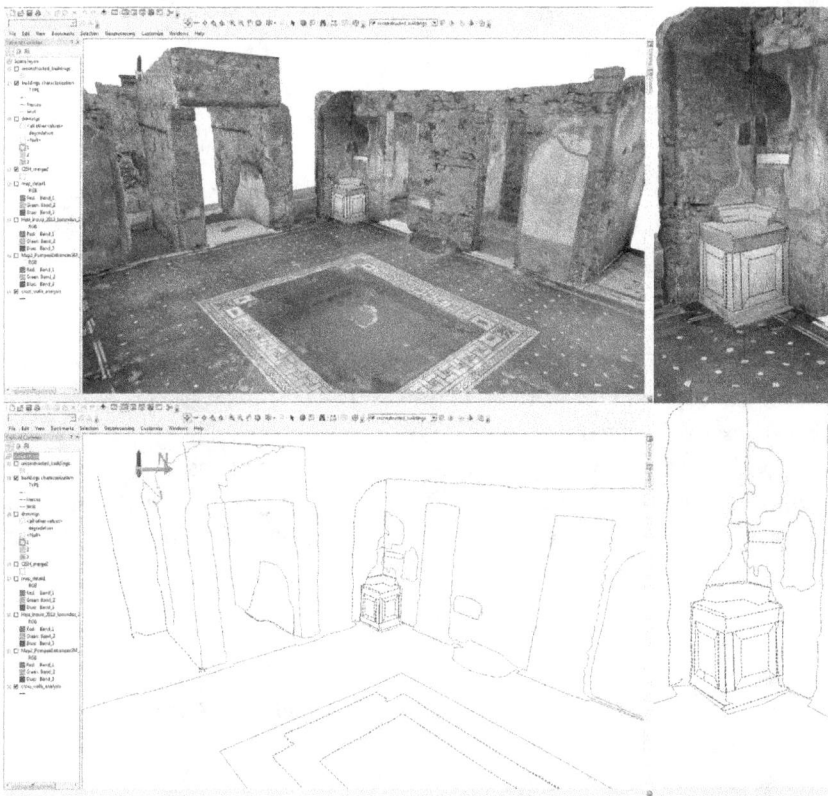

Figure 1.2 Screenshots published by Swedish Pompeii Project showing the polygons and polylines used to characterize the interpretative process. Courtesy of Nicoló Dell'Unto.

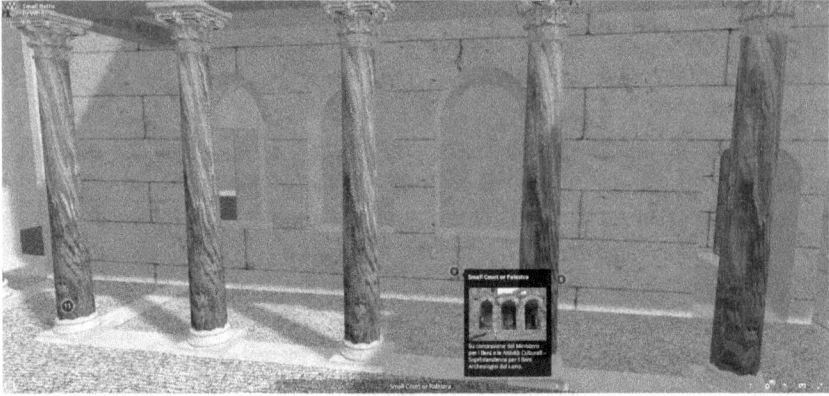

Figure 1.3 Screenshot from Digital Hadrian's Project. Bernard David Frischer, Virtual World Heritage Lab at Indiana University.

abstraction and the photographs of the site in Tivoli, Italy.[20] Each photograph frames a singular moment and a particular view but, embedded within the navigable digital reconstruction space, they create possibilities for reading the material transformation of various types of stones used in the villa (Figure 1.3).

Conclusion

Temporal dimension is hard to capture in conventional modes of architectural representation. One consequence is static renditions of materials, particularly those like stone and masonry construction that embody long histories of change. Digital technologies have been heavily used for modelling and rendering but are still underexplored in terms of how we reconceive drawing as an act. Recent projects on architectural heritage sites begin to explore ways in which material transformation of built work can suggest new ways of representing stone's materiality: in a temporal continuum, examined at multiple scales and representative of scholarly inquiry. These projects deal with aspects of representation in VEs that can transform 'drawing' as a mode of translation and interpretation. They begin to suggest possibilities for how the act of drawing in digital space can in fact tell the stories of making and remaking of an architectural artefact in stone.

Notes

1. Karsten Harries, 'Building and the Terror of Time', *Perspecta* 19 (1982): 64.
2. Jeremy Till, *Architecture Depends* (Cambridge, MA: MIT Press, 2009), 79.
3. Till, *Architecture Depends*, 18.
4. Robin Evans, *The Projective Cast: Architecture and Its Three Geometries* (Cambridge, MA: MIT Press, 1995), 189.

5. Tim Ingold, *Making: Anthropology, Archeology, Art and Architecture* (London and New York: Routledge, 2013), 54–7.

6. Ingold, *Making*, 48.

7. Chantal Conneller, *An Archeology of Materials: Substantial Transformation in Early Prehistoric Europe* (New York: Routledge, 2011), 82.

8. John J. Glessner House, 1800 South Prairie Avenue, Chicago, Cook County, IL, HABS ILL,16-CHIG,17- (sheet 5 of 6), Historic American Buildings Survey, Library of Congress, http://www.loc.gov/pictures/item/il0118/.

9. Jean Baudrillard, *Simulacra and Simulation* (Ann Arbor: University of Michigan Press, 2014,) 53.

10. Paul Emmons, 'Drawn to Scale: The Imaginative Inhabitation of Architectural Drawings', in Marco Frascari, Jonathan Hale and Bradley Starkey (eds), *From Models to Drawings: Imagination and Representation in Architecture* (London: Routledge, 2007), 71.

11. Mark Paterson, 'More-Than Visual Approaches to Architecture: Vision, Touch, Technique', *Social & Cultural Geography*, 12, no. 3 (May 2011): 270.

12. Paterson, 'More-Than Visual Approaches to Architecture', 265.

13. 'Zamani Project', University of Cape Town Zamani Project, http://zamaniproject.org/index.php/home.html (accessed 29 December 2017).

14. Till, *Architecture Depends*, 87.

15. 'SahulTime', Monash University, http://sahultime.monash.edu.au/explore.html (accessed 29 December 2017).

16. 'Virtual St. Paul's Cathedral Project', North Carolina State University, https://vpcp.chass.ncsu.edu/churchyard/resources/ (accessed 29 December 2017).

17. F. I. Appolino, M. Gaiani and Z. Sun, '3D Modeling and Data Enrichment in Digital Reconstruction of Architectural Heritage', in *ISPRS – International Archives of the Photogrammetry, Remote Sensing and Spatial Information Sciences*, XL-5/W2, (2013): 47.

18. Nicolo Dell'Unto, Giacomo Landeschi, Anne-Marie Leander Touati, Matteo Dellepiane, Marco Callieri and Daniele Ferdani, 'Experiencing Ancient Buildings from a 3D GIS Perspective: A Case Drawn from the Swedish Pompeii Project', in *Journal of Archeological Method Theory* 23, no. 73 (2016): 88.

19. Elaine A. Sullivan and Lisa M. Snyder, 'Digital Karnak: An Experiment in Publication and Peer Review of Interactive, Three-Dimensional Content', in *Journal of the Society of Architectural Historians* 76, no. 4 (December 2017): 464–82.

20. 'Virtual Hadrian's Villa Project', Indiana University, http://vwhl.soic.indiana.edu/villa/index.php (accessed 2 January 2018).

2 'The Drama of the Soul': Time, Eternity and Evolution in the Designs of Phoebe Anna Traquair

DR SALLY ANNE HUXTABLE

In 1906, the Irish poet, activist and occultist W. B. Yeats sent a letter to the dramatist, folklorist and theatre manager Lady Augustus Gregory in which he wrote at length on the work and character of the artist and designer Phoebe Anna Traquair:

> She has but one story, the drama of the soul. She herself describes it as captivity, the divine descent to meet it, its liberation, its realisation of itself in the world of spirit . . . She is, herself delightful – a little saint and a singing bird . . . The nearer she reaches the divine, the more passionate become the lines – the more expressive the faces, the more vehement is every movement.[1]

Time and the Victorians

The period 1850–1918 in Britain was an era of intense – and often highly contentious – scientific, religious, philosophical and cultural debate about the very nature and understanding of 'time'. As a consequence of industrialization and the growth of the railways, the measuring of time in everyday life was already moving away from traditional 'cyclical time', governed by the seasons and movements of the sun, towards a more 'linear' notion of time dictated by railway timetables and the working day in factories.[2] However, it was not only everyday life which saw transforming notions of time: the publication of scientific ideas and discoveries such as William Thomson's (later, Lord Kelvin) statement of the 'Second Law of Thermodynamics' (1848) and Charles Darwin's publication of *On the Origin of Species* (1859), as well as the various geological and palaeontological discoveries of the period, all challenged the biblical account of past, present and future. Gradually it was becoming clear that the earth, and the timescale of human existence upon it, was a lot older and longer than biblical exegesis had so far demonstrated, and that this developing notion of Deep Time could not sit with literalist interpretations of Scripture. It was also increasingly believed by many that the world would not end with Armageddon and the Second Coming of Christ but, if one was to believe Kelvin's statement, it was already dying and would end not in conflagration, but in slow entropy. Of course, the established church did not take this well, and in 1860 there was a 'great confrontation over the new theory at Oxford, with the Anglican Bishop of Oxford on one side and Darwin's ally, Huxley, on the other. Taunts were thrown. Someone held a large Bible in the air, loudly insisting on the authority of scripture. A lady fainted. Students cheered. Evolution and the Established Church were at war.'3

Phoebe Anna Traquair

It was amid this ferment of ideas and debates that centred around the very nature of time on Earth, that artistic and design movements such as Pre-Raphaelitism, Arts and Crafts and Aestheticism emerged with sets of ideas which placed the relationship between art and design, and past, present and future at the very centre of their works and beliefs. Rather than what is often lazily assumed by commentators to be movements and ideas based on a sense of misplaced nostalgia – particularly for the medieval world – the artists involved in these movements deliberately reimagined and reconfigured the past as a way of both illuminating the present and of finding ways to offer a vision of a perfected or ideal future. This is undoubtedly true of the work of Phoebe Anna Traquair (née Moss) (1852–1936) who is, arguably, one of the most important, and overlooked, British women artists of the second half of the nineteenth and the early twentieth century, as well as Scotland's first truly professional woman artist of modern times. Born in Dublin, she came to Edinburgh in 1874, having married the Scottish palaeontologist and curator Ramsay Heatley Traquair (1840–1912) in 1873. In 1920 Traquair became the first honorary woman member of the Scottish Royal Academy, reflecting her status as a leading professional designer at a time when art and design was still dominated by men.

Traquair worked with an extraordinarily wide variety of media, encompassing palaeoichthyological drawings, enamelling, bookbinding, embroidery, illustration, illuminated manuscripts, decorative furniture painting, oil and watercolour painting and mural painting. Her famous mural paintings still adorn the walls of the Apostolic Catholic Church (now the Mansfield Traquair Centre), St Mary's Episcopal Cathedral and the mortuary Chapel of the Royal Hospital for Sick Children, and the largest collection of her work is in National Museums Scotland, with another significant collection in the Victoria and Albert Museum. Her designs have often been overlooked as those of yet another follower of Arts and Crafts, but her work not only followed the tradition of artist-designers such as William Morris, she was also deeply influenced by British symbolist artists, particularly the Pre-Raphaelite and Aestheticist work of Dante Gabriel Rossetti (1828–1882), whose artistic style of jewel-bright medievalist watercolours of the 1850s can be seen to have inspired her work. Her vast artistic and design output also drew on that of the Pre-Raphaelite William Holman Hunt (1827–1910), and a 'pantheon' of artists and writers such as George Frederic Watts (1817–1904), Edward Burne-Jones (1833–1898), Dante Alighieri (1265–1312), William Morris (1834–1896), William Blake (1757–1827), Alfred, Lord Tennyson (1809–1902) and Thomas Carlyle (1795–1881), a collection of artists and writers whose work proved so influential upon the artistic movements of the period 1848–1914.

The theory of evolution

Traquair's work is most often categorized, or even dismissed, as yet another unremarkable follower of the ideology of William Morris. However, her ideas, influences and use of complex symbolism transcend this simplistic categorization and demonstrate her interest in, and engagement with, a number of complex ideas and discourses around the relationships between art, spirituality and science, the nature of the soul and selfhood. Traquair's work explores how these might be reconciled with ecumenical Christianity, diverse world mythologies and spiritual beliefs, the scientific and resulting social beliefs of her day. Through her chosen medium of design, Traquair deliberately used myth, imagery and symbolism that directly engaged with these discourses, and which attempted to resolve the seemingly conflicting notions of time and the seismic upheavals they caused in the Britain of the late nineteenth century and the first few decades of the twentieth century.

Some of the earliest artistic work that Traquair undertook was for her soon-to-be husband the palaeontologist Ramsay Heatley Traquair (1840–1912), work that involved making meticulous pencil drawings of the fossil fish that were at the centre of his scientific research and teaching on palaeoichthyology (Figure 2.1).[4] Indeed, she continued drawing these fish fossils for Ramsay. This working partnership with her husband, and their movement in intellectual circles which included luminaries such as T. H. Huxley (1825–1895), Charles Darwin (1808–1882) and the Edinburgh sociobiologist Patrick Geddes (1854–1932), meant that Phoebe Traquair was fully

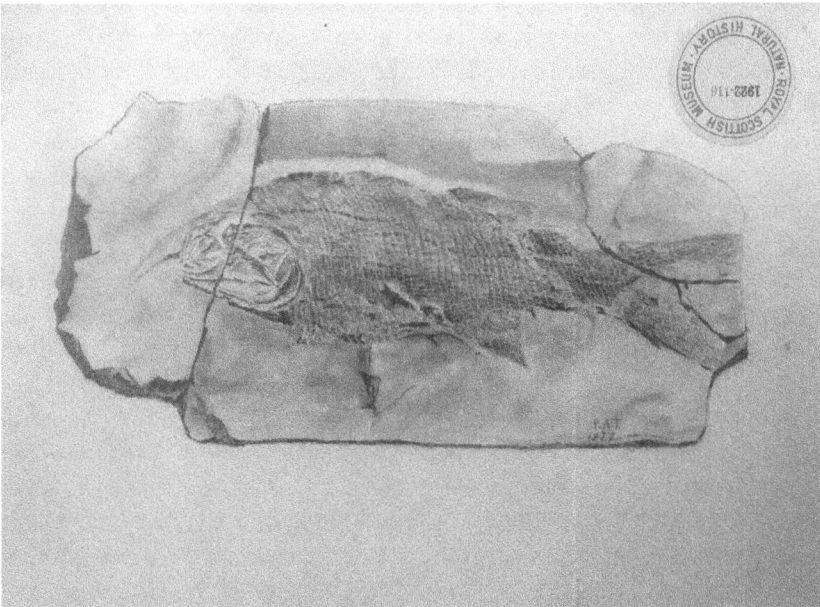

Figure 2.1 Phoebe Anna Traquair, fossil fish drawing, graphite on paper, 1887. Image by the author, by kind permission of National Museums Scotland.

au fait with the science of the age, including ideas about evolution. Nonetheless, she still seems to have been able to fully maintain, and also incorporate, her own spiritual beliefs into this scientific worldview. For example, in two of her mural schemes in places of worship, the interior schemes at the Song School at St Mary's Episcopalian Cathedral in Edinburgh's West End and at the Catholic Apostolic Church in the New Town, she used parts of the murals to depict Creation but made her belief in the fossil record explicitly clear by including an image of a dinosaur in both schemes. However, 'evolution' was not an idea that was confined to the paleontological record during the second half of the nineteenth and the early twentieth centuries. For many, it became an overarching concept that could incorporate the individual, society, 'the nation', politics, economics, spirituality as well as the cosmos, and Traquair was one of a number of designers, writers and artists who attempted to reconcile and articulate this through their work.

Edinburgh Social Union and social evolution

For Traquair – who, it should not be forgotten, was a practising Christian and a member of the Episcopalian congregation near her home in Colinton – the key to incorporating science, mythology and esoteric ideas, ecumenical Christianity and the progressive social agenda of the Arts and Crafts movement, was the notion of evolution in its very broadest sense. From this all-encompassing perspective, all aspects of the physical and spiritual world – of macrocosm and microcosm, of humanity in general, and the individual in particular – were constantly developing and progressing throughout space and time. In this context, design could function as a way of revitalizing and reimagining stories and myths from the past in a way that might offer a vision of these cosmic processes of evolution to which both society and the individual might relate. The notion that society might evolve through the improvement of living conditions, particularly in cities, was, of course, central to much of the progressive political ideology of the end of the nineteenth and the early twentieth centuries. The Arts and Crafts movement, which was built on William Morris's socialist ideals, believed that this could, at least in part, be achieved through art and design.

In Edinburgh, these ideas came together under the auspices of Patrick Geddes, the Scottish evolutionary-biologist, sociologist, geographer and urban planner. In 1884, Geddes founded the Edinburgh Social Union, a philanthropic organization set up to encourage Edinburgh communities to improve their environments. Their first meeting was on 6 January 1885. In particular, the art guild section of the Social Union commissioned artistic decorative schemes for interiors of public buildings. These ideals regarding the relationship between art and social reform chimed closely with those of his good friend Traquair. Geddes's philosophy was based on that of the English thinker Herbert Spencer (1820–1903), who asserted that the notion of biological evolution could be applied to explain the evolution of society. Geddes and the Social Union were responsible for numerous urban improvements in the slums of Edinburgh, and the art guild was responsible for a number of important decorative interiors in the city, including Traquair's stunning murals for the Mortuary Chapel of the Royal Hospital for Sick Children in Sciennes (1885–1886 and 1896–1898) and the Catholic Apostolic Church in Mansfield place on the edge of the New Town (1893–1901). Art and design were seen to be important ways of improving the environment and people's well-being by offering them beautiful and uplifting images and designs to contemplate. As projects that combined evolution, social progressiveness and art, these mural schemes – as well as her murals for the Song School at St Mary's Episcopal Cathedral which, although not commissioned by Edinburgh Social Union, were commissioned for the church by the dean who sat on the art guild of the Social Union – offered a perfect combination to chime with Traquair's ideas and beliefs regarding evolution and society.

The story of Cupid and Psyche

However, at the core of almost all of Traquair's smaller works was the notion of individual spiritual evolution. One story that particularly captured Traquair's imagination was the relatively obscure myth of Cupid and Psyche. The story, which concerns the love of the mortal Psyche (or soul) for the god of love, Cupid, and the seemingly impossible trials that Psyche must undertake in order to win back Cupid's love, after she disobeys instructions and loses it – originated in written form, at least, in the second century text *Metamorphoses*, also known as *The Golden Ass*, by Lucius Apuleius. Like so much classical learning and literature, *The Golden Ass* was rediscovered in Western Europe during the fourteenth century, at which time the story of Cupid and Psyche proved highly popular thanks to its strongly Neoplatonic themes regarding the perfection, or evolution, of the soul and its joining in mystical union with the Divine, or 'the One' from which all things emanate. In this 'theology of love' the human body functions as a microcosm of universe – the 'as above, so below', that is central to this thread of Renaissance thinking. In Neoplatonic thought, physical and spiritual love are both manifestations of the same impulse and, according to the Platonic formulation, we are attracted first to a single beautiful person, then to beautiful people generally, then to beautiful minds, then to beautiful ideas and, ultimately, to spiritual beauty itself, which is the highest rung of the ladder in the progression. Such a philosophy held an attraction for a number of nineteenth- and early twentieth-century Pre-Raphaelites, Aesthetics and artists, designers, writers and poets, such as Rossetti, Pater and Traquair, whose artistic practices were focused upon capturing that sense of beauty through their work, and exploring the ways in which that beauty might aid the evolution of the individual and society.

Traquair captures the essence of the Psyche in her beautiful *Psyche Cup* (1905–1906) (Figure 2.2), which she created in collaboration with her son, the architect Ramsay Traquair (1874–1952). Phoebe Traquair designed and made the jewel-bright enamels that depicted Psyche's story, and delicate floating butterflies, depicting the soul. Ramsay Traquair sourced the iridescent rainbow-like paua or abalone shell, and designed the silver stand with its adularescent moonstones (a stone which, in

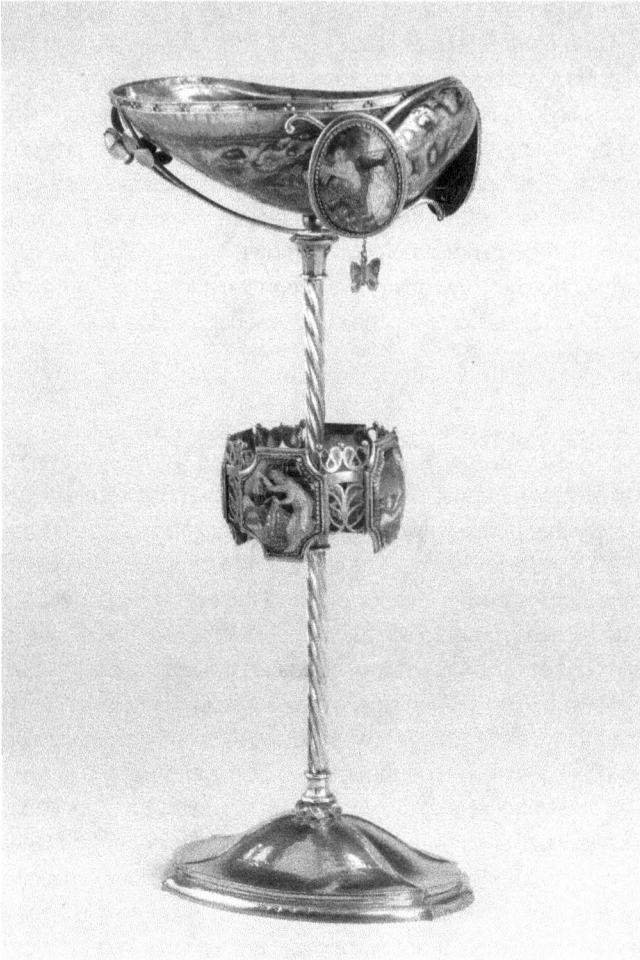

Figure 2.2 Phoebe Anna Traquair and Ramsay Traquair, *Psyche Cup*, paua shell, silver moonstone, enamel 1905. © National Museums Scotland.

gemstone lore, is said to represent love and passion, to restore love between those who have parted in anger, and to act as a protective talisman for those who are on journeys involving water), to create what was a communion chalice dedicated, not to Christianity, but to the sanctity of love.

Another work dedicated to the sanctity of love is Traquair's 1905 portable triptych, *Cupid the Earth Upholder* in which the god of love takes the place of Atlas, and holds up the world (Figure 2.3). Here Traquair presents the theme in the form of an object of personal devotion, much like those used in medieval and Renaissance devotion. Once again we see the deliberate juxtaposition of a Christian – particularly a Catholic – religious form, with a decidedly pagan and/or Renaissance humanist subject matter. The same symbolism of love upholding the earth, which seems to be entirely unique to Traquair, is repeated in an 1895–1905 enamelled necklace of

Figure 2.3 Phoebe Anna Traquair, *Cupid the Earth Upholder* triptych, silver and enamel, 1905–1907. © National Museums Scotland.

the same name in a pendant in the Victoria and Albert Museum, and – alongside a traditional Cupid shooting an arrow and depictions of the Virgin Mary and Christ – in one of the lozenges in another necklace which dates to 1917–1918. A number of more traditional representations of Cupid, either sleeping or shooting his arrow, also appear in Traquair's enamels.

Walter Pater

Although Traquair may have read the Apuleius version of Cupid and Psyche, it is most likely that her designs were more directly inspired by the prose version of the tale, 'The Story of Cupid and Psyche', in the Aesthetic novel *Marius the Epicurean*, originally published between 1881 and 1884, by the art critic and author Walter Pater (1839–1894). The novel is set during the years AD 161–177, and follows the philosophical and spiritual journey of a young Roman man during a time of change and upheaval in the Roman Empire. In particular, Pater saw great parallels between the upheaval caused by the introduction of Christianity to the previously polytheistic empire, and the various contestations and upheavals in his own time, particularly those between the established church and the scientists. In the story, Marius explores various forms of classical philosophy as well as early Christianity, but his 'epiphany' comes in the Sabine Hills, when he is overwhelmed by the sense of 'the One', the Platonic 'Cosmic Mind'. Here, his overarching understanding is that 'the One' is love:

> He would try to fix his mind . . . on all the persons he had loved in life –
> On his love for them, dead or living, grateful for his love or not, rather than on theirs for him . . . In the bare sense of having loved he seemed to find that on which his soul might 'assuredly rest and depend'.[5]

Ultimately, at the very end of his life, Marius comes to the realization that love transcends all. It is the earth upholder.

Traquair was clearly hugely influenced by Pater's ideas, particularly his fascination with, and his own reimaginings of, the kinds of allegorical myths that were central to Renaissance Neoplatonism. This was a theme that ran throughout Pater's work, from his (in)famous essay collection *Studies in the History of the Renaissance* (1873), through to his unfinished novel *Gaston Latour* (published 1896). The story of Cupid and Psyche was the consummate allegory of the perfection of the soul (Psyche) and its joining in mystical union with love or the heart (Cupid). This theology of love is a persistent theme through the decades of Traquair's design and artistic practice, whether in the themes she uses to draw on biblical Scripture and legend, as in her use of the theme of the *Pietà* (the sorrowful Virgin weeping over the lifeless body of her son, Christ) in three of the enamels dating from 1902, 1902 and 1903, respectively, or her three exquisite *Red Crosse Knight* embroideries – inspired by Edmund Spenser's allegorical poem *The Faerie Queene* (1590–1596) – which depict the hero's spiritual transformation through the slaying of the dragon and winning of the love of Princess Una (1907–1914). Traquair's captivation with Pater's Neoplatonic and Aesthetic ideas about spiritual perfection – he believed that the individual might evolve artistically and spiritually through love, art and sensation – can also be seen most fully in her spectacular series of embroideries, the *Progress of the Soul* (1895–1902, National Galleries Scotland), inspired by Pater's 'Imaginary Portrait' Denys l'Auxerrois, a mythological short story exploring the often painful relationship between Dionysian-pagan and Christian beliefs through the birth, life and martyrdom of a godlike young man, who seems to be Dionysius reborn in a Provençal town. It is also interesting to note that the title seems to have been inspired by John Donne's 1612 poem 'The Progress of the Soul', itself a meditation on the soul moving on from the pains of this life to the bliss of the next.

While she was working on the embroideries, it is clear that these ideas were much on her mind, as she wrote:

> The true drama of a soul's development . . . the unconscious living, the awakening, knowledge of good and evil, despair, escape from self-perception of beauty, forgiveness of evil, birth of the new life, there one traces each step through much pain and wanderings, till all is lost forever in a glorious harmony.[6]

In this highly symbolist series of four embroideries, we see the soul/Denys l'Auxerroix undergo this journey. In 'The Entrance' (1895), the young man, dressed in an animal skin, is in harmony with nature and joyfully oblivious to the trials and tribulations that life will bring. In 'The Stress' (1897), the realities of life, and nature itself, in the form of a serpent, have started to impede his progress. In 'Despair' (1899), the young man is dying, hanging from the vines that bring to mind both Dionysius and the Passion of Christ. Finally, we see 'The Victory' (1902) in which he is reborn out of the mouth of the serpent, and held in an embrace by a seraph, a rainbow at their feet marking this ultimate relationship between human love and the love of the Divine.

Dante Gabriel Rossetti and the impossible quest for love

It was not only Pater's ideas on this theology or religion of love that influenced Traquair, but also those of the artist-poet Dante Gabriel Rossetti (1828–1882), whose output was undoubtedly a huge influence on both. As literary scholar Jerome McGann brilliantly discussed in *Dante Gabriel Rossetti and the Game that Must Be Lost*, Rossetti's entire literary and artistic output was built around an impossible quest experience and represents an archetype of perfect love which was the artist's own soul.[7] Unlike Pater or Traquair's Denys/soul figure, the soul/love figure of Rossetti's vision was, however, always represented in the form of a woman, as with his short story 'Hand and Soul', in which a Renaissance artist (Rossetti's alter ego) encounters his soul in female form (1847), and his most famous work *The Blessed Damozel* which he first published in poetic form in 1850 (subsequently revised in 1856, 1870 and 1873) and painted (1875–1878, Fogg Museum of Art). One particular work by Rossetti that heavily influenced Traquair (as well as Margaret Macdonald and Charles Rennie Mackintosh) was Rossetti's poem 'Willowwood' (1868–1869), a symbolist poem set in a ghostly wood, which functions as a mournful paean to steadfast faithfulness in the face of lost love. Traquair illustrated the poem very much in the style of Rossetti's medievalist watercolours of the 1850s, in four exquisitely detailed illuminated manuscript pages (1890). She returned to the subject matter again in 1910, when she decorated the Robert-Lorimer designed piano case for Frank Tennant of Lympne Castle, Kent with a scene from 'Willowwood' above the keyboard, scenes from the Old Testament 'Song of Songs' around the sides, and a lid with a tree of life on one side and Psyche's encounter with the god Pan during her quest to win back the love of Cupid. The 'Willowwood' section, much like the earlier manuscripts, takes great influence from Rossetti's works of the 1850s, particularly his depictions of scenes relating to the work of the poet Dante Alighieri (1265–1361), the writer who, with his central theme of Amore (Dante's transcendent love for Beatrice), influenced Rossetti's work more than any other. Although it is clear that Dante had not read Plato's dialogues on love, it is known that he had read a Latin translation of the philosopher's dialogue *Timaeus* (c. 360 BC), a work which outlines the idea of an eternal world of 'perfect forms' of which the physical world is only a flawed echo.[8] The whole universe, both flawed and perfect, is a living creature as well as the creation of a divine craftsman or demiurge.[9] It seems clear that this Platonic idea of a world of ideal forms was, at least in part, influential on Dante's concept of an idealized 'Amore', and was therefore a significant inspiration for the work of both Rossetti and of Traquair and their notions of perfect love.[10] Here, again, we see the idea of the human soul journeying and/or evolving through the power of love, an idea which had itself evolved through time – from the classical Greek dialogues of Plato, and their echoes in the medieval poetry of Dante, through the Renaissance humanism of figures like Marsilio Ficino, filtered through the Dante-inflected poetry, and art of Rossetti and the Renaissance-revival writings of Pater, finally to the designs of Traquair where they are assimilated with her own mysticism. All complex strata of human layered though the cultural and material history of humanity.

Conclusion – Traquair and syncretism

Of all the great debates of the mid-to-late nineteenth century, perhaps the debates over time and their implications for the cosmos, planet, society and individual were among the most controversial and potentially seismic. Phoebe Anna Traquair was certainly not alone among designers, artists and writers trying to draw on various historical ideas, philosophies, beliefs and art forms to attempt to make sense of the tumult. However, Traquair's work offers some of the first real attempts to create, and then use, a language of design in order to reconcile these seemingly irreconcilable paradigms. In doing so she draws on the histories of ideas, mythology and art to create new myths for a new world, combining her mix of cosmic and personal vision with love as a spiritual as well as a social and erotic force.

Traquair's *Willowwood Piano*, among other works that bring together diverse spiritual and intellectual paradigms, can also be seen to function as an object that

Figure 2.4 Phoebe Anna Traquair, 'Psyche Meets Pan' (detail) *Willowwood Piano*, 1910. © National Museums Scotland.

embodies her approach to time, that is, her attempts to design syncretic themes to reconcile the conflicting discourses of time and meaning tied up in science, history, myth and religion (Figure 2.4). The piano designs bring together the Old Testament Song of Songs, a book about desire that blurs the boundaries between erotic love and longing for the Divine; the story of Psyche meeting Pan while on her seemingly impossible quest to win back Cupid; and Rossetti's lover on his quest for unobtainable lost love in the otherworldly *Willowwood*. These three seemingly disparate elements of Greek myth, Old Testament and nineteenth-century Pre-Raphaelite myth-making are tied together with the Tree of Life, on the top side of the piano lid. With that tree, abundant with the fruits of Creation, Traquair makes clear her belief that science, myth and scripture ultimately branch from the same roots, and those roots are love. As Traquair herself wrote in 1893: 'Perfect harmony, is that not what we all strive after? Seek deeply and is it not perfect, union with the Divine.'[11]

Notes

1. W. B. Yeats to Lady Gregory, London, 13 June 1906, in J. Kelly and R. Schuchard (eds), *The Collected Letters of W. B. Yeats*, Vol. IV, 1905–1907 (Oxford: Oxford University Press, 2005), 417–18.

2. The classic Marxist historical account of the changing nature of time in the nineteenth century is E. P. Thompson (1967), 'Time, Work-Discipline, and Industrial Capitalism', *Past & Present* 38: 56–97.

3. J. Conlin, *Evolution and the Victorians – Science Culture and Politics In Darwin's Britain* (London: Bloomsbury, 2014), 4.

4. All of the objects by Phoebe Anna Traquair that are discussed in this chapter are in the collections of National Museums Scotland, unless stated otherwise. They can be viewed online at https://www.nms.ac.uk/explore-our-collections/search-our-collections/.

5. W. Pater, *Marius the Epicurean: His Sensations and Ideas*, Vol. II (London: Macmillan, 1895), 244.

6. E. Cumming (1993), *Phoebe Anna Traquair* (Edinburgh: National Galleries of Scotland, 1993), 199, 65–6, Cat. 38.

7. J. McGann, *Dante Gabriel Rossetti and the Game that Must be Lost* (New Haven, CT: Yale University Press, 2000).

8. Beatrice explicitly refers to Plato's *Timaeus* in *Paradiso 4*. See T. Barolini (ed.), *Digital Dante*, Columbia University Libraries, https://digitaldante.columbia.edu/dante/divine-comedy/paradiso/paradiso-4/ (accessed 5 February 2018).

9. Crane, Gregory (ed. and trans.), Plato, *Timaeus*, 28a–30d, *Perseus Library*, Tufts University. http://www.perseus.tufts.edu/hopper/text?doc=Perseus%3Atext%3A1999.01.0180%3Atext%3DTim.%3Asection%3D30d (accessed 3 February 2018).

10. J. S. Black and P. A. Traquair, *Dante, Notes and Illustrations* (Edinburgh: Privately printed by T. & A. Constable, 1890).

11. Cumming, *Phoebe Anna Traquair*, 28.

3   Time aboard the Ghan: Alice Springs to Adelaide, March 2016

DR ANNE BURKE

I arrived early at the station, instinctively bypassing the canapés and drinks before checking in my luggage and heading out on to the platform where the Ghan lay waiting. Glinting in the sun, it stretched a full kilometre in length, and was topped by twin red locomotive engines ready to head south. It was shortly before midday, and hot. Other passengers were already milling around, and set up centre stage was an Aboriginal guitarist playing against the backdrop of a huge landscape photograph of the red desert, branded in one corner with the Ghan logo. I wondered how I knew his presence was tokenistic – what it might all be like if it wasn't. On a raised rock-like plinth in front of the guitarist and facing the train was the sculpture of a proud camel and its bare-chested rider, a tribute to the Ghan's namesake, the so-called Afghani but, more often than not, Pakistani cameleers, who had serviced the development of the route north from the 1870s onwards. Keeping pace with the slow building of the railway, they gradually shifted their tin mosques and homes, 'Ghan towns', to the next railhead, until, by the 1920s, they were finally displaced by both road and rail. In Alice Springs, palm trees grown from tossed-aside date stones still offer a culinary reminder of the cameleers, marking the spot where their Ghan town once stood.

Here, in this busy departure scene, were subtle indications of time and design interacting in the corporate management of the experience of travelling the Ghan: its pitch for luxury travel, the assertion of historical time and space in contrast with the modernity of the train, the continuity of Ghan rhetoric with its expansionist, colonial roots. As with the general hubbub on the platform, all of these elements are in continual interplay, symptomatic less of a strategic position than the kinds of assumptions that underpin, in the main, postcolonial Australian identity.

It took one hundred and twenty-four years for the railway to fully extend north across the continent, from Adelaide to Darwin: it was only in 2004 that the tracks for the whole route were finally laid and the first complete crossing made. From 1924 onwards, the Old Ghan, or the Ghan Express, had plied back and forth between Adelaide and Alice Springs, and for a short time a railway had existed between Darwin and the town of Katherine, before the cyclone of 1974 finally forced its demise. In the intervening years, countless commissions and feasibility studies were carried out, but it was not until the millennium that faith in the economic viability of the route for purposes of freight finally motivated its completion. With the road and the airways providing relatively cheap and fast travel, any sense of the Ghan functioning as a passenger service for commuters or local travellers has long gone: what is on offer instead is a high-end luxury holiday, a 'journey beyond', as Great Southern Rail's slogan has it, calling up all the tropes of a quintessentially Australian experience:

> Being spirited across one of the world's most ancient landscapes in absolute luxury is an adventure in itself, but what lies beyond the train is very much a part of this epic journey. It is here, in this glorious untamed outback where you will gain a very real sense of the spiritual connection Indigenous Australians have for the land, as well as an understanding of the awe it was held in by early explorers. (Great Southern Rail: 'Journey Beyond, Australia's Great Train Holidays', April 2016 – March 2017)

At the time I travelled, three levels of fare were available: platinum, gold and red – short for 'red-eye', a reference to the embodiment of time that the cheapest level of travel highlights. I met someone in Darwin who had come the other way and complained of his swollen feet, for, while there were ample fully reclining seats, there were no footrests, not at least without improvization. The red service has since been discontinued altogether, but the difference in fares at the time (red a quarter of the price of gold; and gold two-thirds of the price of platinum – 'the ultimate in transcontinental rail travel') corresponded to levels of service, from the size and luxuriance of the cabins to the inclusivity of excursions and refreshments, hence the canapés and drinks at Alice, to say nothing of footrests. Each service level (the term 'class' is not used) had its own dedicated lounge and dining area: the exclusive Platinum Club for the ultimate experience; the Queen Adelaide Restaurant and Outback Explorer Lounge for gold service; and the Matilda Café for red. There was just one accommodation carriage for the red service and it was located right at the front of the train, sandwiched between the baggage carriage and the Matilda Café, beyond which the rest of the train was strictly out of bounds (Figure 3.1).

As I boarded the train, a guard ticked my name off a list firmly fixed to a clipboard. He was wearing what I later read in the on-board magazine, *Platform*, was the new crew uniform, complete with Akubra, good quality, short-sleeved cotton, striped shirt and dark slacks. Designed by Julie Grbac, tasked with meeting the needs of the working crew as well as Great Southern Rail's appeal to the iconic, the collection was inspired by R. M. Williams, a brand associated with functional but classic clothing emerging from the heart of the outback: nothing could be more Australian, as Grbac suggests. Seats were allocated, and when I found mine I panicked as it was strategically positioned at the point right between the long picture windows, with no direct view out. It had been something of a logistical feat to be able to join the Ghan at Alice, including specifically flying in to Darwin and making a twenty-two-hour journey by Greyhound bus from there, so this set me back. I asked the guard if I could swap to one of the empty seats. He said no. Thus, even before the train pulled off, I had set myself up in the pistachio green, American diner-styled Matilda Café, dizzy at the

Figure 3.1 View from the Ghan. Anne Burke, 2016.

prospect of so many empty tables to choose from, trying out a few seats on either side of the carriage, folding the tables away and then back down again. I went to collect some things from my own seat, just in time to catch the tail end of a briefing on what was and wasn't permitted on route to Adelaide: eating our own food was fine, but please, no throwing dregs down the toilet, lest they block; and absolutely no entry beyond the Matilda Café. In the middle of the night we would be stopping for a star-gazing break at the Manguri rail siding where we could get off and stretch our legs. We would see a bonfire way down the other end of the train, but we were not to approach it, please, nor were we to walk beyond our designated stretch of the train. I was waiting for a handout but there wasn't one.

Riding the train through Alice, running alongside the Stuart Highway and the Todd River, horn belting as we passed through Heavitree gap, was the liveliest part of the journey; a momentary flurry of activity before the town gives way to relentless desert outback, with observable, recognizable features in the landscape few and far between. I had gone on a walking tour in Alice with the historian Linda of Foot Falcons. We sat down in the middle of the Todd, or the Lhere Mparntwe as known by the Arrente people, while she read me a poem and told me what it was like on the rare occasions the river had water, and about the annual Henley-on-Todd regatta, which uses bottomless boats in a running race along the dry river bed. Robyn, a water expert working at the time for the Centre for Appropriate Technology had told me that these were ancient rivers carved out by water routes in place long before the mountain ranges had formed. From the train, I could see small groups of Aboriginal people sitting here and there in cool spots among the trees and bushes that lined the edges of the river bed. Traffic queues formed along all the intersections with the rail track; I watched someone throw garbage out of their truck window. We passed the Aboriginal hostel on the edge of town and the turning out to the Ilparpa Claypans, a series of water pools on a plateau at the edge of the south MacDonnell range where Robyn had taken me, another sacred place for the Arrente custodians. It was all about water here: over the Easter weekend we had driven 160 km to bathe in a creek and sip tea made in a billy-can.

After Alice, it would be at least another eighteen hours – dawn at Port Augusta – before we would see familiar signs of industry and habitation. An announcement was made, soon after leaving, regarding a time change: 'Ladies and gentlemen, the time in Adelaide and aboard the Ghan is now 2.07.' We had crossed no border and were still in the Northern Territory, a few hours yet from South Australia, but were already coordinating time with our journey's end: unconnected to the space we were passing through, we were essentially now in railway time, a capsule or pod of Adelaide. Always seemingly arbitrary, the timing of this adjustment of clock time with our entry into the 'outback' suggested that there was nothing here to keep pace with, an oblique reference to a sense of the land as empty, consistent with the concept of terra nullius, used to justify the colonization of Australia.

From the mid-1840s onwards, the southern colonies of Victoria and South Australia were in a race to find and colonize what they assumed would be fertile land in Central Australia, allowing them to extend their territories, and so their wealth and power. The land had been circumnavigated already, with slight inroads made in the northern regions, but the centre remained unknown. In 1862, the Scotsman John McDouall Stuart became the first explorer to establish a route all the way up to the north coast. A surveyor by trade, he had arrived in 1839 aged 23, just three years after the colony of South Australia had been formed, cutting his expeditionary teeth as an underpaid draftsman on Captain Charles Sturt's 1844 quest to find the inland sea. By 1858, he was leading the first of what would be six expeditions, financed primarily by wealthy entrepreneurs in competition with the colonial administrations, culminating in his eventual success in being the first to forge a route all the way north. In contrast with the more encumbered expeditions of Sturt and the legendary figures Burke and Wills, Stuart was single-minded in approach, increasingly minimalist and hardened, relying on few people, scant supplies and total control of his team. On one of his later expeditions, he did issue a list of rules and regulations, including no journal writing, for this would entail the production of precious knowledge that could undo his own later claims. Stuart kept meticulous records himself at the end of each day; they were so accurate that the men laying the telegraph lines ten years later were able to work directly from his notes.

I had stayed in a motel right at the start of Stuart's Highway when I was in Darwin, the consequence of last-minute planning on my part. I had booked online, choosing the place on account of it being midway between the town and the beach, the best of both worlds, or so I thought. It was Smithie, the taxi driver, who broke it to me that the beach was frequented by crocodiles and loners and that being even a twenty-minute walk from the town centre was hard work in the heat. The only redeeming feature of the location was the romance of looking down a highway I knew led all the way to Adelaide. It was also what made a certain book catch my eye in the Northern Territory Art Gallery shop: *Mr Stuart's Tracks: The Forgotten Life of Australia's Greatest Explorer*, a biography by John Bailey. I felt connected to Stuart somehow and was quickly gripped by Bailey's accounts of his forays north, which I continued to read as I slowly made my way south, first along his highway to Alice, where in book time I think Stuart and I crossed paths, and then on to Adelaide on the Ghan. By that time I was recognizing the people after whom he had named significant features in the landscape: the McDonnell Ranges, Chamber's Pillar, Finke River. Richard McDonnell was the governor general of South Australia in 1860, the year Stuart reached the mountain range, and John Chambers and William Finke were the entrepreneurs who had financed his trips.

They say that between expeditions Stuart drank himself into oblivion, a sure way to cope with the various illnesses and diseases he had contracted. By the time I arrived in Adelaide, I had discovered that, despite his enormous achievements, he had not been able to sustain a living in Australia and had gone back, penniless and sick, to a sister in London, where he died at the age of 50. While his remains lie buried in Kensal Rise cemetery, his memory is etched into the cartography of recent Australia, through the names he attributed to features as well as through features named after him: in addition to the highway, Alice Springs was initially known as Stuart's Town, before it took up the name of Alice, who was married to Charles Todd, the man who oversaw the laying of the telegraph line on the back of Stuart's carefully noted tracks.

The decision to build the railway across Australia came in 1877, not long after these successful endeavours. The heat and the dryness of the land made it exceedingly difficult to traverse, but of course it was not 'empty'. Stuart's diaries record his encounters with the Aboriginal people, and an increasing body of literature now documents the early stages of colonialism from the Aboriginal perspective. In the first chapter of *The Songlines*, written in 1987, before the railway extended north from Alice, Bruce Chatwin introduces us to Arkady, the attractive 'timeless bushwalker' of Russian descent, who became his guide and social conduit to the Aboriginal communities around Alice. In Chatwin's account, Arkady was employed by the chief railway engineer to liaise with 'traditional landowners' in the identification of sacred sites along the proposed route north to Katherine and Darwin beyond.

Back on the Ghan I was transfixed; I could not peel my eyes from the land, constantly scouring it in an attempt to take it in, searching for recognizable features, like looking for dolphins, or whales, at sea: some cattle, a series of watering holes, outcrops of irregular rock, trees – desert oak and eucalyptus, tumbleweed, acacia bushes and always dusty reddish-brown earth; and etched on all I could see was some element of the Ghan itself – a reflection of a window blind, or a light, or its shadow even – to remind me of where I was looking from, what it was that framed this particular viewing experience. There was nothing uniform about the landscape, but its endlessness was mesmerizing in itself and it made my eyes sting. I thought of the coach driver on the trip to Uluru that I had taken, five hours each way – the longest day trip on earth, he called it; at school he had been chided for staring out of the window all day – you won't earn a living like that, his teacher said, but he had proved her wrong. After a while, an announcement: in ten minutes time we would be crossing the Finke River; I braced myself, didn't want to miss it. This was the Larapinta, as it had been known since long before Stuart was wandering these parts. It was dry and wide and sandy, but densely tree-lined all the way. What Robyn had said was true: like the growth of desert plants beneath the ground, not above, the water-course runs beneath the river bed, not the other way round.

A few hours later, another announcement would similarly serve to punctuate time and space. In five minutes time, on the left hand side of the train we would see the *Iron Man* sculpture created in 1980 by the rail workers marking the laying of the one-millionth concrete sleeper on this new standard gauge track, the one that we were now hurtling along (Figure 3.2). An ungainly testament to the monotony of labour, the relentless materiality of time marked out sleeper by sleeper, the *Iron Man*'s elongated body is made out of train track with what looked like an animal skull for its head. Later came the third and final announcement from the tannoy, telling us that in five minutes time, ladies and gentlemen, we would be crossing the border into South Australia, which we could see marked again, on the left hand side of the train. We were traversing an ancient land and the only points of reference attested, directly or obliquely, to the colonial, expansionist period. The Ghan promotional material had promised more of an insight into its secrets, but any closer encounter with the Aboriginal experience was, it seemed, packaged around optional excursions

Figure 3.2 The *Iron Man*. Anne Burke, 2016.

for premium and gold service passengers into the red country, namely to Uluru. I was reminded of the guitarist at Alice with his backdrop, but also of James Northfield's travel poster for the Ghan's east-west counterpart, the Indian Pacific, where the black man similarly stands in for the land: clad in a thong with spear in hand, he looks up in awe at the train as it speeds past against a starlit sky, the evocation of progress and modernity cutting right through the old markers of time, reaffirmed by the slogan 'Save days – by the Trans-Australian Railway'; and in the corner of the poster, an insert of a plushly furnished dining car.

The good thing about travelling on the red service was that the rail manager, Bruce, took his breaks in the Matilda Café and fed us bits of information about the train and its history. It turns out that Great Southern Rail rents the Tarcoola–Darwin section of the track as well as the locomotives from the owners Genesee & Wyoming, an American company, so that the drivers are with Pacific National, not Great Southern Railways like the rest of the crew. The original Ghan trains were all made in Britain, but when they built the new standard gauge route 200 km east of the old route, all the old trains were sent to Tasmania, where they still use narrow gauge. I wanted to ask more about the owners, but at the mention of gauges the conversation got hijacked. Apart from a shared fascination among the passengers with where we were, the conversation inevitably reverted to stories of previous train journeys. Trundling towards sunset across the Central Australian desert, in a 1950s American-style diner car, everything from the Orient Express to journeying across the Bolivian altiplano or the Russian steppes was invoked. In this sense, every train journey seems to reference another, defined by both its own particularities and its continuities with the wider railway community.

In Melbourne, I happened upon a video work *Phantom Ride*, by Daniel Crooks, that seemed to speak directly, and eloquently, to this wider referencing process. The train is a recurring feature of Crooks's work, and this piece focuses on the tracking device central to cinematic time and its literal connection with the train track. It's a composite piece, made up of extracts filmed along disused train tracks in South Australia, in sidings, tunnels and in the open landscape. The camera position adopts that of the front of the train, gliding through the collaged landscape at a uniform speed, moving always towards a distant portal, an insert of a new frame that gradually increases in size, the closer we get, until it envelopes the full screen, absorbing us into this new section of track. Mirror-like, there is never a clear point without a portal in the distance and each portal contains a smaller portal within it, like a mirror within a mirror within a mirror (Figure 3.3).

Knowing I was English, Bruce came and told me later that Ronnie Corbett had died – we lamented, and I managed to get a bit more out of him about the scheduling of the train, which was determined by Genesee Wyoming, not the Ghan – the Ghan was small fry; this route was all about freight and the stop at Manguri siding was actually to allow a freight train to pass; the Ghan was piggybacking on this by turning it into a feature of the journey, a stargazing stop. By the time we reached Manguri, there was a good sense of solidarity at the red end of the train – we were enjoying

Figure 3.3 *Phantom Ride*, Daniel Crooks, 2016. Courtesy the artist, Anna Schwartz Gallery, Melbourne and Starkwhite, Auckland.

ourselves and wondered why anyone would pay more than we had to take this route. It turned out that a bonfire had been put on for us after all, a small one, at our end of the train, almost reducing the temptation to walk back down the track to the larger one at the other end; almost, but not quite.

I slipped into the darkness and walked the length of the train, catching glimpses of the insides of the cabins, the dining cars. They were serving champagne and truffles by the bonfire and I listened in to the night sky talk given by one of the train hostesses; a little laser torch she was using to pick out the constellations stopped working half way through but she got to Orion's belt, the pan, the Southern Cross and the brightest planet, Jupiter. She was explaining how long it would take her laser light to reach the star she pointed to and then how long its light in turn had taken to reach us. I couldn't keep up with the calculations – I was still distracted by her laser light, and the only note in my book reads – 60 zillion years? 12 zeros? Whatever the mathematics, this was another pointer to time, a way of making sense of the vast expanse before us.

She ended by drawing on another, contrasting approach, recounting an apparently indigenous Australian story – although with no mention of whose people or where it came from – about the moon and its cycles. There was a man who kept eating so much and getting so fat that his wife would get angry and chop bits off him, and then he would come back and start eating again, and so the cycle would continue. She laughed the story off, saying she thought it was grounds enough for divorce. It wasn't even a moonlit night, but she had done her bit, the gesture to another primordial way of thinking had been made, however authentic or lacking in context it may have been. I wandered back to the front of the train, reminded of a journey I made one Christmas, on the River Paraguay, when also I was travelling third class, in

Figure 3.4 Near Port Augusta. Anne Burke, 2016.

a hammock slung from the open deck of a river boat, where the Guarani people were similarly used to serve the function of tourist entertainment, but that's another story.

With darkness came respite for my eyes at last; I could close them, free from the task of absorbing all that was seeable in this strange landscape. I woke with the sunrise just north of Port Augusta, the Flinders Range visible in the east (Figure 3.4). Soon came the telltale signs of life at the margins of something recognizably urban: farmyards hoarding broken-down cars, graffiti-tagged freight trains, then gradually dwellings and so on. In the Matilda Café, Bruce was pointing out where his house was, way over there on the other side of the salt flats – it would be a few hours yet before he arrived home. Two more announcements were made – one reaching us red-eyed passengers mistakenly, inviting us to tune in to the information channel on our headphones if we wanted to learn more about where we were passing through; but at our seats we had no headphones. The final announcement stated quite simply, 'Ladies and gentlemen, the scheduled time for arrival in Adelaide is a quarter to one.' We were running an hour and fifteen minutes behind schedule, but that was nothing for a journey of just under 1,500 miles and no one seemed to care.

Before disembarking, Bruce gave me permission to see what lay beyond the Matilda Café. I walked the length of the train, on the inside this time, trying out a few of the lounge seats for comfort and peering into cabins while crew members stripped the beds, folding them back into ottomans (Figure 3.5). After so many hours on the train, I decided to walk to where I was staying in Adelaide, the other side of the city parks, but when I got there I found I had left my glasses on board. On my way back again a car tooted its horn – it was Bruce, finally on his way home. The station had

Figure 3.5 Twin cabin on the Ghan. Anne Burke, 2016.

an air of abandon about it when I arrived, with only a few straggling passengers remaining. My reading glasses had been found and, along with them, a bag full of 'sunnies' also left behind – there must have been fifty or so pairs, all makes and sizes. The guard asked me if I wanted some. I didn't, but it made me think of all those eyes, all that looking.

References

Bailey, J. *Mr Stuart's Track: The Forgotten Life of Australia's Greatest Explorer*, Sydney: Pan Macmillan Australia, 2007.

Chatwin, B. *The Songlines*, London: Pan 1988.

Choi, T. Y. 'The Railway Guide's Experiments in Cartography: Narrative, Information, Advertising', *Victorian Studies*, 57, no. 2 (2015): 251–84.

Clark, I. D., and F. Cahir (eds). *The Aboriginal Story of Burke and Wills: Forgotten Narratives*, Collingwood, Victoria: CSIRO Publishing, 2013.

Crooks, D. *Phantom Ride* [video], 2016, https://www.youtube.com/watch?v=4FrOoxz71Zg (accessed 21 January 2018).

Grady, I., and D. Fuchs. *The Ghan: Australia's Grand Rail Journey*, London, Sydney and Auckland: New Holland, 2015.

Great Southern Rail, 'Australia's Great Train Holidays', April 2016–March 2017, [Travel brochure], n.p., n.d.

Great Southern Rail, 'Putting Our Best Foot Forward', *Platform* 35 (Summer/Autumn 2016): 10–13.

Great Southern Rail, 'Great Southern Rail Uniform Launch', 1 February 2016, https://www. youtube.com/watch?v=M2Ge8yghwCs&feature=youtu.be.

Jones, P. G., A. Kenny and South Australian Museum. *Australia's Muslim Cameleers: Pioneers of the Inland, 1860s-1930s*, Kent Town, South Australia: Wakefield Press, 2010.

Northfield, J., and M. Hetherington. *James Northfield and the Art of Selling Australia*, Canberra: National Library of Australia, 2006.

Ryan. S. 'Sublime Utility: Early Tourism Propaganda and the Cairns-Kuranda Railway', *Journal of Australian Studies*, 29, no., 86 (2005): 37–45.

Schivelbusch, W. *The Railway Journey: The Industrialization of Time and Space in the Nineteenth Century*, Oakland: University of California Press, 2014.

Sterk, G. *The Ghan Memorial* [Sculpture], 1980, Alice Springs Railway Station, http://monumentaustralia.org.au/themes/technology/industry/display/80046-the-ghan-memorial (accessed 21 January 2018).

Stokes, E. *To the Inland Sea: Charles Sturt's Expedition 1844–45*, Melbourne: Hutchinson of Australia, 1986.

Section 2
Centuries, Decades, Years

Chapters in this section consider 'the archive' as the physical embodiment of (official) memory and look at the ways in which the nature of the archive is changing in the digital age, prompting us to consider how notion of 'network time' might influence our practice as historians. The collective memory-making implied by the formation of the 'archive' is a political act: deciding what to keep and how to organize it has a direct relevance for both design historians of the future and design practitioners of the present.

Here we touch on the ways in which structures of time are in some way related to structures of power. That the notion that 'time' is a construct and can therefore be interrogated is perhaps particularly pertinent to discussion of design in relation to national identity. As Fallan and Lees Maffei have noted, scholars such as Ernest Gellner, Benedict Anderson and Eric Hobsbawm 'sought to dismantle the idea of the nation as natural or inevitable', arguing instead for nations as constructs, 'the results of concerted engagements in the invention of tradition (Hobsbawm and Ranger 1993) and imagined communities (Anderson 1983), albeit with a regrettable emphasis on high culture (Gellner 1983)'.[1] Benedict Anderson argued that the development of the idea of 'homogenous empty time' was necessary for the formation of a sense of national identity.[2] He argued that in the nineteenth century, time became understood to proceed in a linear fashion, in equal and measured units, equally available to all. While subsequent historians have taken issue with Anderson's analysis, it nevertheless provides a useful starting point for discussion, offering a rational, secular and 'modern' framework on which to build a national narrative of progress.

A neglect by some historians of the more 'everyday' aspects of national identity has been criticized by historians such as Tim Edensor, who argues for the need for greater attention to popular culture. He suggests that aside from its spectacular and official aspects, 'national identity is grounded in the everyday, in the mundane details of social interaction, habits, routines and practical knowledge'.[3] For Edensor, notions of time, of national identity and of the design of everyday objects can clearly be seen to intersect. This idea is developed by Jessica Jenkins in her chapter on post-reunification Germany. Jenkins is interested in the ways in which collective memory operates in the former German Democratic Republic (GDR) via the preservation or erasure of key pieces of public art. The designed environment of streets and buildings, Jenkins argues, are part of the political discourse of collective remembering and forgetting. This is something that has a particular kind of resonance for the former East Germany. As Boyer notes:

> In political and cultural discussions of the East, talk of transformation and futurity has been rendered into tropes of stasis and pastness.[4]

The fall of the Berlin Wall symbolized a loss of a particular kind of future that was promised under socialism, hence any discussion of the past, the present and the future is deeply problematic.

Carlos Bártolo explores the Portuguese government's use of an everyday and familiar item, the pottery cock, derived from the nation's peasant culture, to fashion a new symbol of nationhood and modernity. Bártolo argues that the Portuguese cock came to be seen as an embodiment of the nation's morals and virtues, the product of a mythical past, and part of an attempt by the government to erase the present and halt the regular progression of time. Here, an attention to the temporal dimension of design can reveal the way in which ideas about a nation's past, present and future are wrapped up within the design of one familiar and apparently inconsequential object.

In his chapter on High and Over, the house designed by Amyas Connell for Bernard Ashmole, Michael Findlay draws attention to ways in which time can be seen to fold in on itself in our reading of this one architectural example. Findlay's suggestion is not simply that Connell drew on the work of Piranesi and of other evidence of Roman architecture in his design of High and Over. Instead, he draws attention to the deep connections between modernist architecture and the classical world, and to High and Over's complex relationships with past, present and future as a consequence. Here we have another echo across time, since the work of Giovanni Battista Piranesi was discussed by Seher Erdoğan Ford in Chapter 1 in relation to historical practices of architectural depiction.

Emily Candela's chapter points to the recent phenomenon of the online auction site eBay, which enables users to buy and sell objects, thereby turning unwanted items into desirable collectibles. Candela prompts us to consider how design historians might deal with the assumptions about time and timelessness embodied in notions of so-called retro-designed objects. Her discussion centres on the 'atomic' ball-and-rod furniture that characterized the mid-twentieth century's faith in scientific progress and the nuclear age. These magazine racks and coffee tables were regarded as low-status objects at the time, yet now seem to have gone through a transition process from what Michael Thompson termed 'rubbish' to the category of 'durable', meaning recognized as increasing in value.[5] Perhaps more than a discussion of retro, however, Candela's contribution draws attention to the ways in which eBay acts as an unofficial 'museum' or 'archive', in counterpoint to the official classification systems with which we are familiar. On the one hand, historians such as Raphael Samuel might have applauded eBay's ability to act as a repository of popular memory and popular history-making.[6] Yet, Candela's point is that eBay's users are in a sense its subjects rather than the reverse, and that this has implications for researchers, requiring us to reconsider the ways in which we conceptualize both the future and our engagement with the past.[7]

Discussion of the archive leads us to John Potvin's chapter on the queer archive, and a consideration of the notion of chrononormativity. Potvin argues that the inclusion of queer theories into the practice of design history is long overdue, and in one sense his contribution is a call to arms. But the relevance of his argument to the theme of time is much more than one of 'timeliness': design history, he suggests, continues to be based on heteronormative assumptions about time and our relationship with the designed world. Once again we are reminded that 'time' is not neutral or inevitable but is a socially constructed metaphor, albeit one that has become so all-encompassing that we frequently overlook it.[8] Potvin draws on the work of Elizabeth Freeman, who argues that 'queer time' subverts the dominant notion of time and history that assumes a consequential narrative. 'Heteronormative time' assumes that individuals' lifetimes are structured around the goals of heterosexual marriage and the production of children; these assumptions have become so pervasive that they underpin many aspects of society including healthcare, gender roles and – importantly in this context – our relationship to both past and future. Freeman's preference would be 'to elaborate ways of living aslant to dominant forms of object-choice, coupledom, family, marriage, sociability and self-presentation, and, thus, out of sync with state-sponsored narratives of belonging and becoming'.[9] Just as women's domestic labour exists in opposition to the rigidly commodified notion of factory time, so queer temporalities also offer a place of resistance to dominant temporalities. There are clear implications here for design historians, as Potvin demonstrates.

Notes

1. Kjetil Fallan and Grace Lees-Maffei, *Designing Worlds: National Design Histories in an Age of Globalization* (New York: Berghahn Books, 2016), 3.
2. Benedict Anderson, *Imagined Communities: Reflections on the Origin and Spread of Nationalism* (London: Verso, 2016).
3. Tim Edensor, *National Identity, Popular Culture and Everyday Life* (Oxford: Berg, 2002).
4. Dominic Boyer, 'Ostalige and the Politics of the Future in Eastern Germany', *Neoliberal Historicities* 18, no. 2 (2006): 361.
5. Michael Thompson, 'The Filth in the Way', in Susan Pearce (ed.), *Interpreting Objects and Collections* (Routledge, 1995), 269–78.
6. Raphael Samuel, *Theatres of Memory: Past and Present in Contemporary Culture* (London: Verso, 1994).

7. Marquard Smith, 'Theses on the Philosophy of History: The Work of Research in the Age of Digital Searchability and Distributability', *Journal of Visual Culture* 12, no. 3 (2013): 375–403, doi:10.1177/1470412913507505.

8. Barbara Adam, *Timewatch: The Social Analysis of Time* (Cambridge: Polity Press, 1995), 91.

9. Elizabeth Freeman, *Time Binds: Queer Temporalities, Queer Histories* (Durham: Duke University Press, 2010), xv.

4 As Good as Apple Pie? Post-Unification Germany and the Reception of Public Art from the Former German Democratic Republic

DR JESSICA JENKINS

In March 2011, a local councillor in the town of Plauen, situated in the former East Germany, was invited to inspect a freshly renovated primary school. Dismayed to discover a socialist-era mosaic on display, he asked:

> Does the town administration believe, that it serves the basic free and democratic educational mission of the school to put on show symbols of a totalitarian organisation and state without commentary?[1]

The mosaic in question depicts a narrative typical of mid-1960s socialist realism in the German Democratic Republic (GDR). In a sequential narrative from the reconstruction, through agriculture and industry, young pioneers, peace and the Soviet Union, it enters the 1960s with new tropes of space travel and modern communications. The depiction of a young couple wearing track suits and headphones, bending over a radio as well as the astronaut were to demonstrate alignment with achievements in the West. The 'symbols' to which the city councillor alluded were not those of the space race or pop music, but the hammer and sickle, visible on a Soviet flag, and the young pioneer flag.

The local press jumped on the story, pursuing artists and politicians for their opinions; suddenly the artwork required a 'solution'. However, it seemed that no one else saw the mosaic quite in same terms as the councillor. The head teacher of the school said nobody had ever objected to the mural before, and she had been there since 1967. When one of the two artists who created the mural, Lothar Rentsch, was persuaded to give his opinion, he downplayed the significance of the work, saying, 'That was our era. That was the way it was.'[2]

This chapter looks at examples of works of art – statues, sculptures and murals – in public spaces of the GDR and traces the way in which their reception has adapted as the fields of meaning around them have changed. I argue that both the removal and the retention (or in some cases resurrection) of works of art and design in public spaces have served the need to project a national consensus on the GDR's past. My premise is that the federally sponsored project of 'working through' or *Aufarbeitung* of the GDR's past is better understood as 'constructing' the past, and that material culture, including the built environment, has been central to this highly contested project.

The British liberalist historian Timothy Garton Ash claimed that Germany has developed 'the gold standard for dealing with a difficult past'.[3] In stark contrast, one of those engaged with this 'working through', Ilko-Sascha Kowalczuk, claimed in 2016 that *Aufarbeitung* was not only paralyzed but that its failure also helped to explain the resurgence of the extreme right in East Germany.[4] As the project of 'working though' the past sought a wholesale repudiation of the GDR and embrace of a new national identity, this was undoubtedly thrown into crisis by the emergence of 'nostalgia' (*Ostalgie*) for the East in the early 2000s. However, with the increasing temporal distance to the GDR, a greater acceptance of divergent narratives on the GDR is accommodated within establishment public history.

This chapter identifies three phases in the national project of 'working through' the past: first, what I call the 'trashing phase' until the mid to end of the 1990s; second, the 'crisis' of 'nostalgia', predominantly in the 2000s; and third, the approximately post-2010 'adjustment' phase. Through an examination of some cases of works of art in public spaces, we can see how the original remit to wholly repudiate the GDR heritage has been adjusted to accommodate changing economic and social needs. The overarching requirements within the geopolitical and economic context to support capital investment, to develop a public 'heritage' acceptable both internally and externally, and to temper the social, psychological and economic impact of unification in depleted communities has allowed for the rehabilitation of some artists and some works of art in public spaces which were initially discredited.

The term *Aufarbeitung* was given to the six-year-long (1992–1998) government-led official investigation into the 'history and consequences of the Socialist dictatorship in East Germany'.[5] The principal government agency, the Federal Foundation for the Working through of the SED Dictatorship, was set up with legally binding aims to promote public awareness of the 'communist tyranny'.[6] The foundation has an explicit anti-communist positioning as its legal premise. Before any 'reworking' of the past in order to reach 'internal unity' could begin, any favourable attitudes to the GDR or communism more generally were systematically excluded.

The asymmetry of the need to conduct detailed examination of the past of (only) the GDR in order to construct an all-German identity for the present was predicated on the *naturalness* of Germany unity, and the *naturalness* of the West German democratic model for the two merged states. This asymmetry did not go unremarked in the early phase, but dissent had no traction in the seismic changes taking place in the geopolitical order.[7] Political scientist Frank Unger, speaking in 1990, claimed that the myth of reunification was as ingrained in the West German mindset, as indisputably good, as 'motherhood or apple pie'.[8] When East Germany unexpectedly collapsed into the lap of the West, consensus that this could be projected as the natural and correct course of history was pre-programmed.

Whatever the historical inevitability of this outcome, the new Germany was unprepared for the many questions that opened up in the course of the accession of East to West. The early 1990s' period of the 'trashing' of the GDR was fuelled and legitimized by the media, and soon fed into debates around East German literature, art and architecture. The *Bilderstreit* ('dispute about art') stemmed from the establishment view that East German art had no place within the new national culture. This fed only indirectly into assessments of works of art in public spaces because such works were not even perceived to fall within the category of art. On unification, East German art was removed from museums, with prominent GDR artists widely condemned as 'state artists' who, as such, were not artists at all. This denigration reached its lowest point in 1999 at the notorious Aufstieg und Fall der Moderne exhibition in Weimar, where a mass of paintings from East Germany were hung frame against frame, without differentiation against black plastic. One commentator summed it up as a 'Trash-Event'.[9]

Across the towns and residential complexes of the GDR, the process of trashing and reconstruction began immediately after reunification – it was an 'inevitable consequence' of the capital flows, but it was also ideologically motivated. The aforementioned commission for *Aufarbeitung* used ideological and moralizing rhetoric to condemn the architecture and urban design of the GDR as symptoms of a discredited system.[10] The perception of the East German built environment as a disaster best swept away as soon as possible was manifest in the planning discussions. In Dresden, for example, architects agreed in 1990 'to demolish as many buildings as possible from the last forty years, and so to extinguish the past, and to reconstruct the past from the previous era'.[11] Residential areas suffered steep population losses, but the demolition of living complexes was not purely due to economic rationale; as Weizman argues, '"shrinking" [seemed to be] part of a plan to re-appropriate the city by erasing the "unfamiliar" fabric of a competing ideology.'[12]

I have chosen two examples of the way in which this trashing period of the 1990s saw the urgent need to remove and recontextualize works of art in public spaces that were seen by political decision makers as explicit signifiers of the GDR regime. The Lenin statue on the crossroads that was Leninplatz in East Berlin was removed in October 1991 despite vociferous efforts to save it. The monument lost its protected status on the grounds that the statue stood for 'personality cult and subjection to dictatorship'.[13]

Among the initiatives to save GDR monuments was the forum of (West German) Art History Students, who argued in May 1990 that to remove the monuments would be a 'blanket discrediting the historical value of the persons depicted, making their ideological value equal to that of those who commissioned them'.[14] In other words, they wanted to distinguish between the 'ideological value' of Lenin et al. and that of the GDR authorities. This would have implied a shift in the indexicality of the monuments, a shift which had not been implied by calls for their demolition. To remove the monuments was not only to make part of history no longer visible, but it also suggested that icons of Marxism–Leninism had agency in a reunified Germany. The premise was that the monuments were a reminder of a discredited regime rather than that they might act as heroic icons for Berlin citizens. The working group Socialist Monumental Art argued that there was a danger that 'once again, repression will determine historical self-understanding', a reference to a perceived failure to acknowledge the Nazi past.[15] In the same vein, the prominent historian of art and public monuments, Hans Mittig, argued for retaining visible testimony even to the difficult past in order to leave open the possibility of debate.[16] Such arguments failed to convince decision makers of the need to clear the landscape in order to forge a new democratic German identity.

At the time of German unification, the interiors and exterior public spaces of the former East Germany were replete with murals, mosaics, modular structures, ornamental works, tapestries, stained glass, sculptures, fountains and play apparatus.[17] Hundreds of less prominent works of art on and within buildings simply disappeared under the bulldozer, fell into disrepair or were situated in spaces that were abandoned. It was more often the case that works were regarded as culturally and economically 'worthless', and thus not worth saving from the re-modelling required by planners and investors, than politically 'dangerous'. Highly visible and explicitly political works were identified by local authorities in the 1990s as requiring a re-signification in line with the new era, and generally artists were enlisted in this process – evidence of the considerable investment in Germany in the 'soft power' of the arts.

Before its demontage, the Lenin statue was subject to an artist's intervention, even before reunification. In September 1990, artist Krzyszstof Wodiczko projected onto it a photomontage image of a Polish shopper gathering consumer goods. The projection, one of seventeen in East Berlin, costing a reported 1.5 million Deutschmarks, was also not without controversy, and is an early example of the way in which sanctioned artistic interventions created a liminal phase for works during the period of rapid change.[18]

While it is unsurprising that a centrally located statue of Lenin was promptly removed after the fall of the Wall, I would like to turn now to the fate of a mural that was essentially treated as politically equivalent to a statue. Max Lingner's 1953 mural *Aufbau der Republik* (Building the Republic) depicts a joyful socialist realist story of the optimism of youth in the new East Germany. It is positioned at a site in Berlin that was a focal point of the 1953 violent suppression of protests by East German workers, which was to become an important event in the East–West propaganda war. As part of the process of staking out new commemorative moments in the process of reconstructing the past, the site was chosen by the Berlin Senate in 1993 for a new work to commemorate the victims of the uprising (Figures 4.1 and 4.2).

The new work by Wolfgang Rüppel presents a reportage image from the 1953 protests set into the ground and sealed under highly reflective glass. Lingner's mythic 1953 representation, an assertion of the then present and future, was countered in 1993 by a montage of highly rasterized press photographs which seem to show 'what it really looked like' in 1953.

The counter-narrative equates the original work with the kind of 'truth of image' proposed by the mimetic idea of socialist realism and, in doing so, assigns to

Figure 4.1 *Aufbau der Republik* (Building the Republic), painted ceramic mural by Max Lingner (1953) (background) and part of memorial to the events of 17 June 1953 by Wolfgang Rüppel (2000) (foreground), Detlev-Rohwedder-Haus, Berlin. Photo © Jessica Jenkins 2010.

Figure 4.2 *Aufbau der Republik* (Building the Republic), painted ceramic mural by Max Lingner (1953). *Detail*. Photo © Jessica Jenkins 2016.

Lingner's 1953 celebratory piece the agency assumed by socialist realism. Rüppel's 1993 photographic work reasserts the Western lens on the events. If this potentially opens a reflection on the Cold War propaganda war, this reading is deflected by the additional explanatory material at the site, which affirms Rüppel's work as a reply to the propaganda image of 1953. What was intended in the early 1990s in the tradition of commemoration – in the sense of binding memories into a common moment of the present – loses its purpose in its need to reply to Lingner's work. As a result, Rüppel's work marks 1990s' Germany more than it does the Germany of 1953. Rüppel's work may have seemed appropriate at the time but today looks as pedagogical as the Lingner piece.

By the late 1990s, the institutionalized trashing of the GDR and the exclusion of its culture from German history created a crisis for the general process of *Aufarbeitung* in the form of a popular cultural backlash in the form of so-called *Ostalgie*, a neologism of 'East' and 'nostalgia'. It is not possible to recount the many forms and development of *Ostalgie* here, which has in itself spawned a whole field of cultural historical and ethnographic scholarship.[19] However, what had begun as a pop cultural phenomenon of re-enacting East German culture in the late 1990s was identified as having huge commercial potential, and mutated. In the view of leading historians, *Aufarbeitung* was 'thrown back years'.[20] It became clear that *Ostalgie* was more than its commercial exploitation, that it was indicative of a sense of estrangement in the new Germany. In turn, *Ostalgie* became embedded into public discourse as a derogatory term employed to dismiss any favourable memories of the East German past.

'Nostalgia' has a pejorative connotation of a foolishness, which does not well characterize the sense of dislocation which fed a public revival of interest in the East German past. 'Nostalgia' in its etymological origin as a longing for 'home' rather than a longing for 'the past' is a better characterization of the counter-narratives that came as such a shock to the standard bearers of the official *Aufarbeitung*.[21] That material culture and the built environment should emerge as contested territory in remembering the GDR must come as a surprise; it was understood to be the disaffection of most East Germans with the material offerings and decrepit urban spaces of the GDR in the late 1980s which hastened the demise of the socialist state. It was an extraordinary détournement that the designed artefacts of the GDR should take on a compensatory role in the face of a sense of loss. The so hopelessly earnest and inadequate culture, once so laughable – the plasticky goods, the outmoded music, the poor imitations of Western brands, the badly printed graphics, the cheaply built housing, the state commissioned works of art became the object of affectionate memorialization. The effects of the passage of time on all of this *design* could not be more pointed. It is obvious to point out that objects change their signification from one generation to the next, the mundane becoming something affectionately remembered, but in the case of the GDR these attachments seemed counter-rational and contradicted the hegemony of the post-1990 history-writing project.

The school mural story offers an illustration of how counter-narratives disrupted official history-writing. The newspaper framed the discussion around acceptable

Figure 4.3 Bundesarchiv, Bild 183-F0809-0201-001 / CC-BY-SA 3.0 GDR Foreign Ministry Building, Architectural collective of Joseph Kaiser, 1967. Demolished. Photo © Peter Straube, Berlin.

responses. Opinions on the artistic quality of the mosaic were not given in the articles: the debate circled around whether the symbolism was harmful and must be either removed or balanced by means of an explanatory plaque or other educational measure, or redundant and thus harmless; a local artist interviewed vented his anger at his experience of political state patronage of artists. Online, however, the discussion was more wide-ranging – one local citizen framed the media speculation on the mosaic as provocative sensationalism, proposing:

> Everyone will have their own image of this country, [the GDR] and will know of its weaknesses, mistakes and injustice, and will when they look back without prejudice, also remember its good sides.[22]

The 'good as well as bad' feeling about the GDR represents a majority view among former GDR citizens, with opinion polls consistently showing only a small minority saying it was very good or very bad.[23] This is in stark contrast to the 1990s premise of *Aufarbeitung* which was that a wholesale repudiation of everything the GDR stood for was a necessary prerequisite to national unity. By the time of the Plauen school mural commotion in 2011, it was evident that there had not been unequivocal embrace by East Germans of all that the West had to offer, but equally that the GDR as a political entity belonged to the past. With the ideas of communism safely consigned to history, the political establishment could afford to be a little more generous; a limited space was opened up for curated, recontextualized and re-signified works of art in public spaces. Arguably, it was not the mural, but the councillor who was out of step with the times.

In the next examples, we will see how this space that was opened up nonetheless worked to maintain the larger project of national consensus. Works of art have not been revalidated in their original sense or purpose. Instead, value has been extracted from some significant pieces where they can be integrated within acceptable cultural myths, or where they offer commercial heritage value within a clearly delineated space. Further, some works have been repurposed to enhance a sense of local ownership of place, which simultaneously helps to renew economically depleted areas where there is no 'historic' architecture of yore to reinstate.

An acceptable cultural myth, although not immediately recognized as part of the heritage of Eastern Germany, is twentieth-century post-war modernism. The renewal of interest in modernist architecture and design as 'heritage' is not confined to Germany, of course, but recognition of the so-called *Ostmoderne* by the 2000s came, in many cases, too late. The fate of works of the prominent East German artist Walter Womacka provide an interesting case. Womacka's mosaic *Unser Leben* is well known in Berlin due to its scale and prominent position facing Alexanderplatz. The 125-metre frieze wraps around the Haus des Lehrers, a building designed together with the domed congress hall by Hermann Henselmann in 1964. This architecture was significant at the time for its explicit reference to international modernism. After years of neglect and increasing disrepair in the 1990s, the Haus des Lehrers was, by the 2000s, revalued as an icon of modernism, and the frieze, distinctly socialist realist, came under protection.

Before the renovation took place, the building was given over to an artistic intervention in September 2001, a digital-light project called 'blinkenlights', which was a hacking, delocalized discourse of cool. Blinkenlights was a progression from the 1990s light projections in East Berlin, but both of these light events offered up the surfaces of former icons of the GDR cityscape for a liminal moment before their reabsorption into the new mainstream.

Haus des Lehrers and its mural were fully restored in the mid-2000s; the promotional material draws on the building's modernist heritage, but also acknowledges the socialist promise of the 1960s – 'A dazzling vision of the future and a prominent symbol of a new age' in order to promote the prestige of the building as an 'iconic' site for current-day businesses. An extended description of Womacka's frieze describes the ideological intentions, such as: 'These ideals included supporting developing countries to fight for political and economic independence. A key motivation behind this was the mission of bringing socialism into the world.'[24] Such a public effort to present the historical context of the art work helped not only to increase the value of the real estate but also to serve the interest of curious visitors to Berlin. In this case, the mural is privileged due to its coupling with the 'heritage' modernist architecture, and its location in the centre of eastern Berlin.

The fate of another set of three Womacka murals situated in the conference room of the former foreign ministry at the administrative heart of East Berlin demonstrates

Figure 4.4 *'Der Mensch gestaltet seine Welt'* (The Person Creates Their World). Mural by Walter Womacka in the former Ministry for Foreign Affairs of the GDR (murals and building now demolished).

how much had changed since 1995. The *Berliner Zeitung* reported at the time that Womacka's work was destroyed due to a 'lack of interest'. The building, equally an interesting exponent of modernist architecture, by Joseph Kaiser, was described as a 'blunder' and demolished to make way for a restoration of the 'historic' Schinkelplatz.[25] The much more fluid, Picasso-like drawings of Womacka's works *Der Mensch gestaltet seine Welt* were not politically charged, and were less visible, but scant consideration was given to the integrated art works or their potential value (Figures 4.3 and 4.4).

There are several interesting examples where works of art have been repurposed to enhance a sense of local ownership of place, while simultaneously divesting them of their original purpose and political meaning. Among other examples, this is evident in the rhetoric around Lev Kerbel's enormous Karl Marx bust in the centre of Chemnitz, and in the re-signification of Sigbert Fliegel's flame monument in the centre of Halle old town. In the local authority of Berlin Marzahn, selected works of art from the 1980s – none of which are political – have been retained and validated alongside new commissions in residential complexes largely populated by the older generation.

This sense of art as a local identifier of belonging has been most evident where an artist identified with a particular place has been rehabilitated. One of the most important examples is the work of Willi Neubert who, like all prominent GDR artists, was denigrated as a 'state artist' in the 1990s. During this period, his work was removed from public view. Neubert, originally a metalworker from the small steel industry town of Thale, pioneered the use of industrial enamelling for murals; his work, often leaning heavily on modernist form-making, had in the GDR period been installed in prominent locations.

In 2000, the mayor of Thale, Thomas Balcerowski, negotiated the retrieval of a major work which had been put in storage in Suhl for public redisplay in Thale. Balcerowski explained to me that he was determined to honour this 'son of the town'; the works 'created under the political circumstances of the time', were a 'milestone in Thale's earlier [industrial] history'.[26] Here in a town which, like all the former industrial towns of East Germany, suffered huge working-age population losses after unification, the importance of place, historical connection and personal connections to the artist overcame the stigma attached to GDR public art.

Figure 4.5 Willi Neubert, *Kampf um den Sieg des Marxismus Leninismus* (Struggle for the Victory of Marxism Leninism), 1977. Enamel painted on tiles. The work was retrieved from storage in the town of Suhl and transferred to the artist's home town of Thale. Photo © Jessica Jenkins 2010.

Such reinstatements of artists and artwork in a localized context have taken place across the former GDR – while artists have been dismissed as 'state artists' in the national discourse, at a local level opportunities are found to celebrate them, to quietly restore works which give some sense of identification in otherwise depleted landscapes. The story of the school mosaic in Plauen was concluded at least for the time being when the majority vote on the council was against the addition of a plaque to explain the mural. The same arguments were rehearsed – from the residual potency of the symbols to their relative unimportance. When the artist Lothar Rentsch died in May 2017, he was feted in the local press as a wonderful artist, without a mention of the GDR. With the GDR safely consigned to history, it has been possible to absolve some of its artefacts and their makers from their alleged 'complicity'. There is evidence that East German art is beginning to return to the museums today; the status of works of in public spaces is dependent on where they can accommodate the functions of heritage-making and local identification.[27]

As Germany enters its third decade of the post-Wall era, the examples I have shown of rehabilitation of some remaining works of architectural art indicate how the increasing temporal distance to the GDR permits a greater tolerance within mainstream decision-making bodies. While there continues to be controversy at all levels over the interpretation of the GDR, the project of consensus has acknowledged that there were a multitude of experiences of the socialist state. The publicly sponsored history project still set the limits of the acceptable discourse but those limits are broader than in the 1990s phase of *Aufarbeitung*.

Notes

1. Piontkowski Thomas and Reißmann Martin, 'Debatte um Wandbild aus DDR-Zeiten', *Vogtland Anzeiger*, 25 March 2011, http://vogtland-anzeiger.de/Vogtland_Anzeiger/cms-nachrichten/entgegengesetzt/debatte-um-wandbild-aus-ddr-zeiten.html (accessed 25 March 2011).
2. Plauener Künstler hält Debatte für überflüssig', www.spitzenstadt.de, 29 April 2011, https://www.spitzenstadt.de/plauen/1-nachrichten/plauener-kuenstler-haelt-debatte-fuer-ueberfluessig.html (accessed 25 March 2011).
3. Timothy Garton Ash, 'Germany Can Show Reborn Arab Nations the Art of Overcoming a Difficult Past'. *The Guardian*, 16 March 2011, https://www.theguardian.com/commentisfree/2011/mar/16/germany-overcoming-past-arab-dictatorships (accessed 25 March 2011).
4. Kowalczuk, Ilko-Sascha. 'Historikerstreit über DDR-Forschung, Die Aufarbeitung ist gescheitert', 20 April 2016, TAZ, Berlin, http://www.taz.de/!5293270/ (accessed 1 November 2017).
5. 'Enquete Kommission des deutschen Bundestages Aufarbeitung der Geschichte und Folgen der SED- Diktatur in Deutschland', 1992–1998.
6. Die Bundesstiftung zur Aufarbeitung der SED-Diktatur.
7. Konrad H. Jarausch, *The Rush to German Unity* (Oxford: Oxford University Press, 1994).
8. How Do You See Germany? Symposium organized by the BFI/ Goethe Institut, London, 26–27 October 1990. Taken from the author's notes.
9. Hanno Rauterberg, 'Kesseltreiben in Weimar: Aus Bilderstreit wird Bilderkampf: Wie eine Ausstellung den Ost-West-Konflikt schürt.' Zeit Online. 27 May 1999, http://www.zeit.de/1999/22/199922..b7._fortsetzung.xml (accessed 1 November 2017).
10. Tobias Zervosen, 'Denkmalpflege und geschichtspolitischer Diskurs', in Mark Escherich (ed.), *Denkmal Ost-Moderne, Aneignung und Erhaltung des baulichen Erbes der Nachkriegsmoderne* (Stadtentwicklung und Denkmalpflege, Band 16) (Berlin: Jovis, 2012).
11. Meinhard Gerkan (ed.), *West-Östlicher Architektenworkshop zum Gesamtkunstwerk Dresden* (Hamburg: Christians,1990), cited in Tanja Scheffler, 'Dresden. Vom schnellen Scheitern der sozialistischen Städtebaukonzepte. Der Weg zurück zur historischen Stadt', in *Deutschland Archiv* 45, no. 4: 666–80, http://www.bpb.de/geschichte/zeitgeschichte/deutschlandarchiv/147752/dresden-das-scheitern-der-sozialistischen-stadt?p=all.
12. Ines Weizman (2010), 'The Destruction of Participation . . . and of Housing in Leipzig-Grunau', *The Neoliberal Frontline: Urban Struggles in Post-Socialist Societies*, Zagreb, 4 December–7 December 2008, 3 October 2010, https://issuu.com/tiranaworkshop/docs/petrescu (accessed 1 November 2017).

13. CDU Senator Volker Hassemer, October 1991. For a detailed discussion of the 1990s debates on the fate of monuments, see Russel Lemmons, 'Imprisoned, Murdered, Besmirched: The Controversy Concerning Berlin's Ernst Thälmann Monument and German National Identity, 1990–1995'. in Arnold-de Simine Silke (ed.), Memory Traces: 1989 and the Question of German Cultural Identity (Bern: Peter Lang, 2005) 309–34.

14. Resolution, 44. Kunsthistorische StudentInnen, Conference, Berlin, 23–27 May 1990. 'Resolution zum Erhalt der sozialistischen Denkmale im der DDR', in Correspondence to Hermann Raum, Getty Research Institute, DDR Collections, Series XXXIV: Hermann Raum papers, 1945–1992, Box 217, Folder 15. Correspondence, manuscripts & newspaper articles, Socialist Monuments Debate, 1990–1991.

15. Ibid.

16. Hans-Ernst Mittig, 'Zur Eröffnung der Ausstellung', in Erhalten – zerstören – verändern? (Berlin: nGbK: 1990), 8–15. Text to accompany the exhibition: Erhalten – zerstören – verändern? Denkmäler der DDR in Ost-Berlin 11 August–7 September 1990, NGBK, Tempelhofer Ufer 22, Berlin. Mittig's seminal work on this subject was Hans Mittig, Kunst und Alltag im NS-System: Albert Speers Berliner Strassenlaternen (Giessen: Anabas, 1975).

17. See Jessica Jenkins, 'Visual Arts in the Urban Environment in the German Democratic Republic: Formal, Theoretical and Functional Change, 1949–1980', dissertation, Royal College of Art, London, 2014.

18. L. B. 'Monumental' in Sonntag (16 September 1991): 1.

19. Anna Saunders and Debbie Pinfold, Remembering and Rethinking the GDR: Multiple Perspectives and Plural Authenticities (Hampshire: Palgrave MacMillan, 2013) Daphne Berdahl, On the Social Life of Postsocialism: Memory, Consumption, Germany (Bloomington: Indiana University Press, 2010); Maria Todorova, Augusta Dimou and Stefan Troebst (eds), Remembering Communism: Private and Public Recollections of Lived Experience in Southeast Europe (Budapest and New York: Central European University Press, 2014); Jonathan Bach, 'Consuming Communism Material Cultures of Nostalgia in Former East Germany', in Olivia Angé and David Berliner (eds), Anthropology and Nostalgia (New York and Oxford: Berghan, 2014); Jason James, Preservation and National Belonging in Eastern Germany: Heritage Fetishism and Redeeming Germanness (Hampshire and New York: Palgrave Macmillan, 2012).

20. Ulrich Mählert et al. (eds), DDR-Geschichte vermitteln, Ansätze und Erfahrungen in Unterricht, Hochschullehre und politischer Bildung (Berlin: Metropol, 2004), 10.

21. Boyer, 'Ostalige and the Politics of the Future in Eatern Germany'.

22. Reader's comment online to the article cited in Endnote 1.

23. See e.g. statista.com. 'Wie beurteilen Sie rückblickend das Leben in die DDR?' https://de.statista.com/statistik/daten/studie/13027/umfrage/beurteilung-des-lebens-in-der-ddr/ (accessed 1 November 2017).

24. Mosaikfries 'Unser Leben Die berühmte Bauchbinde', https://www.hausdeslehrers.de/geschichte/der-fries/#c1388, WBM Wohnungsbaugesellschaft Berlin-Mitte mbH.

25. Paul Ulrich, 'Wie das alte DDR-Außenministerium ohne Dynamit dem Erdboden gleichgemacht wird Bagger fressen sich durch den Beton'. *Berliner Zeitung*, 5 August 1995, https://www.berliner-zeitung.de/16921296 (accessed 1 November 2017).

26. Letter to the author in response to an enquiry about the retrieval of Neubert's work. Thomas Balcerowski, Mayor of Thale, 8 March 2011.

27. Catherine Hickley, 'East German "Arseholes" Are Reappraised', in *Art Newspaper Review* (February 2018): 6–7.

5 The Story of a Portuguese Cock and Other Knick-Knacks: Heritage, Propaganda and Design in a Far-Right Dictatorship

CARLOS BÁRTOLO

This chapter examines the development of two elements of the Portuguese visual identity: the Barcelos cock and the typically Portuguese decorative rustic style developed in the 1940s. Both examples occurred during the Portuguese dictatorship that lasted almost fifty years (1926–1974) and are the outcome of a more or less direct influence of the aesthetic and ideological policies of a regime that attempted to establish a new national identity. As with other far-right regimes of the interwar period, the Portuguese dictatorship promoted a policy of deep isolationism that opposed corrupting foreign influences – democracy, liberalism, capitalism, socialism, modernity and internationalism in general. In order to promote this nationalist culture, the regime sought in its own history and traditions, elements that would allow it to create a new nation, distinct either from foreign models or from previous national ones, an intention revealed in how it would name itself: *Estado Novo* (New State).

These two examples can thus be read as paradigmatic of the concept of the 'invention of tradition' developed by Hobsbawm and Ranger in 1983.[1] This is implicit in the way they were created from pre-existing elements which, after being moulded and sanitized, would become something autonomous. It is also implicit in the way that, as soon as they were recognized as part of the country's visual identity, a possible link with their point of origin was withdrawn and another mythic past recreated. Here time could be perceived in its most pliable form: both in terms of how from a contemporary moment it is possible to travel back in time to hand-pick stimulus used to ground images of an ideal present and/or future; and how this recreated present, a reaction to modernity, is announced as new and modern, thus severing the connection with the recent past, considered impure and decadent.

Lost in these atemporal realms between reform and reaction, past and present, modern and tradition, some correlations with the theories of fascism developed by Roger Griffin could also be found.[2] According to Griffin, the ideal of national rebirth – starting point common to all these multiple movements – would have been part of the modernist attempt to achieve a new ideal society, a substitute for the decaying present (in patent contrast with the Marxist approach). In these cases, fascism would pursue an alternative modernity that rejected the current one founded, from the eighteenth century onwards, on progressive liberal democratic principles. In trying to define which actors were responsible for the development of these processes of national identity – from the local craftsman to the governmental policy – one should not forget the role that design – or approaches of a proto-design – could have had in these,[3] especially since this period was the one during which design emerged as an autonomous professional and artistic discipline in Portugal, a practice acknowledged officially only in 1960.[4]

A rediscovered nation

As a small country on the edge of Europe, Portugal always suffered influences from more prominent centres of artistic development, be it the adjacent but despised Iberian kingdoms, the blooming Italy and Flanders of the Renaissance, the absolute power of France or the later industrious England. Despite Portugal's distinctive Moorish heritage, the foremost acquaintance of exotic worlds of Africa, Asia and America that occurred during the Portuguese discoveries in the fifteenth and sixteenth centuries,[5] and the occasional development of almost-idiosyncratic decorative styles during prosperous periods, the national disposition usually abided by 'the common error according to which we [the Portuguese] perceive that everything that comes from abroad is better', as stated in 1675 by Duarte Ribeiro de Macedo, the secretary of the Portuguese ambassador to the court of Louis XIV.[6]

Only at the end of the nineteenth century did a nationalistic awareness lead to the appearance of the first ethnographic studies.[7] This movement followed the universal trend of the arts and sciences, itself a consequence of similar developments in the political sphere. For the first time, the Portuguese vernacular material world – the products of the simple peasant – were looked upon and analysed, even if still understood as the mere work of the uneducated. As art critic Ramalho Ortigão notes,

> It is in these free and spontaneous works of the people that more purely and brilliantly the tendencies and artistic dispositions of a race are revealed. The altar jewels made by request of rich orders or blessed kings are subaltern documents. The people are the custodians, the guardians and the cultists of the traditions, style and taste of a country. We maintain that a simple yoke of oxen from Minho or a ewer, like those with which Coimbra's women use to get water from Mondego river, have more artistic character and more ethnological value than the patens and monstrances of King João V all together.[8]

The primitiveness of this production – in its rough purity – would gradually be admired and used as source of inspiration by a thriving generation of Portuguese modernist thinkers and creators. This happened in accordance with the infatuation of the avant-garde generation with the local European folklore, as also with African, Mesoamerican and Oriental arts, all perceived as artistic productions still untainted by civilization.

A naïf cockerel

The story of the Barcelos cock – the colourful glazed clay figure nowadays recognized as a symbol of Portugal – begins roughly at the same time when Amadeo de Souza-Cardoso, Eduardo Viana, Almada de Negreiros and others artists such as Sonia and Robert Delaunay (who briefly lived in Portugal during the Great War) discovered, and were enchanted by, the diversity of colours and shapes of the peasants' artefacts. They were especially attracted to useful ware and colourful toys made by potters from Barcelos, a small town in the north province of Minho.

These colourful toys were hand moulded by the wives and children of the potters, helping to fill up the empty interstices of the kiln. They were sold cheaply at fairs and markets alongside earthenware glazed pans, pots and ewers. Their shapes were inspired by daily life – objects, animals, characters or fantasy creatures – and they usually included a whistle at the base. Children happily, and noisily, played with them until they broke, making them yearn for the next fair. Of this fauna, Rocha Peixoto, one of the earliest ethnographers, wrote:

> However, the cock exceeds in number and variety all other fauna specimens. He's the best accomplished on the magnificence of its posture, on the emphasis of details, or in the care on its modelling. Of the bird's overall impression, this one stands out, with its dominant and virile attributes. Proud and majestic, vigilant and seductive, all the people celebrate it, in tales, superstitions or songs.[9]

Due to their popularity, these small cock whistles were initially made into different shapes, as registered in Rocha Peixoto's studies published in 1900. They steadily developed in size and decorative features until the proud and vigilant pose of a cock almost crowing prevailed above all. Later, probably as a derivation of the technique of making ocarinas or bird water whistles, this figure began to be moulded at the wheel by the potter, with a hollow body that allowed them to reach bigger dimensions.[10] Consequently, they evolved from a simple child's toy to a decorative domestic object, sometimes doubling as a toothpick holder or money box, or a gift offered during courtship. These developments occurred from the end of the nineteenth century to the first decades of the twentieth century. At this time, they were still made by their original creators free of direct external influences. However, this anonymity was about to cease as the Barcelos cock was increasingly noticed throughout the country.

A cosmopolitan cock

In 1931, António Ferro, a writer and journalist associated with the modernist milieu, organized the Fifth International Conference of Dramatic and Musical Critique in Lisbon. It was attended by some figures of the European intellectual elite: Luigi Pirandello, Émile Vuillermoz and Robert Kemp, among others.[11] Following a veiled propaganda agenda, the conference included a journey throughout the country to savour its original and picturesque atmosphere. For one of the conference dinners at Estoril Casino, the art and cinema director Leitão de Barros, one of Ferro's collaborators, created a musical event presenting folkloric music and dance from the north provinces. Preparing the event, Artur Maciel and Leitão de Barros wrote to the painter Manuel Couto Viana:

> Leitão de Barros decided to offer the conference participants, clay figures from the North – Famalicão, Barcelos? He gave me a letter that I annexed to this one . . . I think you know what I mean. It is those decorative figures that one can only buy at county fairs: red and primitive bulls, cocks . . . Acquire those that look more tasteful. Some are large, very curious looking; once Leitão de Barros bought some at the fair of Our Lord of Matosinhos's pilgrimage.
>
> . . .
>
> There should be larger figures, but some small ones too. Of the largest, some time ago I've seen cocks, very large. Buy different models, but tasteful! . . . The figures will decorate the tables and should be offered to the congressmen. The most vivid and variegated colours.[12]

The success of the congress was partly due to the publicity it received in the press, which was in part controlled by Ferro and Barros, who were also the directors of the main illustrated magazines. This was a step towards Ferro's political notability as one of the major cultural agents. Two years later, the far-right dictator of the recently consolidated Estado Novo regime, Prime Minister Antonio Oliveira Salazar, appointed him as the director of the Secretariado de Propaganda Nacional-SPN (National Propaganda Bureau). During the next two decades, Ferro strove to promote Portugal's new regime within and beyond the country's frontiers, and also to implement his Política do Espírito (Policy of the Spirit). This consisted of a program that established culture as one of the nation's foundation stones, promoting an organic vision of a new society, which was nevertheless based on traditional values.

To achieve this, the SPN developed numerous activities based on more or less accurate ethnographic studies that were, to a certain extent, merged with modernist aesthetics. This presented a recreated vision of a perpetually perfect, bucolic society, the nation's bedrock. For the first time, the homogenized mass of the Portuguese people (or the recreated version of its character and art) was officially praised and presented as an ideal of innocence and purity instead of, as previously, an ignorant and primitive horde incapable of keeping up with progress.[13] As it was then stated in the last page of SPN's book *Arte e Indústrias Populares* (Popular Arts and Industries), 'The life of People, in its conception of Art, is the most human manifestation of the spirit.'[14]

The cheerful Barcelos clay figures were regarded by the ethnographic section of the SPN as flawless examples of this glorified artisanal production. They were chosen to accompany these propaganda efforts and were presented all over the world, with the proud cock achieving more and more prominence. Reacting to increasing external demand, the Barcelos potters developed its size, colour and decorative details. Therefore the cock appeared everywhere: on mantelshelves of modernist

Figure 5.1 Barcelos cocks on display at the Popular Arts Room of the Portuguese Pavilion, Paris International Exhibition, 1937. Photo Mário Novais. Col. Estúdio Mário Novais. Courtesy of Calouste Gulbenkian Foundation-Art Library [CFT003.103317].

architects' cottages, in living rooms designed by renowned decorators, in state-run hotels built by the regime as examples of good taste and at the privately owned hotels that accordingly followed them.[15] Furthermore, the cock was used as a common denominator to illustrate the Portuguese popular arts and, in a more official role, travelled from the northern county fairs to folkloric markets organized by the SPN in Lisbon, where the poor pottery merchants offered it to the president of the Republic during the visits that marked these propaganda events. In 1948, the cock proudly crowned the top shelves of Minho province's museographic display at the newly inaugurated Museu de Artes Populares (Folk Arts Museum), and was immortalized on Thomás de Melo's modernist mural that till today decorates the room.

In the 1950s, after being interpreted by many artists, the clay figure was for the first time subjected to a redesign by someone unrelated to the vernacular pottery. According to a later study, the local artist Manuel Gonçalves Torres, would

give the Barcelos' cock the first touches of charm and elegance. From then on, the cock became more erudite and snobbish. Today there is already a wide range of models that, while respecting the original features and its type, are, however, a varied collection that want to follow progress without abandoning the original character. This has been criticized, but the truth is that these new cocks are sold extraordinary well and the primitives have a negligible sale.[16]

The particularities of his intervention are not clear but, during the 1950s, the overall form became leaner, curvilinear, and some detailing features were systematized, so much that they lost the original naivety. At the same time, matte black pigment became the main background colour and the applied moulded details disappeared, so that the ornamentation subsisted only in painted patterns with bright colours. At the end of the decade, moulds would be used to increase the production of the object that was now the potter's bestseller, resulting in a sturdier silhouette of the bird. A more attractive and long-lasting glazed finish became the norm, generally decorated by a red heart painted on its tail and wings. To help establish its newly found national fame, the cock began to be associated with stories of Saint James and the pilgrimage route to Santiago de Compostela. These stories were familiar all over Europe, but were now relocated to Barcelos, a city on one of the pilgrimage routes. This association was based on the representation of a crowing cock existent in the city's medieval pillory. The evolution was now justified by concocted historic and religious traditions, and a new past was fabricated for the cock, superseding the penniless whistle toy origins.

A politically engaged fowl

From the mid-1950s onwards, depictions of these standardized modern cocks – now produced in large scale at Barcelos's artisanal potteries to be sold throughout the country – appeared everywhere, from official tourist posters to all kind of supports and materials, for both serious purposes and as kitsch souvenirs. Later, designers made variations following their style or new trends, more or less obliged to work with what now was increasingly assumed to be a national symbol.[17]

In spite of the pseudo-industrial development, some potters continued to throw the clay on the wheel, creating figures in harmony with their personal impulses and more in tune with the cocks produced in the first half of the century, while a new generation of ethnographers was emerging during the 1950s detached from the regime ideals (sometimes even opposing it). Freer from political agendas, they worked in harmony with worldwide scientific guidelines, in tandem with a new generation of artists and art theorists, thus regarding this authorial production as the genuine one in relation to the bastardized standard modern versions. Nevertheless, for the common man, the standard version was the only one; he was oblivious of other versions – the earliest or the recent one.

Near the end of the dictatorship, the modern Barcelos cock suffered the expected consequences of being progressively perceived by everybody as a son of the regime, thus appearing in political cartoons as one of the kitsch symbols of the fascist period. Other authors continued to use it to depict the stubborn, resilient and sometimes resentful character of the Portuguese people. After the 1974 revolution, the cock remained generally despised by the modern cultural elite that, after four decades of fascist regime, was able to look forward rather than backward, free of the repressive and reactionary attitudes of an authoritarian regime that was never afraid to use censorship, or even violence, to achieve its isolationist goals. Yet the Barcelos cock continued to survive in the hands and pockets of the tourists avid for local souvenirs. It would reassume its national icon status during the 1980s, first in the hands of ironic postmoderns and, in recent years, newly reappropriated by younger generations, oblivious of the cocks' fascist past.

During the dictatorship, ethnographic studies were responsible for a lot more than just the modern Barcelos cock, a case explained here in a more detailed manner due to its popular elevation to the status of a national symbol. However, one should highlight again that most of its formal evolution was due to its original creators, the innocent potters of Barcelos distant from design concepts or industrial processes. In other cases, erudite artists, now called designers, and subsequently the industry, had to appropriate and transpose these inspirational inputs more quickly and bluntly to the modern world.

An impoverished country and a perfect world

During the 1930s, urban society was more aware of these artisanal objects than, for instance, an item of vernacular furniture or the interior of a rural home. A simple toy or a painted earthenware bowl would be bought in fairs, removed from its world and integrated in the house of its new owner as an *objet d'art* and regarded as modern in its stark primitivism. It was impossible to look at these gay and colourful abstract decorative objects and perceive the reality of the poverty-stricken Portuguese rural world and the crude life of the people who produced them as functional objects.

Nonetheless, the functional use of a rough and harsh item of rural furniture, like a bed, a chair or a chest, always remained evident, as – due to its size, to the formal similarity with contemporary pieces or its compelling use – the detachment from reality was not possible. This would make it difficult to integrate these furniture pieces in the home that the regime imagined for the new Portugal. The government encouraged the formation of a society anchored in this traditional rural world, but one should only take from it candid naivety and proper old chaste moral values, remaining unaware of the poverty and the civilizational delay that drove the majority of the country.[18]

So, when the regime decided to present images of an ideal home, a home that unquestioningly embraced this bucolic rural fantasy, it was also necessary to detach it from the real world. In 1940, for the Exposição do Mundo Português (Exhibition of the Portuguese World), a monumental event celebrating Portugal's history and place in the world, the SPN curated two sections entirely dedicated to the Portuguese people. First, the Pavilhão da Vida Popular (Pavilion of Popular Life) where the traditional industries, arts and crafts were exhibited, alongside artisans working for the audience to see, all displayed in a modernist minimal set that dissociated them from their habitat. There they were shown as well-mannered working characters, dressed in pristine traditional clothes, grateful for living in a regime that presented them as almost well-behaved monkeys behind a fence. This was similar to the colonial section where, for the glory of the empire, indigenous citizens from the

African and Asian territories were displayed in their crude authenticity, some semi-naked, though reverently attending the Sunday Mass like the good Christians they were forced to be.

The other section was Aldeias Portuguesas (Portuguese Villages), a group of houses presenting the different styles of traditional architecture where peasants acted bucolically all summer: working, selling souvenirs or just socializing.

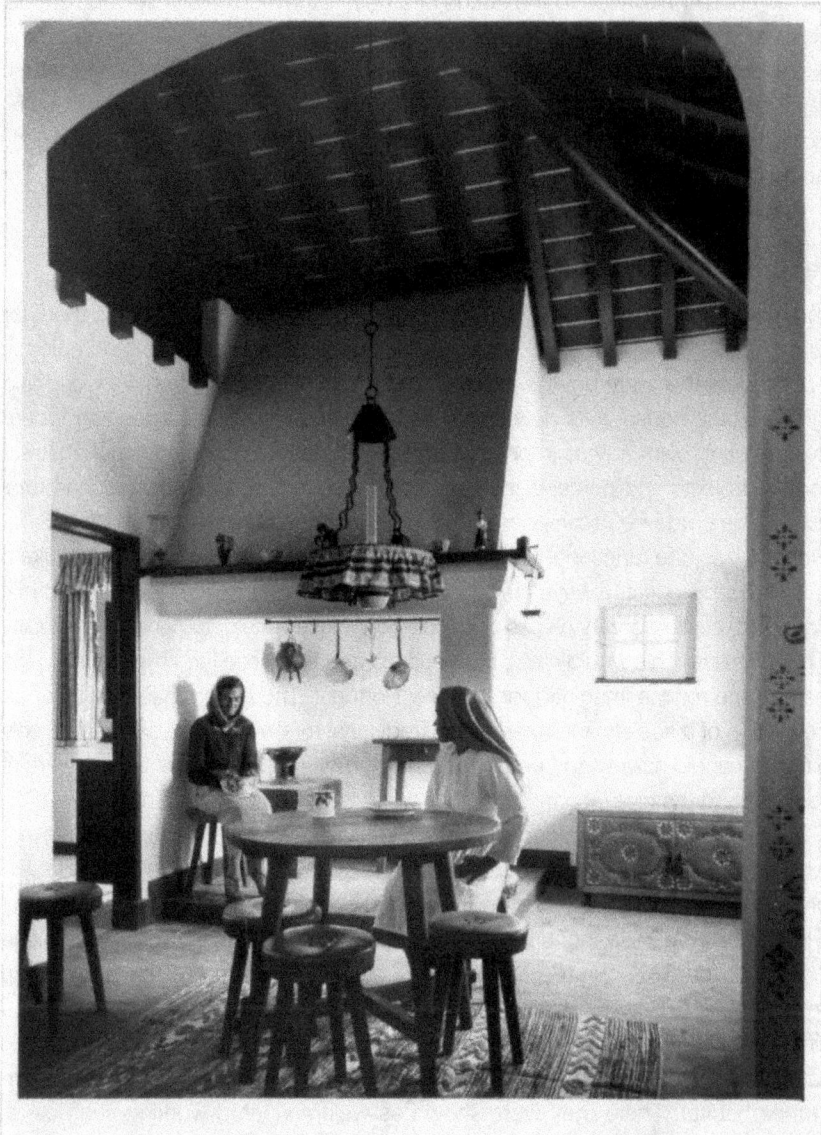

Figure 5.2 A traditional kitchen of the Portuguese Villages at the Exhibition of the Portuguese World, Lisbon, 1940. Photo Mário Novais. Col. Estúdio Mário Novais. Courtesy of Calouste Gulbenkian Foundation-Art Library [CFT003.201751].

A photograph depicting the interior of one of these houses shows a kitchen (Figure 5.2). It lacked all the amenities of the modern world: there was no plumbing, water or electricity, not even the simplest stove. This sanitized version was presented as the home of a clean and honest rural family – the foundation stone of Portugal – perfectly conscious of the unmovable character of its social stratum and following the traditional adage of 'poor, but honourable'. The furniture was sparse but sufficient, and everything looked immaculate, from the trimmed chandelier and the ordered display of objects, to the lime-washed walls and the ceiling's regular beams. Authentic as it looked, almost everything was a designed and manufactured fantasy created for the urban public; impossible to see if one travelled a few kilometres outside of Lisbon.

Our own home

Still in 1940, SPN began the completion of a network of seven small state-run hotels – the Pousadas – throughout the country, covering the obsolete private offer and encouraging the national tourism industry by example. The first decorative programmes of the Pousadas were conceived between 1940 and 1942 by different designers: José Luis Brandão de Carvalho (Marão), Maria Keil (Estrela), Carlos Botelho (Vouga), Veloso Camelo (Alfeizeirão), and Vera Leroy and Anne-Marie Jauss (Elvas, Santiago, Alportel) (Figure 5.3). Their brief established that each hotel should look and feel like a regional domestic home in every respect instead of following general international standards: 'The occasional home that belongs to everyone but that could be our own,' as Ferro said.[19]

The designers looked once more at existing studies and tried to translate it to functional and comfortable spaces, understanding, during the process, the difficulties associated with it.[20] As Brandão de Carvalho mentioned,

Almost all the decorative motifs were searched on the Marão people's art, but everything was adapted to the comfort requirements as the roughness of the furniture and utensils of those mountain persons is a sign of a simple and primitive life, stripped of all well-being. The furniture is nevertheless enhanced by some naïf carvings and the ironwork candid contours.

The linen are sombre because the fabrics weaved on these highlander's looms are not merry and gay. Natural tone wool, without fancy colourings, is enough of a decorative effort.

Iron made lamps and candlesticks are adapted the best way to electric light. Since electricity is a recent invention there hasn't been the opportunity for people to create appliances with artistic and popular appearance.[21]

Different approaches were observed on these experiments: some respecting materials, proportions and techniques, others just adopting local decorative motives through a modernist eye. In some of the Pousadas, the furniture was wholly different from room to room, trying to express a more organic ambience, in others the same effect was produced with decorative customized features on serial pieces and

Figure 5.3 Dining room of the Pousada de S. Braz de Alportel, Algarve; interiors by Anne-Marie Jauss and Vera Leroy, 1942. Photo Horácio Novais. Col. Estúdio Mário Novais. Courtesy of Calouste Gulbenkian Foundation-Art Library [CFT164.52698].

variations on the use of fabrics, linen and decorative objects. Overall, a new decorative style was being developed that appropriated elements of the traditional crafts. In the specific case of furniture, mainly national woods were used, such as pine, elm, ash or oak. The decorative use of explicit joinery details, the hinges and other hardware on coarse wrought-iron complemented the wood work and the applied ornamentation carved or painted using motifs of the vernacular lexicon like the recurrent heart shape, flowers or simple geometric patterns. Scattered all through these interiors, authentic artisanal objects were used to decorate and convey genuine character to the Pousadas, with the Barcelos cock appearing, once again, here and there.

Due to the insistent propaganda of these interior design examples inaugurated between 1942 and 1948, as well as the endorsement by *Panorama*, the official SPN magazine, of other private country homes designed under similar stimulus, the rustic style, or 'estilo Secretariado' (style of the S[ecretariado]PN) as Ferro christened it,[22] was understood as inheritor of 'a fondness for the folk arts that underlies certain aspects of the decorative arts with a national character', differentiating it from the dull, historical national styles, from the imported fashions or from the international modernisms.[23]

The style, at first intended as a model to be consumed by the upper classes in their country houses – like the pieces subsequently manufactured by the high-grade furniture company Olaio – would be more commonly used by the middle class in their urban dwellings. During the 1950s, it would grow in popularity and smaller companies

Figure 5.4 A pantry cupboard with fold-down table and benches for a country house by Thomás de Melo, 1942. Photo Mário Novais. Col. Estúdio Mário Novais. Courtesy of Calouste Gulbenkian Foundation-Art Library [CFT003.065123.ic, CFT003.065124.ic].

copying the trend would downgrade the quality with cheap stereotyped versions that, available for every purse, would be produced until the end of the 1960s.

An enduring rustic Portugal

After the regime's golden years during the 1930s and throughout the war, the victory of the democracies in 1945 and the global post-war development in the 1950s promoted the growth of ideological and political opposition movements. Simultaneously, the progressive cultural elites began to distance themselves from this rustic Portugal, gradually perceiving it as kitsch, fake and manipulative. The blissful dream of the construction of this modern-traditional utopia was coming to an end, as it was systematically more difficult to prevent the global progress invading the country's borders. Nevertheless, a set of traditional stereotypes had already been developed and, step by step, inculcated in the general public an awareness that continued to abide until the 1960s, elevating it to elements of national identity. Most are still recognized today, many decades and political turmoil later, when the temporal distance makes them almost playful and innocuous memories again.

The role of design as a professional practice in the development, during the first decades of the dictatorship, of these two cases of national identity is understandably distinct. The Barcelos cock is definitely a 'bottom-up approach' – using the definition offered by Gimeno-Martinez – created almost exclusively by the common citizen both

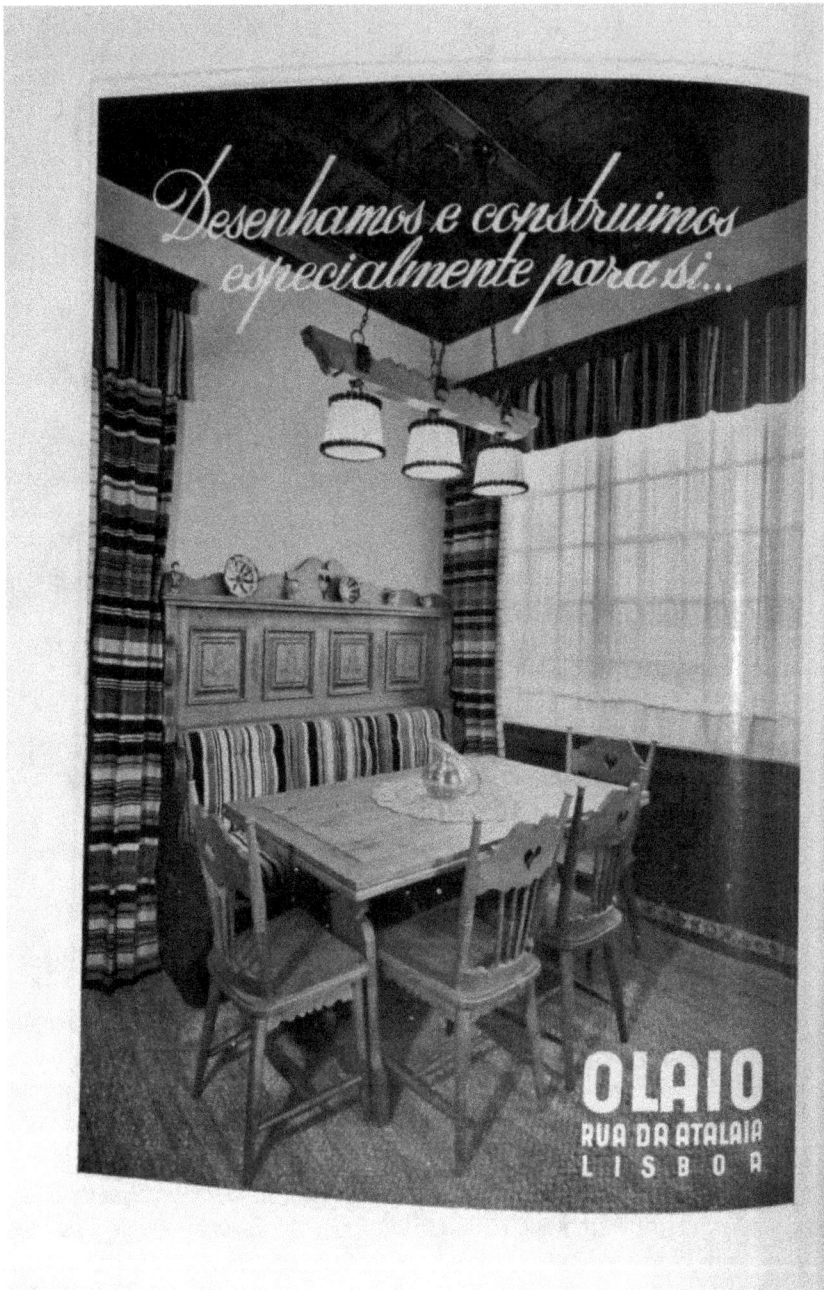

Figure 5.5 An advertisement for rustic-style furniture by José Espinho, produced by Olaio, 1946. In *Panorama: Revista Portuguesa de Arte e Turismo*, vol. 6, no. 27 (1946).

as producer, potter and local artist and as the main consumer responsible for its establishment.[24] It was this anonymous entity that, through unconscious processes, while bumping from time to time with the top ideological decision makers, undertook its development from child's toy to the moment of its definitive shape, when finally the nation acknowledged and sanctioned its existence through official use.[25]

In the case of the rustic style furniture, a different 'top-down approach' was necessary. Recognizing the difficulties in evoking longed-for moral values through images of the traditional Portuguese rural home that, while considered its ancestral cradle, was commonly related with the poverty-stricken reality, the regime – through its propaganda bureau and other official channels – decided to propagate models of a more bucolic and joyful fantasy. For that purpose a group of modernist artists, illustrators, architects and decorators (i.e. designers) was employed. These would recreate a traditional decorative style through the interpretation of the past memories deciphered on ethnological studies developed since the nineteenth century. This ambience of poetic frugal joy defined by obliterating the bad conditions of the peasants' life was then successfully propagated throughout the country and assimilated by everybody as a new image of Portugal.

Finally one should highlight, by means of the following considerations, the dissolution of the natural temporal dimension through these creative political processes. A mythical past was believed to exist unspoilt in the present through the suggestion that the current artefact's production embodied the nation's dormant morals and virtues. There was an effort to erase the present and the regular progression of time through the regime's endeavour to eradicate signs and outcomes of what it considered to be a decadent international modernity, and its search for a valid replacement. Thus the design of a future was based on the values of a past that never existed, accomplished through the development of models for an idealized new society that were established on recreated traditions like the examples presented in this chapter.

Notes

1. Eric Hobsbawm and Terence Ranger (eds), *The Invention of Tradition* (Cambridge: Cambridge University Press, 1983).

2. Roger Griffin, *The Nature of Fascism* (London and New York: Routledge, 1991) and *Modernism and Fascism* (Hampshire and New York: Palgrave Macmillan, 2007).

3. Javier Gimeno-Martínez, *Design and National Identity* (London and New York: Bloomsbury, 2016).

4. Maria Helena Santos, 'Design in Portugal (1960–1974)', in Santos (ed.), *Rehearsal for an Archive* (Lisbon: CML/MUDE, 2017).

5. For a study of Lisbon as 'center of the world' and main entrepôt for rarities, curiosities, luxury goods and wild animals, see Annemarie Jordan Gschwend and Kate Lowe (eds), *The Global City: On the Streets of Renaissance Lisbon* (London: Paul Holberton, 2015), 228–34.

6. Duarte Ribeiro de Macedo, 'Discurso I [Sobre a Introdução das Artes]', in Antonio Lourenço Caminha (ed.), *Obras Ineditas de Duarte Ribeiro de Macedo* (Lisbon: Impressão Régia, 1817), 89.

7. For a study on the Portuguese ethnography history, see João Leal, *Etnografias Portuguesas (1870–1970)* (Lisbon: Publicações Dom Quixote, 2000).

8. Ramalho Ortigão, 'A Exposição de Arte Ornamental', *O António Maria*, no. 4 (2 March 1882): 67.

9. Rocha Peixoto, 'As Olarias de Prado', *Portugalia: Materiaes para o estudo do povo portuguez* 1, no. 2 (1900): 252.

10. For a detailed study on the formal and technical evolution of the Barcelos cock earthenware figure, see João Manuel Mimoso, 'Origem e Evolução do Galo de Barcelos', *Olaria: Estudos Arqueológicos, Históricos e Etnológicos*, no. 4 (2008–2011): 144–61.

11. 'Vº Congresso da Crítica', *O Notícias Ilustrado*, no. 171 (20 September 1931): 14.

12. Artur Maciel and Leitão de Barros's letters quoted in António Manuel Couto Viana, *Gentes e Cousas d'antre Minho e Lima* (Viana do Castelo: C. M. Viana do Castelo, 1988), 123–4.

13. For a study on the importance of the Portuguese folklore as aesthetic definer during Estado Novo regime, see Vera Marques Alves, '«Camponeses Estetas» no Estado Novo: Arte Popular e Nação na Política Folclorista do Secretariado da Propaganda Nacional', PhD dissertation, Departamento de Antropologia, ISCTE, Lisbon, 2007.

14. Luiz Chaves, *Artes e Indústrias Populares* (Lisbon: SPN, 1940), back cover verso.

15. For a study on the 'Good Taste Campaign', see Carlos Bártolo, 'The Good Taste of an Authoritarian Regime', in Priscilla Farias and Paul Atkinson (eds), *Design Frontiers: Territories, Concepts, Technologies* (Mexico: Editorial Designio, 2014), 141–54.

16. João Macedo Correia, *As Louças de Barcelos* (Barcelos: Museu Regional de Cerâmica, 1965), 24.

17. For a detailed study on the evolution of the Barcelos cock from a vernacular toy to a national symbol, see Elisabete Muga Rodrigues, 'O Galo de Barcelos: Do Mito, do Símbolo, do Ícone', MA dissertation, Faculdade de Arquitectura e Artes, Universidade Lusíada, Lisbon, 2008.

18. For a study on the idealized society of Portugal's dictatorship, see Rita de Almeida Carvalho and António Costa Pinto, 'The "Everyman" of the Portuguese New State during the Fascist Era', in Jorge Dagnino, Matthew Feldman and Paul Stocker (eds), *The New Man in Radical Right Ideology and Practice, 1919–45* (London: Bloomsbury, 2018), 131–47.

19. António Ferro, *Turismo* (Lisbon: SNI, 1949), 53.

20. For a study on the design of Pousadas, see Carlos Bártolo, 'Being Modern while Rejecting Modernism, Being Traditional while Dismissing Tradition: A Brief Study of the Portuguese First Seven Pousadas (1942–1948)', in *Tradition Transition Trajectories: Major or Minor Influences?* 9th Conference of the ICDHS 2014 (São Paulo: Blucher, 2014), 213–8.

21. José Luis Brandão de Carvalho, '[Report]. 1941–08. A exigüidade da verba . . .', manuscript accessible at IAN/TT, Lisbon. SNI archiv, cx-1103, PT-TT-SNI/DGT/I/1/1.

22. Ferro, *Turismo*, 113.

23. António Ferro, *Artes Decorativas* (Lisbon: SNI, 1949), 25–6.

24. Gimeno-Martínez, *Design and National Identity*.

25. About the use of the Barcelos cock as national symbol by the Portuguese flag carrier airline in the 1960s, see Pedro Gentil-Homem, 'Where the Clouds Are Far Behind', in Bárbara Coutinho (ed.), *TAP Portugal: Image of a People* (Lisbon: MUDE, 2015), 65–6; 186–203.

6 An Experiment with Time: Modern and Classical Influences in the Planning of High and Over

MICHAEL FINDLAY

High and Over (1929–1931), a country house in Amersham by Connell and Thomson, has long been recognized as marking a key turn in British architecture.[1] Its principal designer Amyas Douglas Connell (1901–1980) was a New Zealand-trained architect who arrived in England in 1923 to join the Atelier at London's Bartlett School of Architecture and compete for scholarships.[2] Connell and his future partner Basil Robert Ward (1902–1974) gained the Rome Prize and Henry Jarvis Travelling Scholarship in 1926. These awards enabled them to travel extensively in Europe and base themselves at the British School at Rome (BSR). The prizes were the pinnacle of the British architectural studentship system, designed foremost to reinforce the classical tradition in architecture.

Prior to this success, Connell and Ward had begun their European travels in 1926 with a trip to Paris to view the Exposition des Arts Decoratifs. As well as Le Corbusier's Pavilon L'Esprit Nouveau that left an enduring impression on them, there were pavilions by Andre Lurçat and a modernist garden, Le Jardin d'eau et de lumière, by the Armenian architect Gabriel Guévrékian (1892–1970). Like other French contemporary gardens, it had little to do with horticulture or the picturesque traditions of landscape design. It was a synthetic garden, sketched with triangles in low relief on the landscape like a two-and-a-half-dimensional diagram.[3] Connell and Ward's visit to Paris armed them with first-hand experience of architectural modernism and set them on a path that seemed diametrically opposed to the tenets of the BSR.

After a triumphal return to New Zealand and a civic reception in Wellington, Connell and Ward arrived in Rome in January 1927, where they were met by the recently appointed director Bernard Ashmole, an archaeologist only in his mid-30s, who had been given the task of reforming the school.[4] The main area of study for architects was the restoration, through drawings, of ancient sites. This was achieved by surveying their ruins and applying details gleaned from archaeological literature and observation of surviving structures. In his first year, Connell studied Michelangelo's Campidoglio, including its Roman remnants, and prepared for his second year project, which was to be the restoration of the Villa of Tiberius on the island of Capri.[5] Connell's analysis of the Campidoglio impressed Ashmole, who later noted in his autobiography that Connell's work allowed him to understand the subtleties of the design 'perhaps more thoroughly than anyone before, except their creator'.[6] Although early in his own career, Ashmole was an astute classical historian, easily able to see through any student efforts to bluff him on his own ground.

Connell took full advantage of the opportunity for travel while holding the Rome scholarship. From his reports to the London office of the BSR we know that he visited over twenty Italian towns and villages to investigate classical and Renaissance buildings and their landscape settings. The list ran to four visits to Capri as well as Naples, Pompei, Paestum, Salerno, Amalfi and Ravello. He explored the hill towns of central Italy as well as Genoa, Florence, Lucca, Pisa, Siena, Venice, Ravenna, Bologna, Padua, Turin and Milan. Connell also visited the Ecole des Beaux Arts in Paris to study restoration drawings, and squeezed in a visit to Germany in 1928.[7] Although unstated in his reports, Connell was visiting buildings by European modernists and reading about their work. Frederick Etchell's 1927 translation of Corbusier's *Vers Une Architecture* was available at the BSR despite the London committee's hostility towards the new style. During this eventful year, Dorothy and Bernard Ashmole began talking with Connell about the site that they had bought at Amersham on the Hill, overlooking the Misbourne Valley. Connell applied for a renewal of his scholarship for a third year in 1928 and was supported by Ashmole although funds were restricted and other students were being turned away. It came as a shock in 1928 when Ashmole announced his resignation, having accepted the position of Yates Professor of Classical Archaeology at the University of London. To the further disappointment of the BSR Committee, Connell resigned his scholarship in December 1928 and followed the Ashmoles back to England.

Connell started on the Ashmole's commission during the BSR summer break in mid-1928, initially sharing a London studio with Herbert Thearle, the Jarvis Scholar in 1926. Ashmole later wrote that an initial proposal for an 'E' shaped house on Elizabethan lines was quickly discounted when architect and clients walked over the 12 acre site together, stopping at a disused chalk pit that formed a hollow in the side of the hill. Ashmole recollected that it was his suggestion to plan the house around three 120 degree wings but that Connell was initially reluctant, seeing difficulties in circulation and the fixed room sizes that would result from the use of radial symmetry.

Connell and Ashmole visited Germany in 1928 and may have seen a competition design by Max Taut (1884–1967) for a Trade Union School at Bernau. Taut's model showed a building on a hillside with a hexagonal core radiating out in two- and three-storey wings. Although unbuilt, the scheme was exhibited with the other entrants at the Bauhaus school at Dessau. A picture of the model was later reproduced in Jürgen Joedecke's *A History of Modern Architecture* in 1959 but it was not widely seen at the time, nor is it well noted in Taut's oeuvre. While the suggestion for the radial plan may have come from Ashmole as he claimed, it seems likely that one or the other had seen Taut's model and found an answer to their planning problems.[8]

An undated sketch plan of this early version of High and Over was made shortly afterwards. Heavily annotated by Bernard Ashmole, it shows that the essential elements of the house and garden were in place by the middle of the year and probably settled before Connell's return to London.[9] It shows the three-winged main house and lodge in their future positions, surrounded by pools and gardens laid out on triangular terraces. The project moved on quickly but the first permit drawings for High and Over, dated November 1928, were not in Connell's hand and were possibly drawn by Stewart Lloyd Thomson while Connell was still in Rome attempting to finish his reconstruction. Thomson, from Melbourne, was a fellow student at the Bartlett School and his pathway through British modernism closely followed Connell's. Their partnership ended somewhat bitterly in 1930, and the later drawings for High and Over are Connell's alone.[10]

The planning of the house showed Connell's strong intention to produce a fusion of classical and contemporary design ideas. While it may have seemed capricious to some, the hexagon had practical advantages. It may be multiplied and composed into a regular pattern or subdivided into equilateral triangles. Roman hexagonal plans were continued in early Byzantine Christian churches and revived later in the Baroque period by Borromini. Hexagonal room shapes were occasionally incorporated into Roman baths and one example, the Sala Trilobata (c.AD400), near the Baths of Trajan in Rome, might be considered as a model.[11] The provision of different sized rooms in a bath is less of a problem than in a house where spaces might range from a lavatory to a library. Connell drew a double square for the main rooms, starting from the spigot of a fountain situated in the centre of the entrance hall. This expanded geometry allowed the complex functions of a house with domestic staff to be fitted into the compact footprint.

Water was central in the planning of the house and garden and the fountain within its hexagonal frame formed the hub of a much larger scheme. The fountain has posed a critical dilemma for those striving to fit High and Over into the conventional narrative of modernism. Connell was not striving after historical revival but a bricolage that combined the lucidity of modernism with classicism and the power of imagination. For that final essential quality he looked to the eighteenth-century engraver Giovanni Piranesi, who wrote in the introduction to his *Prima parte di architetture e prospettive* engravings in 1743 (Figure 6.1):

> I will not tire you by telling you once again of the wonder I felt in observing the Roman buildings up close, of the absolute perfection of their architectonic parts, the rarity and the immeasurable quantity of the marble to be found on all sides, or that vast space, once occupied by the Circuses, the Forums and the Imperial Palaces: I will tell you only that those living, speaking ruins filled my spirit with images such as even the masterfully wrought drawings of the immortal Palladio, which I kept before me at all times, could not arouse in me. It is thus that the idea has come to me to tell the world of some of these buildings.[12]

Piranesi went on to elaborate the lessons in his redrawing of ancient Rome for the readers of his own period, writing:

> If someone compares these aspects with the ancient manner of architecture, he will see that many of them break with tradition, and resemble the usage of our own time. But whoever he is, before condemning anyone of imposture, let

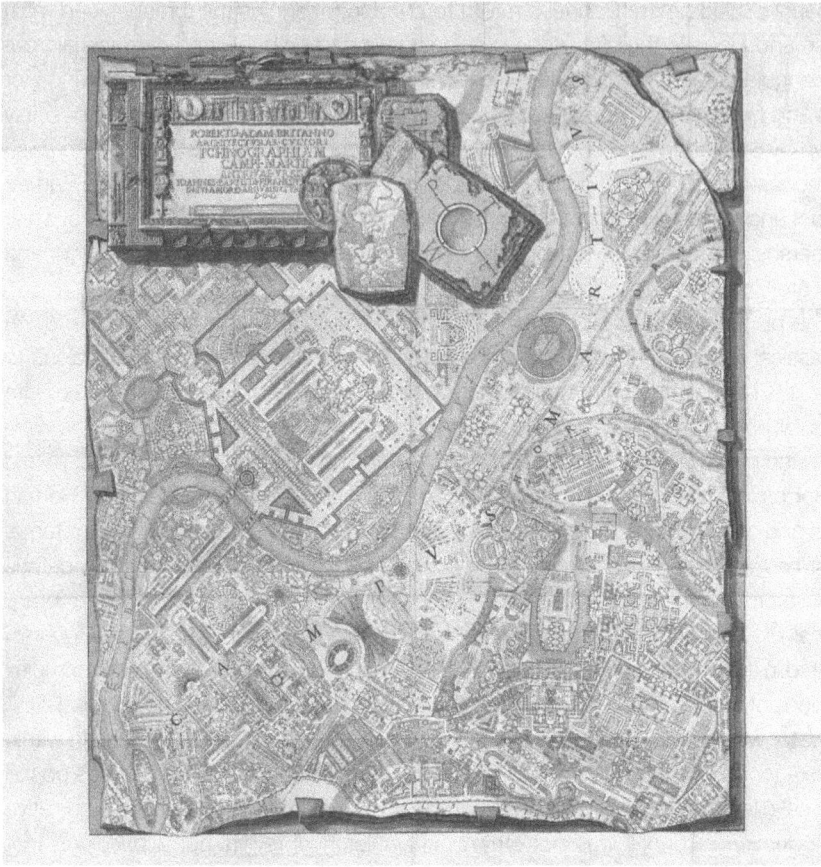

Figure 6.1 Giovanni Battista Piranesi, *Ichnographia of the Campus Martius of the Ancient City* (1757), etching in six plates. The origin of Connell's geometric planning of High and Over may be seen in the star-shaped Officinae Armorum complex at the top right, contained within the three linked Circulus. Image courtesy of the Arthur Ross Collection, Yale University Art Gallery.

him observe the ancient plan of Rome mentioned above [the Forma urbis in the Campidoglio], let him observe the ancient villas of Lazio, the villa of Hadrian in Tivoli, the sepulchres, and the other buildings in Rome that remain, in particular outside of Porta Capena: he will not find more things invented by the moderns, than by the ancients, in accordance with the most rigid laws of architecture.[13]

Parts of Connell's landscape for High and Over seem to appear in modified scales and positions in Piranesi's reconstruction of classical Rome. Piranesi projected a six-pointed star-shaped building on the banks of the Tiber that he named the Officinae Armorum, which was surrounded by circular open spaces for games and sports. The outdoor areas at High and Over were similarly allocated to swimming pools and a fives court with a maze, long lawn and triangular rose garden linked by paths and stairs. The fives court was built into the base of a tall concrete water tower that stood at the highest point of the site, its unconventional profile adding a further level of geometrical complexity to the landscape.

Connell's landscape elements were set in circular plazas connected by straight line segments, a particular geometry that appeared in Piranesi's reinterpretation of Rome but not regularly in the known classical world. As noted by Roman architectural historian Vincenzo Fasolo, Piranesi's Officinae Armorum was 'a triangular and star-shaped system to which it is certainly not possible to find a comparison in classical typology'. This point is reinforced in *The Sphere and the Labyrinth: Avant-Gardes and Architecture from Piranesi to the 1970s*, where, as Italian architect and postmodern theorist Manfredo Tafuri describes,

> the insertion of the of cinae machinarum militarium within the triangle formed by the three large piazzas joined at the Pons Fabianus. The central star, formed by the intersection of two equilateral triangles, appears to be rotated with respect to its natural lying position, so that its vertices, aligned on the cross-axis, terminate in the little side rooms flanking the round site: the whole organism seems to be a kind of clockwork mechanism, in which, however, there is an independence of the parts and a lack of interest in formal qualities.[14]

If this was the effect Connell was striving for, it was not recognized in architectural criticism for the next forty years.

The star form became the central element in the plan for High and Over, its layout replicated in the fountain in the central hall. Can we be sure Connell used Piranesi's plans of Rome as a starting point for the planning of High and Over and its garden? Ashmole's predecessor Thomas Ashby owned a Piranesi folio, which is still held by the BSR, so it is more than likely that Connell knew of it and used it in his planning of the garden. What has not been evident before is the link between Piranesi's creative reimagining of classical Rome and the politics of twentieth-century architecture. Connell's fusion of the aggressively modern into the Piranesi's fantastic world of the ancients was bold and then, as now, quite unique. Those looking for actual classical prototypes would remain unfulfilled, as the sources for the landscape are works of the imagination.

The first published image of the house was in *Architect and Building News* in January 1930 in an article written by Howard Robertson entitled 'An Experiment with Time: A House at Amersham by A. D. Connell'.[15] Robertson's title drew from an influential 1927 book by the Irish aeronautical engineer John W. Dunne (1875–1949) on dreams, precognition and the human experience of time that he termed 'serialism'.[16] Dunne's central notion was that time is eternally present, and that past, present and future are all happening together. It is our presence in the ever-moving now that prevents us from seeing anything else. Dunne's thoughts on the human experience of time were taken up by influential figures like J. B. Priestly and reflected in William Faulkner's well-known observation that 'the past is never dead. It's not even past.'[17] Dunne's theories, though essentially spiritualist in nature, were enticing to critics hoping to see a connection between modernism and the classical world. The author of the *Architect and Building News* articles on High and Over, Howard Morley

Figure 6.2 High and Over. Photograph by Steve Cadman.

Robertson (1888–1963) was principal at London's Architectural Association School. He was already a well-published writer on modernism, often working in conjunction with the photographers Frank Yerbury and Leo Herbert Felton. Robertson made numerous visits to Europe and North America to document early modernist buildings. Robertson keenly awaited Connell's project as it fitted his own emergent perspective on what British modernism might become. Both Robertson and Christopher Hussey writing in *Country Life* identified High and Over as being something different even for a modernist building. It was to be functional but also to answer the client's need for a house that represented the 'lucid and practical ideals of Classical civilisation'.[18] By applying Dunne's metaphysics, Robertson drew attention to how High and Over stood between the twentieth-century technological realm of objectivity and science and the worlds of archaeology and the imagination.

Architectural modernism was moving towards a different use of geometry to that applied by Connell at High and Over, adopting the classically derived grids of Mies Van der Rohe and the humanist proportions of Le Corbusier. The use of particular geometric systems in architecture including symmetry and radial geometry was described by modernist critics as 'formalism' but the term implied different things as modernism developed its aesthetic codes. To describe a building as 'formalist' in the 1930s was to equate it with outmoded Beaux-Arts types of architecture. In *Le*

Figure 6.3 High and Over House and water tower, Amersham, 1934. Image copyright Historic England.

Modulor (1950), Le Corbusier weighed in with his own disapproval of radial geometry and particularly the stellated polygon plans of the Baroque period. Just as the Corbusean grid was handed on to the future, the hexagon that underlay the planning of High and Over stayed fixed in its time. Unlike Van der Rohe's use of temple-like grids in his planning for iconic structures such as the Barcelona Pavilion, Connell's debt to Rome seemed somehow more contrived.

Reading through the often guarded prose from the period in which it was built, a critical pattern emerges that underpins much of what is written about High and Over today. Apart from Robertson and Hussey's lengthy articles and many features in popular magazines, there is not a great deal of critical material on High and Over to read from the 1930s. Aside from brief references in surveys like F. R. S. Yorke and Colin Penn's *A Key to Modern Architecture* (1939), it was largely left to the post-war generation to try and explain what High and Over represented and what its relationship to future architectural development might be. This was related to the development of architectural theory itself and a shift towards more complex critical positions in modernism. Connell's mixed ideology of classical Rome, formal Beaux-Arts planning and the rationality of modernism was seen as a weakness by Yorke, Nikolaus Pevsner and other functionalist critics. The matter of formalism as defined in the period was not an easy subject to coherently address when axial and radial symmetries made their triumphal return to modernism in the second half of the 1930s.

Basil Ward, who designed the four cubic houses that were built on the High and Over Estate in 1934, addressed the Architectural Association in 1956 to launch a special issue of the *Architectural Association Journal* dedicated to the pre-war output of Connell, Ward and Lucas. For Ward, formalism was defined as 'the doctrine of those who tend to design in the abstract, those who make shapes and for whom structure is a means to that end and for whom function is secondary. Formalism is the antithesis of constructivism'.[19] Ward was attempting to square the circle by fitting the work of the practice in the 1930s into constructivism, an alternative category that would allow both science and a certain artistic independence of thought to prevail. To accept the formalist tag suggested that what Pevsner wrote of Connell, Ward and Lucas in his influential *Buildings of England* series was true – that their work was exhibitionistic and intended to shock the public. The accusations of *épater la bourgeoisie* represented Pevsner's belief that Connell's contribution to British modernism was somehow improper.[20]

A letter from architect Peter Smithson in the same issue of the *AA Journal* offered Connell, Ward and Lucas as the only British practice from the interwar period that could be taken seriously in terms of the conditions Britain faced after the war. The disintegration of the British Empire, the moral issues raised by the war and the pressing need to rebuild allowed little room for empty formal gestures. Smithson's frustration and frank language were a challenge to the gentlemanly socialist impulses of post-war modernism reflected in the Festival of Britain and what was termed the New Empiricism, a cheerful form of modernist domesticity strongly influenced by Scandinavian design. The Smithsons looked boldly to a future that they claimed had been sighted in the past by Connell, Ward and Lucas but lost in the facile celebration of the Festival of Britain and adoption of folksy regionalism as a way forward to British architecture. Here was the basis for the rowdy discourse at the Architectural Association in the mid-1950s and the reason for trawling the back catalogue of British modernism for something that was uncompromised by a desire to please the establishment. Out of this critical milieu came Reyner Banham who was the inheritor of Pevsner's critical mantle. Banham linked 'functionalism' to formalist strictures, allowing heterogeneity back into the analysis of modernism and laying the way for Brutalism, postmodern architectural theory and the return of history. Piranesi also made a sweeping return to architectural theory in the 1960s through the work of the American architect Louis Kahn, whose deployment of vernacular planning and classical traditions marked another postmodern turn. High and Over was then situated on two major cross roads in modern architecture, standing over both the transition from Beaux-Arts classicism in the 1920s and the breaking down of modernist theory in the 1960s. This complex relationship with time makes High and Over one of the most challenging and fascinating objects for interpretation in the entire history of British architecture.

Among the obstacles to a better critical understanding of High and Over is the tendency to see modernist buildings in purist isolation from their broader context. Rarely seen in relation to their physical or indeed intellectual environments, similar

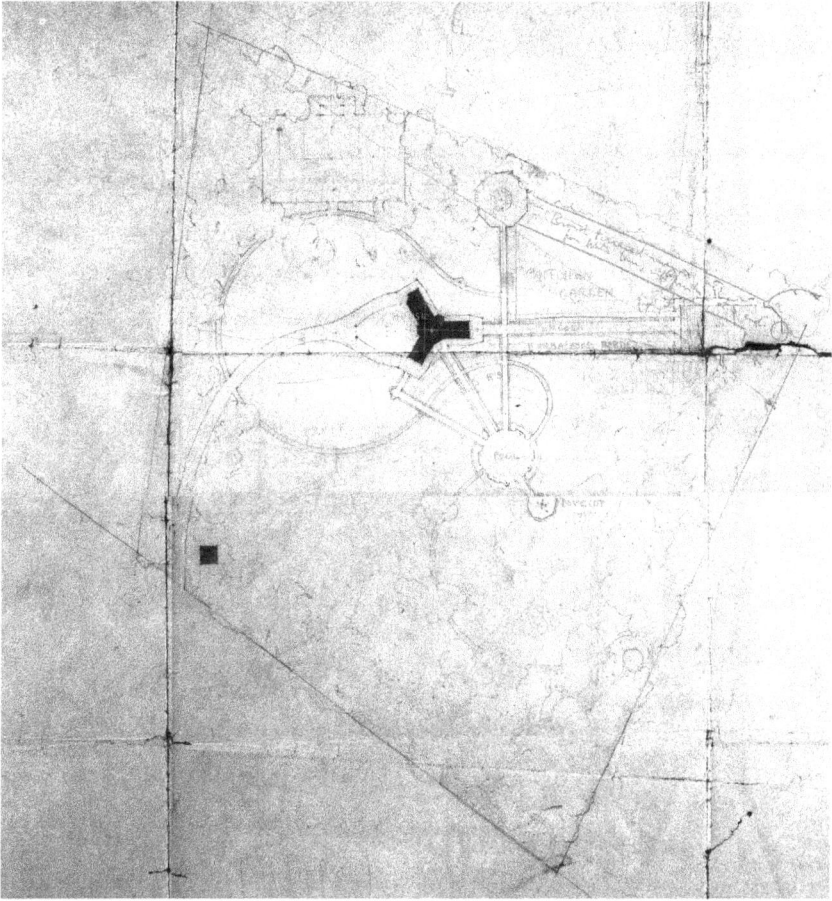

Figure 6.4 Amyas Connell. Sketch plan of High and Over with annotations by Bernard Ashmole. Undated, 1928. Image courtesy of Nelson Philip Ashmole.

and repetitious claims about buildings based on an analysis of a few well-known views and a floor plan can supply little more than a simple sketch of a building's significance. Working back through the critical analysis of High and Over through almost a century – the building was conceived an extraordinary ninety years ago – it emerges into fuller view as a sign on a path not taken towards a British modernist architecture bearing classical values, not a muddled compromise but a powerful, syncretic and original conception.

Notes

1. Alan Powers, *Britain: Modern Architectures in History* (London: Reaktion Books. 2007).
2. Dennis Sharp and Sally Rendell, *Connell, Ward & Lucas: Modern Architects In England 1929–1939* (London: Frances Lincoln, 2008).

3. E. Vitou, 'Gabriel Guévrékian', Grove Art Online (Oxford: Oxford University Press), www. oxfordartonline.com.

4. Andrew Wallace Hadrill, *The British School at Rome: One Hundred Years*. (London: British School at Rome, 2001).

5. Amyas Connell, Application for the Renewal of Scholarship for Second Year, The British School at Rome, Faculty of Architecture, undated c. 1927, British School at Rome Archives, A. Connell File.

6. Bernard Ashmole and Donna Kurtz (eds), *Bernard Ashmole: An Autobiography*. (Los Angeles: Getty Trust Publications, 1995).

7. Amyas Connell, Application for the Renewal of Scholarship for One Year, The British School at Rome, Faculty of Architecture, undated June 1928, British School at Rome Archives, A. Connell File.

8. The image is published on page 111 of Jürgen Joedecke, *A History of Modern Architecture* (New York: Frederick A. Praeger, 1959). Neither Connell or Ashmole talked about Taut's model so the conjecture is mine.

9. Amyas Connell, Sketch plan of High and Over annotated by Bernard Ashmole, undated 1928, courtesy of Bernard Ashmole.

10. Thomson's contribution to High and Over is hard to establish. He made no claim for the design but probably did more than help Connell prepare the initial drawings.

11. A diagram of the Sala Trilobata can be found in M. W. Jones, *Principles of Roman Architecture* (New Haven, CT: Yale University Press, 2000).

12. Giovanni Piranesi, *Prima parte di architetture e prospettive* (Rome, 1743), dedicatory letter to Sig. Nicola Giobbe quoted in Manfredo Tafuri, *The Sphere and the Labyrinth. Avant-Gardes and Architecture from Piranesi to the 1970s*. Trans. Pellegrino d'Acierno and Robert Connolly (Cambridge, MA: MIT Press 1987).

13. Ibid., b2.

14. Ibid., 35.

15. Howard Robertson, 'An Experiment with Time', *Architect and Building News* 123 (3 January 1930): 12–13.

16. J. W. Dunne, *An Experiment with Time* (London: Faber, 1927).

17. William Faulkner, *Requiem for a Nun*, act 1, scene 3 (New York: Random House, 1951).

18. Christopher Hussey, 'High and Over, Amersham, Bucks: The Residence of Professor Ashmole', *Country Life* 60, 19 September 1931: 302–7.

19. Basil Ward, 'Connell, Ward and Lucas', in D. Sharp (ed.), *Planning and Architecture: Essays Presented to Arthur Korn by The Architectural Association* (London: Barry & Rocliffe, 1967).

20. Nikolaus Pevsner, *London 4: North: The Buildings of England* (New Haven, CT, and London: Yale University Press, 2002).

7 Making 'Atomic' History: Consuming Historical Narratives in the 'Unofficial' Digital Archive

DR EMILY CANDELA

In 2014, an article entitled 'Let's Get Spherical', in the UK-based *Vintage Explorer* magazine proclaimed, 'The design world . . . is again awash with atomic balls!'[1] The revival of the 'atomic balls' to which the magazine refers concerns the twenty-first-century fashion for a kind of post-war household furnishing distinguished by a 'ball-and-rod' form, often comprising metal rod and wooden or rubber ball-feet or finials (Figure 7.1) Today, the so-called atomic magazine racks, chairs, coat hooks and other objects sharing this distinctive construction serve as archetypes of a brand of future-facing, optimistic post-war British design for collectors, aficionados, historians and museum-goers alike. But the passage of time and changes in the technologies mediating post-war ball-and-rod objects have corresponded with great shifts in the status of these furnishings since the period of their original production. Their most recent resurgence as a commodity has seen them eagerly snapped up by retro enthusiasts in Britain, for whom online platforms, principally eBay, constitute an important site of consumption.[2] The contemporary life of these 'atomic' objects on eBay constitutes an important stage in their long and dynamic history as a commodity, one that illuminates the site's character as a contemporary technology of archivization with the power to shape, collapse and overlay historical timelines.

This chapter focuses on the mediation of ball-and-rod objects for sale on eBay's UK site, eBay.co.uk, in the mid-2010s, when this research was carried out.[3] It explores the role of ball-and-rod furnishings within popular narratives about the post-war past and its design and science today. But it is also about larger questions concerning eBay's role in the development of popular memory, particularly where design histories are concerned – questions that the twenty-first-century history of 'atomic' furnishings make difficult to ignore.

Retro consumption is an important way in which those who are not professional historians engage with narratives of the past. In recent decades, this function has been taken up by online platforms. In her ethnographic study of contemporary British retro, Sarah Elsie Baker writes of the recent shift in retro exchange from 'spaces like jumble sales to ones like eBay'.[4] eBay has reshaped British retro consumption, contracting geographies, providing a database of current retro commodities, and altering how sellers describe objects.[5] On eBay, second-hand exchange

Figure 7.1 British ball-and-rod magazine rack sourced from eBay, most likely produced between the late 1950s and early 1960s, and in a style sold at Woolworths in the period. © Emily Candela.

is structured by technologies and interactions that did not shape previous forms of retro consumption. The site's operations as an online shopping application are therefore crucial to understanding the solidification and mediation of the historical narratives in which ball-and-rod objects have been embedded as twenty-first-century commodities.

eBay is a site of 'public history', one of the places in which history is 'made' – or 'written' in a metaphorical sense – outside the penning of texts by historians working in academia. 'Public history', a designation broader than 'popular history', includes history texts written for non-academic audiences, museum display, documentaries and films, historical re-enactment, and forms of second-hand consumption.[6] Yet, aside from a few key studies that examine or acknowledge eBay as a platform for the consumption of histories and the 'narrativization' of objects, there is little in-depth research on eBay as a site for the generation and communication of histories – especially design histories.[7] The narrativization of ball-and-rod objects on eBay, however, prompts questions about the digital public histories mediated by designed objects from the past, and about the practice of design history at a time when issues of who, and what, writes history become more pressing.

Icons and archetypes

British iterations of the ball-and-rod style, produced primarily from the late 1940s through early 1960s, became attached early on to the 'contemporary' or 'Festival' style promoted by the government-sponsored Council of Industrial Design (CoID) in the early 1950s. This association, which endures today, was due in part to the 1951 Festival of Britain debut of designer Ernest Race's ball-footed Antelope chair, which maintains a status in academic histories and museum collections as an icon of post-war British design. Later in the 1950s, after the style had fallen out of favour with the CoID and the modernist design establishment generally, retailers, including Woolworths, began selling cheaper, mass-produced ball-and-rod furnishings. These account for many of the ball-and-rod objects produced in the period, and are the 'atomic' furnishings most commonplace on eBay today.

In their twenty-first-century lives as second-hand commodities, ball-and-rod objects – primarily the cheaper, marginal furnishings, such as magazine racks – are among the archetypes defining the 'mid-century modern' style. Their recent re-emergence as a retro commodity coincided with the latest retro revival of the 1950s. Beginning in the late 2000s, this has seen the period reimagined through fashion, period television and film, advertising and the consumption of post-war and reproduction 'mid-century modern' designed objects by both committed collectors and those with a casual affection for retro home accessories. Although there is no published academic research dedicated specifically to ball-and-rod furnishings, surveys of post-war British design, across different genres of history-writing, almost always picture at least one.[8] With their spindly rods and often colourful balls, these objects embrace the visual hallmarks often associated with post-war British 'contemporary' design. They have also become emblematic of the period's scientific discoveries; ball-and-rod furnishings are frequently described as 'molecular' or 'atomic', suggesting that their motif is a kind of science-inflected ornament.

In the post-war period, however, a single name to describe the style did not consolidate around it. In the design press, magazines and in manufacturers' and retailers' advertisements, they were frequently described simply as furnishings with 'rods' and 'balls' or 'knobs'. And very often, these outlets included no text at all accompanying ball-and-rod objects. Their relative marginality as commodities at the time is demonstrated further by the fact that they were frequently marketed as something consumers were not expected to buy for themselves but rather would purchase as gifts. In the 1950s, for instance, Heal's advertised ball-and-rod furnishings in their 'Presents for Particular People' catalogue, in which shoppers were entreated to 'find gifts to please your most exacting friends' (Figure 7.2).[9] Post-war sources,

Presents for Particular People

The buying of presents is a highly individual art which requires the careful study of the recipient's taste and interest. At Heal's, with five floors of presents to choose from, you can do your shopping for all the family and find gifts to please your most exacting friends.

This catalogue has been arranged so that many presents of unusual character can be found, floor by floor, and department by department, starting with the Craftsman's Market on the Fourth Floor, and finishing with the Electrical Department, in the Basement.

For those who are unable to visit Heal's, it is hoped that this catalogue and the enclosed order form will help the choosing of presents at home.

The Fourth Floor THE CRAFTSMAN'S MARKET

COTTON CUSHION COVER, CM/S 480
Hand-woven in red, emerald or yellow, trimmed white ric-rac. 14" × 18". *(Postage 1s.)* £1. 17. 6
CUSHION (for above), CM/S 483
Filled with down and feather. 14" × 18". *(Postage 1s.)* 10s. 6d.
WASTE PAPER BASKET, CM/MW 140
Wicker with black or red metal frame (15½" high overall). *(Packing & Postage 2s.)* £1. 8. 3
MAGAZINE RACK, CM/MW 96
White metal and natural walnut. 19¼" high × 15" long. *(Packing & Carriage 5s.)* £2. 17. 9

HANGING PLANT BASKET, CM/MW 150
Wicker, with small glazed terra cotta bowl. 15" high overall. *(Packing & Postage 2s. 6d.)* 11s. 0d.
FLOWER POT HOLDER, CM/MW 64
Natural cane with hook for hanging, 5" diam., 5¼" high. *(Postage 1s.)* 9s. 6d.
(Without hook for standing 9s. 0d. *Other sizes* 10s. 0d., 10s. 6d., 11s. 0d., 11s. 6d.)
FLOWER POT HOLDER, CM/MW 149
Bamboo and string; 4⅜" × 4⅜". *(Postage 1s.)* 8s. 0d.
(Also with hook for hanging 8s. 6d. *Other sizes* 9s. 0d., 9s. 6d., 10s. 0d., 10s. 6d.)

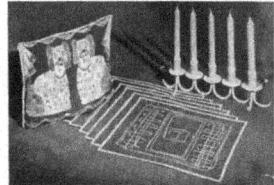

LINEN TEA COSY, CM/L 7005
Staffordshire poodles design in white on pink, gold or grey ground. *(Postage 1s.)* £1. 11. 6
TABLE MATS, CM/L 9005A
Hand-printed linen in white on elephant grey or yellow ground, set of six, each 14" × 11¼". *(Post Free)* £2. 14. 0
CANDELABRA, CM/MW 99A
Black or white painted wrought iron to take five candles. *(Post Free)* £2. 7. 6
(There is a large selection of candles to be found in the Metalware Department)

Figure 7.2 Heal & Son Ltd, 'Presents for Particular People' catalogue, 1953, detail of page 2. © Archive of Heal & Son Limited, Victoria and Albert Museum.

such as this, present a rather different picture of these objects and their status. Once the peripheral furnishing with 'knob' feet, a possible gift for a picky friend; now an archetype of post-war 'atomic' design.[10]

While researching the post-war British history of ball-and-rod furnishings, I discovered that aside from the more well-known high-end examples of the style, like Race's Antelope chair, ball-and-rod objects are rarely found in conventional archives and museum collections. Consequently, as many historians who research artefacts absent from the traditional archive do, I turned to the 'unofficial' archive, that is, eBay. I typed 'atomic' into the bar at the top of the webpage and clicked the blue 'Search' button. An abundance of coloured balls and thin metal rods shaped into magazine racks, coat hooks, rubbish bins, plant stands and other furnishings appeared – the very objects that were so resistant to the word 'atomic' in period sources, and were largely absent from conventional archives.

It was in this 'unofficial' archive where the appellation for ball-and-rod objects most closely resembled their characterization in many secondary sources. On eBay, ball-and-rod objects have been almost universally identified with the keyword 'atomic'.

The results of systematic searches carried out in 2015 for the term 'atomic' across the whole site and in eBay's 'vintage/retro' category indicated this: nearly half of the items in the first one hundred results for any search using the keyword 'atomic' were ball-and-rod objects, which constituted a larger proportion of the listings summoned by the search term than any other single type of object in these sets of results.[11]

As in the museum, on eBay the lives of historical artefacts involve their submission to particular modes of categorization. These affect the kinds of narratives about the past in which they are embedded. In this case, the keyword 'atomic' was central to the narrativization of the ball-and-rod objects I observed on eBay, due to the way in which keywords on eBay function as indexes for informal categories. One sense in which the term 'atomic' is used on eBay is as shorthand for a period, the 'Atomic Age' (in line with the liberal use of the word in 1950s' retro culture generally). The shifting results list generated by any search using the keyword 'atomic' doubles as an informal historical category, the 'Atomic Age', defined by the artefacts appearing on the page. The strong link between ball-and-rod objects on eBay and the tag 'atomic' afforded them a prominent position within this informal category, where their abundance generated a retrospective sense of their popularity and archetypal status in the post-war era.

The profusion of ball-and-rod furnishings on eBay speaks less to their actual post-war lives, however, than to the mechanisms of their arrival on eBay. The generation that originally consumed ball-and-rod objects in the post-war period is ageing; a 25-year-old in 1958 would have been 82 in 2015, one year older than the UK's average life expectancy.[12] A marginal furnishing, such as a Woolworths magazine rack, is rarely treasured as an heirloom or keepsake when its original owner passes away or moves home. Instead it is likely to be cast off, often landing eventually on eBay. There it joins a collection of other objects like it, their numbers generating the illusion of post-war popularity. As Zoe Trodd writes on eBay, 'junk becomes a counterhistory'.[13] This is the past as what consumers from the period have discarded.

Although ball-and-rod objects accounted for most of the results of searches carried out using the keyword 'atomic', they shared this category with other now-archetypal 1950s and 1960s domestic furnishings (Figure 7.3). These included kidney-shaped coffee tables, glassware with starburst patterns and furnishings with thin splayed legs. The combined visual representation of these archetypes within eBay's seemingly endless results lists contributed to the ball-and-rod's narrativization on the site. Scrolling through the 'atomic' category represents a mode of consuming history that differs greatly from encountering a ball-footed object in the home of a post-war consumer or in a charity shop, likely surrounded by furniture from multiple periods. On eBay, as they drift upwards on the screen, ball-and-rod objects are cut off from the contexts that might have defined them in the past, and inserted into a vision of post-war material culture in which its own past is invisible. The artefacts of the 'atomic' category suggest the most unlikely of post-war British homes: one in which everything is new.

1960's retro atomic sputnick white magazine rack original coloured ball feet

£14.00
0 bids   Ended (Tomorrow, 20:00)

£21.00
⚡Buy It Now
+ £13.00 postage

VINTAGE RETRO 1960'S/70'S SPUTNIK ATOMIC WALL HANGING COAT HOOKS / HAT RACK

£45.00
Buy It Now
or Best Offer
+ £5.00 postage

ATOMIC vtg 1950s SET OF FOUR STAR MINI TUMBLER GLASSES ORANGE BLUE YELLOW 60s

£15.00
⚡Buy It Now
Free Postage

Retro pink yellow small 50s vase atomic design vintage mid century

£15.00
Buy It Now
or Best Offer
+ £3.50 postage

Figure 7.3 Screenshot from the results list of a search using keyword 'atomic' in ebay. co.uk's 'Vintage and Retro Collectables' category, accessed 20 July 2015. Image courtesy of eBay.

Ball-and-rod objects have re-emerged as commodities before, during 1950s retro revivals in the mid-1970s, mid-1980s and late 1990s. Their identification as 'atomic' was stronger on eBay in the mid-2010s, however, than in the literature associated with these previous revivals. In the 1970s, for example, British critic Bevis Hillier identified ball-and-rod objects by the term 'cocktail cherry'.[14] He surmised that the style referenced the 'breaking-down of matter into atoms and molecules', which, he wrote, were 'often imaged by "cocktail cherry" type models'.[15] In the 1980s, 'atomic' appeared as an adjective for ball-and-rod objects in some collectors' guides, such as US author Cara Greenberg's influential *Mid-Century Modern*.[16] But collectors' guides published in the 1990s and early 2000s still do not show the strong solidification of a definitive term for ball-and-rod furnishings.[17] Alongside 'swizzle stick', 'cocktail cherry' still appears, perhaps due to its use in Hillier's 1975 book, which is well-known within British retro collecting circles.[18] The 2003 Miller's buyer's guide, in some ways a precursor to eBay as a source for the current value of collectibles, uses no specific terminology for the style.[19]

That eBay's recent link between ball-and-rod objects and the term 'atomic' (or a single name generally) is stronger than in collectors' guides of previous retro revivals may be due in part to the way in which eBay has altered the mediation of retro commodities. Baker writes that brand names, such as 'Eames', are used in a fluid fashion on eBay, and with a frequency not witnessed previously in collecting cultures.[20] This use of brand names is one way, Baker observes, that the identification of objects on eBay is mirrored in retro culture more generally.[21] 'Atomic', in the case of eBay's ball-and-rod objects, is similarly deployed as though it is a 'brand' – as a shorthand classifier advertising and making easily identifiable a large group of commodities. And this strong attachment is evident in recent British retro culture outside eBay as well, as evidenced by its use in publications such as *Vintage Explorer* magazine, and more recent collectors' guides; a 2009 Miller's guide references 'the rod and ball atomic-style', for example.[22]

It is impossible to state with certainty that eBay is solely responsible for the strong contemporary attachment between ball-and-rod furnishings and the term 'atomic', but it is clear that eBay's design facilitates and solidifies such linkages. This is due to the way metadata functions on the site. Metadata is the information (like the tag 'atomic') attached to data online – including eBay auctions and 'Buy It Now' listings – that makes such data searchable. The algorithms governing how metadata is searched determine what a user sees online.

Like most marketplaces, eBay has its own systems and conventions for displaying goods. Central to its display of objects is the way metadata operates in its database. eBay's software indexes, searches and displays items based on tags, keywords, price and geographical data entered by users so that potential buyers can more easily locate desired objects. Not all metadata is immediately visible to Internet users, but on eBay some metadata is in plain sight, such as the titles accompanying items for sale. These are especially significant because eBay's search engine's default mode trawls keywords in titles, rather than words, in item descriptions. Many guides to selling on eBay therefore emphasize the title's importance, advising sellers to anticipate buyers' search terms in their titles.[23] Conversely, consumers are enlisted in using the language of the object's mediation, because an effective search involves anticipating sellers' tags. This cycle in which sellers and potential buyers anticipate each other's terminology ultimately leads to the universalization and solidification of terminology for ball-and-rod furnishings on eBay, principally the tag 'atomic'.

In her study of eBay item descriptions for nineteenth-century *cartes-de-visite*, Trodd points out that the historical narrativization of collectibles on the site is part of the seller's strategy.[24] Most ball-and-rod objects on eBay lack extensive item descriptions but, by carefully titling their auctions, sellers capitalize on the potential of the visible metadata in titles to double as a tool for communication. Title tags are used to limn histories of ball-and-rod objects. Within the laconic, awkward compositional style common to the eBay title's bargain-aesthetic, a vocabulary of keywords has congealed around ball-and-rod furnishings. Title terms orbiting the most prevalent tag 'atomic' have included 'sputnik', 'mid-century modern', 'kitsch', and sometimes 'molecular' or 'Eames' (possibly a reference to the Eames's 1953 'Hang-It-All' ball-and-rod hooks, or simply shorthand for a picture of 'Atomic Age' design dominated by US archetypes). For example: 'ATOMIC LAMP FINIAL MID CENTURY MODERN

STYLE SPACE NEEDLE'; 'Original 1950s Festival of Britain style shop mirror 24"x14" molecular'; 'Vintage Retro Magazine Rack, Atomic Feet, Original Condition'. Ball-feet were sometimes singled out as 'atomic' specifically (as in 'atomic feet'), thus introducing a second, more specific meaning of the term 'atomic' on eBay; in addition to further solidifying the archetypal position of the ball-and-rod motif in the larger 'Atomic Age' category, this usage of 'atomic' suggested a resemblance to ball-and-spoke models of atoms in molecules.

The solidification of terminology on eBay, designed to lubricate commerce on the site, has in this case also solidified ball-and-rod objects' associations with a post-war history of science. Many titles for ball-and-rod objects reference notions of 1950s and 1960s period style with a strong emphasis on post-war science and technology as optimistic, future focused, anodyne and – unironically – integrated into the home. Titles such as 'Gumball Atomic Space Age Magazine Rack' suggest an age of technological and scientific discovery stripped of any inkling of danger or destruction that the 'atomic' might otherwise connote. In this sense, eBay's image of the past replicates aspects of post-war narratives about science that were deployed, for instance, in many public science exhibitions in Britain. Historian Sophie Forgan has shown that exhibitions at the Science Museum and the 1951 Festival of Britain focused on science as safe, largely omitting references to destructive applications. In this period, she writes, 'official institutions such as the Science Museum eschewed all mention of the bomb' in discussions of atomic physics.[25]

Period style in the case of eBay's ball-and-rod objects becomes tethered to an analogous notion of 'period science'. Just as design histories based on notions of period style understand objects through a progression of visual styles indelibly linked with period designation over other historical contexts, ball-and-rod objects on eBay are categorized and understood through a notion of the period's most well-known and mythologized areas of scientific novelty: nuclear, molecular and space sciences. The historical narrative of these 'atomic' designed objects on eBay thus contributes to what historian of science David Edgerton has described as an 'innovation-centred timeline' of the history of science and technology that can obscure a picture of what was actually used, experienced and consumed in a period in favour of a teleological, positivistic presentation of progress.[26]

In these processes of narrativization, eBay is, of course, part of a larger ecology of retro consumption, past and present. There are, no doubt, elements of a feedback loop operating between eBay, collector's guides and other spaces of retro consumption. But, as noted above, eBay is the go-to site for many collectors in a landscape in which much retro exchange now takes place online. Furthermore, eBay articulates narratives in a way that simply was not possible in markets for second-hand objects that were not word-searchable, such as vintage shops and car boot fairs. The ball-and-rod object's link with the keyword 'atomic' on the site makes this clear; it is funnelled into narrow historical categories, solidifying its archetypal status within the site's novelty-focused 'Atomic Age' narrative. eBay replicates aspects of existing popular memory, but strengthens and streamlines them for wide dissemination through the action of its software, shaping stories of second-hand objects on- and offline.

Making history

Through its display design and indexing functions, eBay acts not only as an e-commerce platform, but also as a digital archive with a powerful narrativizing influence. As this study demonstrates, however, many of eBay's modes of narrativization differ from those operating in traditional historical writing. The narratives explored here, for instance, depart from the conventions of the linear prose text (and from the methodologies of professional history practice). Instead, the stories generated through the display, categorization and indexing of objects more closely resemble the narrative style of the archive. In this 'unofficial' archive, Jacques Derrida's observation that 'archivization produces as much as it records the event' holds just as much as it does for traditional archives.[27]

Narratives emerge from the interaction between eBay's software, which traffics in keywords and categories, and the buyers, browsers and sellers who use it. This prompts a rethinking of social historian Raphael Samuel's statement, published in 1994, that if history was viewed 'as an activity rather than a profession, then the number of its practitioners would be legion'.[28] The rise of online media adds new complexities to the politics of knowledge at the heart of questions about public history, as it has increased access to the tools for making and consuming history beyond academic forums for some publics, and has introduced new technologies to the process of 'making' history.[29]

There is a contemporary strain of dynamic, digital archive that emerges on commercial sites with user-generated content.[30] These include, for instance, the collections of photographs on Flickr and Facebook's stores of personal information. eBay is also one of these. And although it provides space outside the often-insular sphere of academia for participation in history, this private space in many respects does not constitute a 'democratic' platform for the production of histories. In addition to the fact that access to and participation on the site is delimited in numerous ways, the narratives generated and disseminated there are shaped by ideas inscribed in what communication scholar Michele White calls eBay's underlying 'organizational logic' (represented, for instance, by features such as its in-built item categories).[31] eBay users are, in many ways, subject to the platform rather than the converse. This dynamic does not remove people from the equation, however: human actors, such as eBay's product managers and user interaction and experience designers, play a role in making public design histories in the 'unofficial' digital archive.

As the mediation of ball-and-rod objects on eBay indicates, historical narratives on the site are, in many ways, problematic. But there is nevertheless reason for historians working in academia to engage with such public histories. First, public history can provide perspectives on the past that 'official' histories might miss.[32] In this case, for instance, eBay's 'atomic' narrative is one populated by the mass-produced ball-and-rod objects that constitute much of the post-war biography of this class of furnishings, but which are missing from most archives and museum collections, and from histories that spotlight the role of high-end designers such as Race and the Eameses.

Second, an understanding of public history narratives is clearly key for historians engaging in dialogues outside of academia. And as Ludmilla Jordanova has argued, even those who do not can benefit from understanding the operation of what she calls popular 'myths', because of their sheer power in the present. 'When we talk about historical myths,' she writes, 'we are not so much contesting what happened as drawing attention to the intense affect that surrounds certain views of the past.'[33] Indeed, in this case, the twenty-first-century retro consumption of ball-and-rod objects is a channel through which historical narratives of both design and science enter popular culture, and their circulation operates as a part of larger dynamics of public history-making. They are embedded, for instance, within narratives of innovation-focused histories of science that have been critiqued for their dominance in public elsewhere, such as in museums of science and technology.[34]

The case of post-war ball-and-rod objects on eBay reveals yet another reason for historians to engage further with the operation of historical narratives outside the academy. Such understanding is not only key to the practice of historians concerned with the wider ramifications of their work, but also necessary for the academic work itself. Historians are part of many 'publics' comprising the audience for public histories. Academic design historians have worked for decades to move past the influence of connoisseurial approaches, and have, in many respects, succeeded at this endeavour. There is an enduring relevance, however, to critically examining the field's traditional links – and sometimes-blurred boundary – with new cultures of collecting and connoisseurship, and the technologies underpinning them.

Notes

1. Colin Pill, 'Let's Get Spherical', *Vintage Explorer* (February/March 2014): 40.
2. 'Retro' here refers to the revival of post-war styles of a 'long' 1950s, encompassing the late 1940s and early 1960s.
3. 'Mediation' in this context corresponds to what Grace Lees-Maffei calls the 'mediating channels' between producers and consumers, which include retailing and advertising. Grace Lees-Maffei, 'The Production – Consumption – Mediation Paradigm', *Journal of Design History* 22, no. 4 (2009): 354.
4. Sarah Elsie Baker, *Retro Style: Class, Gender and Design in the Home* (London: Bloomsbury, 2013), 107.
5. Baker, *Retro Style*.
6. Hilda Kean and Paul Martin (eds), *The Public History Reader* (London: Routledge, 2013).
7. Zoe Trodd, 'Reading eBay: Hidden Stores, Subjective Stories, and a People's History of the Archive', in Ken Hillis and Michael Petit (eds), *Everyday eBay: Culture, Collecting, and*

Desire (London: Routledge, 2006), 77–90; Ken Hillis, 'Auctioning the Authentic: eBay, Narrative Effect, and the Superfluity of Memory', in Hillis and Petit, *Everyday eBay*, 167–84; Baker, *Retro Style*; Michele White, *Buy It Now: Lessons from eBay* (Durham: Duke University Press, 2012); Sharon Zukin, *Point of Purchase: How Shopping Changed American Culture* (London: Routledge, 2004).

8. See e.g. Christopher Breward and Ghislaine Wood (eds), *British Design From 1948: Innovation in the Modern Age* (London: V&A, 2012); Jonathan M. Woodham, *Twentieth-Century Ornament* (London: Studio Vista, 1990); Lesley Jackson, *Contemporary: Architecture and Interiors of the 1950s* (London: Phaidon, 1994).

9. Heal & Son, 'Presents for Particular People', 1953–1956, 2. V&A National Art Library Trade Catalogues Collection.

10. There is insufficient space for a detailed post-war history of ball-and-rod furnishings here. Research informing this section is covered in my doctoral thesis, 'Mid-Century Molecular: The Material Culture of X-ray Crystallographic Visualisation across Post-war British Science and Industrial Design', PhD dissertation, Royal College of Art and the Science Museum, 2016.

11. As a result of eBay search experiments carried out between 2013 and 2015 testing the relationship between ball-and-rod objects and several keywords, I hypothesized that they were most strongly linked to the keyword 'atomic'. Between May and July 2015, I analyzed the frequency with which ball-and-rod objects appear in results lists generated by searches using the keyword 'atomic' through data gathered weekly throughout this three-month period.

12. Office for National Statistics, National Life Tables, United Kingdom, 2012–2014, 23 September 2015, http://www.ons.gov.uk/ons/dcp171778_416983.pdf (accessed 26 September 2015).

13. Trodd, 'Reading eBay', 88.

14. Bevis Hillier, *Austerity/Binge: The Decorative Arts of the Forties and Fifties* (London: Studio Vista, 1975), 159.

15. Ibid.

16. Cara Greenberg, *Mid-Century Modern* (New York: Thames and Hudson, 1984), 45.

17. Paul Rennie, *Miller's 20th-Century Design Buyers Guide* (Kent: Miller's, 2003); Madeleine Marsh, *Miller's Collecting the 1950s* (London: Miller's, 1997); Christopher Pearce, *Fifties Source Book: A Visual Guide to the Style of a Decade* (London: Quarto, 1990).

18. Marsh, *Miller's Collecting the 1950s*, 35, 78; Pearce, *Fifties Source Book*, 135.

19. Rennie, *Miller's 20th-Century Design*.

20. Baker, *Retro Style*, 101.

21. Baker, *Retro Style*.

22. Judith Miller, *Miller's 20th Century Design: The Definitive Illustrated Sourcebook* (London: Miller's, 2009), 146.

23. Cathy Hayes, *The Easy eBay Business Guide: The Story of One Person's Success and a Step-by-Step Guide to Doing It Yourself* (London: Right Way, 2014).

24. Trodd, 'Reading eBay'.

25. Sophie Forgan, 'Atoms in Wonderland', *History and Technology* 19, no. 3 (2003): 182.

26. David Edgerton, *The Shock of the Old: Technology and Global History Since 1900* (London: Profile Books, 2006), xi.

27. Jacques Derrida and Eric Prenowitz, 'Archive Fever: A Freudian Impression', *Diacritics* 25, no. 2 (1995): 17.

28. Raphael Samuel, *Theatres of Memory* (London: Verso, 1994), 17.

29. Meg Foster, 'Online and Plugged In?: Public History and Historians in the Digital Age', *Public History Review* 21 (2014): 1–19.

30. See Marquard Smith, 'Theses on the Philosophy of History: The Work of Research in the Age of Digital Searchability and Distributability', *Journal of Visual Culture* 12, no. 3 (2013): 375–403.

31. White, *Buy It Now*, 8.

32. Samuel, *Theatres of Memory*.

33. Ludmilla Jordanova, *History in Practice* (London: Arnold, 2000), 103.

34. Edgerton, *The Shock of the Old*.

8   A Queer Feeling and Its Future in/for Design History

DR JOHN POTVIN

My research in general, and this chapter more specifically, is motivated by the ambition to provide a long overdue intervention into the state of Design History in which the study of sexuality has been systemically ignored and upon which queer theory has seemingly left no discernible trace twenty-five years after it first made its appearance in academic circles and activist networks. What fascinates me is how sexuality continues to be either taken for granted in the case of gay men as interior designers or simply omitted in the case of lesbians. As architect and essayist Joel Sanders once claimed: 'If the history of the professional decorator has been neglected, the subject of homosexuality and interior decoration has been largely ignored.'[1] In the *Journal of Interior Design*, Mark Hinchman has more recently noted, even if in passing, that 'one might think, [. . .], that the issues of design, sexuality, and identity would interest historians [. . .] but this [. . .] remains largely unexpressed'.[2] In key Design History texts by leading scholars focusing on the field's methodologies, historiography and its possible future directions, sexuality as a path of inquiry has consistently been missing.[3] This fact becomes even more distressing when one considers that the majority of these texts, which proclaimed to provide the blueprint of the future of Design Studies, were written during the most dire period of the AIDS crisis and the development and consolidation of queer theory itself. Yet, neither the texts nor their authors hint at queer theory's and sexuality's potential for the study of design and its histories. In short, the complex relationship between the practices and histories of design and sexuality remain the love that dare not speak its name. To what can we attribute this glaring lacuna?

Undoubtedly, the easiest way out of this dilemma is to simply blame the archives. But this would prove short-sighted. By moving in and out of time, this chapter seeks to ask, rather than definitively answer, what a queer design archives might be and concurrently how might we queer Design History and its archival landscape. As a result, without providing a definitive answer, I pose the following series of questions:

- What is a scholar to do when faced with an absence of images and notebooks? Is affect an effective means to fill in blanks, as some have suggested?

- How can queer theory and the study of sexuality more broadly help to shape the design archive?

- How might a queer-activist reading and intervention into historico-archival material provide the groundwork for a future Design History?

- Still excluded from Design Studies and Design History, what is the future of a queer design archive?
- What or how might queer theory intervene in our tacit understanding of the time and temporality of design?

In short, what is the queer future of the design archive and Design History itself?

Speculative and theoretical, my ambition is to queer Design History and its archives as much as it is to locate a queer feeling within and for the archive and history of design. Given the current state of Design History, both, I suggest, are required and equally of value as they offer a necessary critique as well as a recuperative exercise. Within the brief space of this chapter I aim to question, provoke and call upon my reader to help flesh out a long and sadly forgotten history. Finally, by exploring and moving forward queer theory's more recent attention to queer futurity, this chapter attempts to fold into the narrative of Design History a queer concern for history and its future impact on the discipline and its archival landscape.

Scholarship in many ways parallels how designers and their pedagogues speak of design problems and design solutions, a structural logic that portends to find concrete answers to tangible human needs and demands. Not unlike traditional academic 'rigour', with its pretensions to near mathematical precision, design problems call for quantifiable solutions and tangible outcomes, reliant on empirical data. In this context, it can come as no surprise that queer theory and its ambiguous applicability provides a challenge to the so-called rigours of academic and industrial praxis. As the late queer scholar José Esteban Muñoz simply yet cogently queer-ied: 'Who owns rigor?' Muñoz provides the answer by claiming that it is to 'institutional ideology' that we owe our understanding of a notional rigour.[4] Queer theory all too often is seen as being too preoccupied with the surfaceness of style and taste and is victim, like feminism before it, of 'lacking historical grounding and conceptual staying power [. . .]. Work and thinking that does not employ and subscribe to traditionalist scholarly archives and methodologies,' Muñoz asserts, 'are increasingly viewed as being utterly without merit. Work that attempts to index the anecdotal, the performative, or the ephemeral as proof is often undermined by the academy's officiating structures.'[5]

Queer leanings

I begin my excursion through queer theoretical territory by way of a slight diversion; one I hope will situate what I see as a much larger discussion and historical current, one which cannot, however, be fully fleshed out within the scope of this brief chapter. In a review of my recent book *Bachelors of a Different Sort: Queer Aesthetics, Material Culture and the Modern Interior in Britain*, one reviewer wrote: 'Potvin prefers to explore the "mood" of these domestic spaces and some of the ways in which their inhabitants experienced them, although much of the experiential material comes from accounts offered by the ephemeral visits made by guests and/or the carefully orchestrated performances of the occupants.'[6] While I must confess to originally being affected by the author's use of 'mood' in ironic quotation marks as well as the seemingly dismissive idea that the experiential is largely derived from so-called guests, I soon realized that the nerve it hit spoke to a larger concern at stake. For me, the idea of 'mood' and other cognate terms made me think about what constitutes the histories of design and the material world, and perhaps more specifically its objects, subjects and the methodologies best suited to understand this rich history. At the same time, it also seemed to pit 'mood' against 'rigour' and empirical fact. On another level, the nerve it hit, I might further suggest, is one activated all too often by a common experience: one of justification in the face of an inhospitable, unaccommodating and incomplete archive which, by its very nature, leaves little, if any, room for marginal histories, however understood. Like many other marginal groups, the queer men I have studied in the past, and continue to investigate, did not leave extensive records, personal impressions or deep archives, seemingly the 'stuff' of rigour. Some made painfully clear their desire to have their records and archives destroyed posthumously. The Welsh artist and pedagogue Sir Cedric Morris (1889–1982) comes to mind in this context given that he made explicit his desire for all his letters, diaries and sketches to be destroyed following his death.[7]

Material legacy is a critical facet of the design archive and the site of deep tension, trauma and loss within queer identity and historiography. Elizabeth Freeman offers the notion of chrononormativity to describe the 'use of time to organise individual human bodies toward maximum productivity'.[8] For Freeman, chrononormativity is the twinned outcome of industrial capitalism and the birth of the sexual deviant, historical realities of the mid- to late-nineteenth century. Following the self-perpetuating necessities of capitalism and its normalizing tendencies, chrononormativity sees its concern 'beyond individual anatomies to encompass the management of entire populations'. The resulting effects are 'teleological schemes of events or strategies for living such as marriage, accumulation of health and wealth for the future, reproduction, childrearing, and death and its attendant rituals'.[9] For the dissident queer subject, whose lack of progeny prevents inheritance and eventual cultural legacy, chrononormativity further enables an absence through the measuring, embodiment and progressive heteronormative stages of proper, diachronic and teleological time.

Rather than lamenting the lack of archival abundance and archival opacity, I read the partial or at times full lack of visual or textual remnants of the spaces and the objects of queer design as products of personal legacies, the effects of history and the architecture of the archives, which I believe in turn compels a different sort of looking, especially as it concerns the history of the professional decorator, for example. In a different context, Peggy Phelan has made a plausible case for the power of invisibility and the potential agency that remaining unmarked might hold. She writes: 'The binary between the power of visibility and the impotency of invisibility is falsifying. There is real power in remaining unmarked; and there are serious limitations to visual representation as a political goal.'[10] Residing in the unmarked, where moods, atmospheres, feelings and the ephemeral give or enhance the meaning and significance of spaces and objects provides a hidden language for a community outside and yet within the bounds of normative structures and meanings; below the radar, if you will. Moods, atmospheres and feelings are sometimes all we have as historians, and all too often they come from within but also from outside a community, a reminder that certain types of lives – queers in particular – have always been subject to a scrutinizing, surveying gaze.

As feminist queer scholar Anne Cvetkovich asserts, 'Forged around sexuality and intimacy, and hence forms of privacy and invisibility that are both chosen and enforced, gay and lesbian cultures often leave ephemeral and unusual traces.'[11] This certainly becomes abundantly clear in any investigation of the domestic interior. These so-called ephemeral and unusual traces provide an alternative or queer way through Walter Benjamin's well-cited notion of the 'traces of inhabitation'. For Benjamin, faced with the effects of industrial modernity, the bourgeois sets out to 'compensate for the absence of any trace of private life in the big city. He tries to do this within the four walls of his apartment. [. . .] Indefatigably, he takes the impression of a host of objects. [. . .] He has marked preference for velour and plush, which preserve the imprint of all contact. [. . .] The traces of its inhabitant are moulded into the interior'.[12] In another context, Benjamin also concludes that 'photography made it possible for the first time to preserve permanent and unmistakable traces of a human being'.[13] The advent of the modern/ist interior was greatly facilitated by and earned its success almost entirely due to the rich photographic culture it generated.[14] As a critique to the hermeneutics of archival evidence, it might be prudent not to fall into the trap of the visibility of representation.

How the so-called traces of inhabitation, the material evidence of being in the world, is outlined, analysed and interpreted is a rather complicated and tense site for the queer subject. Ephemeral traces such as moods, gossip and innuendo are important facets of queer object relations. As Muñoz importantly notes,

> Queerness is often transmitted covertly. This has everything to do with the fact that leaving too much of a trace has often meant that the queer subject has left herself open for attack. [. . .] Queer acts, like queer performances, and various performances of queerness, stand as evidence of queer lives, powers, and possibilities. [15]

> Cvetkovich also writes:

> Lesbian and gay history demands a radical archive of emotion in order to document intimacy, sexuality, love, and activism, all areas of experience that are difficult to chronicle through the materials of a traditional archive. Moreover, gay and lesbian archives address the traumatic loss of history that has accompanied sexual life . . . and they assert the role of memory and affect in compensating for institutional neglect [. . .]. Memories can cohere around objects in unpredictable ways, and the task of the archivist of emotion is thus an unusual one.[16]

What this suggests is an alternative pathway into the design archive; a method that takes into consideration the important ways instinct, affect, mood and feeling can and do affect the history of design and the modern interior.

Professional insinuations

In one of two foundational essays from 1895, American decorator Candice Wheeler was among the very first to claim interior decoration as a suitable and natural profession for women. For her, the domestic realm was already largely understood to be the purview of women, themselves relegated to its confines. However, it was less social realities than a seemingly inherent instinct that gave women their clear advantage. According to Wheeler, 'the apparently instinctive knowledge which women have of textiles, and which men have not, the intimate knowledge of the conveniences of domestic life – conveniences which may also be used as factors in a scheme of beauty – are great advantages to women who make this choice of a profession'.[17] Even before Wheeler's brief but effective treatise extoling the virtues and social significance of legitimate professional women, Jacob von Falke asserted that 'taste in women may, on the contrary [to men], be said to be natural to her sex. She is the mistress of the house in which she rules and which she orders like a queen.'[18]

Not long after, Elsie de Wolfe also affirmed that the domestic interior and its decoration was not the domain of men:

> We take it for granted that every woman is interested in houses – that she either has a home in course of construction, or dreams of having one, or has had a house long enough wrong to wish it right. And we take it for granted that this American home is always a woman's home: a man may build and decorate a beautiful house, but it remains for a woman to make a home of it for him. It is the personality of the mistress that the house expresses. Men are forever guests in our homes no matter how much happiness they may find there.[19]

De Wolfe's choice of words reveals her ambition to legitimate women's cultural and social position more broadly and more specifically in relation to the home and its decoration; an endeavour she, among others, deemed worthy of recognition. However, two short years later, Frank Alvah Parsons proclaimed, 'The house is but the externalized man; himself expressed in colour, form, line and texture. To be sure, he is usually limited in means, hampered by a contrary and penurious landlord or by family heirlooms, and often he cannot find just what he wants in the trade; but still the house is his house. It is he.'[20] For Parsons, the home is the material manifestation of male subjectivity.

By the turn of the century, the professional decorating press set out to define the characteristics of the type of character best suited to a profession that 'appeals to many people who have an inclination for the artistic, and it will appeal to many others who think they see in it possibilities of easily acquiring the ability to produce an income by a genteel vocation'.[21] Designations such 'artistic' and 'genteel', especially within a context of decoration, could only designate two types of people: women and effeminate men. David M. Halperin emphatically reminds us that 'effeminacy deserves to be treated independently because it was for a long time defined as a symptom of an excess of what we would call heterosexual as well as homosexual desire. It is therefore a category unto itself.'[22] It is the effeminacy attributed to homosexuality that proves problematic in a cultural context that ensures and sanctions preferred and hegemonic masculinity as distinct from its (feminine) other. The gay decorator's 'effeminate manners and voice hinted [and] provided a foil for the "real" man – productive, reproductive, and resolutely heterosexual'.[23] The effeminate male decorator quickly became a menacing, hybrid figure who was neither true decorator nor true man.

In 'Interior Desecration', Dorothy Rothschild narrates the fictional story of an afternoon encounter at the home of Mrs Endicott with a fictional friend, 'one of our most talented interior decorators', who was responsible for its decoration. Alistair St Cloud is 'pale and tall and slim, and he droops a bit, like a wilted lily. He is always just a little weary. He has phenomenally long nervous hands, white and translucent, which are used principally for making languid gestures for though his voice is sweet and low like the wind of the western sea, he speaks but seldom.'[24] Throughout the interiors, 'the delicate touch of Alistair was visible'. Oversaturated, Rothschild is consumed by the sensational decoration St Cloud has orchestrated. Physician and social critic Max Nordau feared the affective response to decadent and aesthetic decorative objects and interiors when he claimed that, for men like St Cloud, 'everything in these houses aims at exciting the nerves and dazzling the senses. The disconnected and antithetical effects in all arrangements, the constant contradiction between form and purpose, the outlandishness of most objects, is intended to be bewildering.'[25] Rothschild continues: 'He paced the floor, one delicate hand on his hip, one pressing his forehead, behind which great thoughts leaped and surged. But inspiration did not come with exercise.'[26] The image evoked is that of the 'genteel' and 'artistic' decorator. St Cloud embodies the characteristics of the female decorator, whose instinct, taste, affect and feeling are the only means through which to conjure interior décor.

From instinct to feelings

In *The Art of Decoration*, Mrs H. R. Haweis made clear that 'if taste means sensibility and judgement, there may be unhealthy sensibility and prejudiced judgement'.[27] For her part, Wheeler clarified this relationship along gendered lines, asserting that 'now, truth compels me to confess that the man decorator – if he is not a mere man of trade, as many of them, alas! are – will follow the purpose of the – architect. Perhaps this is because he is more widely educated, and is less interested in and impressed by individual things; he *feels* them less strongly.'[28] Periodicals like *The Upholsterer* and *Interior Decorator* lamented the need for greater education as a means to ameliorate and legitimate the profession. Yet for Wheeler it was precisely education that disabled men from feeling objects as strongly as women did. The male decorator's lack of feeling, for Wheeler, aligned him perfectly with male architects, and yet for architects too much feeling – or emotion – left a man vulnerable to suspicion of effeminacy. As

I have argued elsewhere, the simple and short, yet powerfully suggestive use of 'too' has long been deployed as a highly charged index of queer decadence and excess.[29] It is precisely, however, this excess, this overflowing of *too* much feeling where I think an important, though misplaced, history within decoration and design resides.

Following Raymond Williams's notion of the 'structures of feeling', which acknowledges the material dimensions that shape feelings, Muñoz points out that 'the ephemeral work of structures of feeling, is firmly anchored *within* the social'.[30] I wish to conclude by arguing for the important role 'feeling' seems to have played in these early and formative decades of the profession – at least within the Anglo-American context – best exemplified in a cartoon from 17 July 1926 in the *New Yorker*. In it, a young man and woman sit side by side on a settee, he with a noticeably cinched-in, wasp-like waist. The caption underneath reads as a question from the female companion who asks: 'I hear you are an interior decorator. Tell me, how does it feel?' As a question, it may appear simple and perhaps even mundane, but it speaks volumes about the dubious role of the male decorator. Perhaps it is even a trick question. For, at once her question points to an overall sense of professional attainment and pride, the haptic implications of decoration, a clear (homo)sexual innuendo even and yet, at the same time, speaks to Wheeler's, among others', gender bias that affords only women with affective potential. However, in addition to the particular professional dimension of the cartoon, there is also that question of gender, one that harkens back to another similarly dubious and amusing picture from the late nineteenth century. Featured in the 14 June 1879 issue of the satirical periodical *Punch*, a cartoon by Georges Du Maurier depicts a young 'Fair Aesthetic' gazing longingly, almost desperately, at the man to whom she has just been introduced and who is to serve as her dinner companion. Wistful and in earnest, she asks: 'Are you intense?' Intensity, after all, is everything, for it is the affective embodiment of the 'art for art's sake' mantra espoused by the willowy, lily-like Aesthetes, male and female alike. However, her companion is the embodiment of the straight-faced, straight-backed indifferent man, who does not even acknowledge her. He is not a kindred spirit, but rather a man without aesthetic inclination or, more exactly, without feeling. In English, to be intense refers to a number of intersecting definitions according to the *Oxford English Dictionary*. First and foremost, it refers to 'a quality or condition: Raised to or existing in a strained or very high degree; very strong or acute; violent, vehement, extreme, excessive; of colour, very deep; of a feeling, ardent.' It also describes 'feeling, or susceptible to, intense emotion or affection. Also, manifesting intense emotion or excitability, esp. in aesthetic or intellectual contexts.' Her companion for the evening exhibits neither signs of excess or ardent, aesthetic feeling, neither emotion nor affection and, finally, he is neither earnest nor ardent. Indeed, he is the perfect foil to the decorator represented decades later in the *New Yorker*, whose real currency is indeed his feelings. For, without feeling he is simply another straight (up) and respectable man, but with it he is definitively queer.

In the end, feeling, that is, the queer affects of decoration and design itself, as a seemingly integral ingredient of interior decorating, doubles upon itself and offers both a feminist intervention and yet at the same a queer interpolation into the twentieth-century Anglo-American professional interior design landscape. Queer modernist designer and architect Eileen Gray once stated that 'one must build for man, so that he may rediscover for himself the joy of feeling'.[31] Indeed, what I might assert is a queer history of design is not to be found necessarily in specific objects or entire spaces, but in those moods and feelings we have so long been told to repress throughout history and which require a different type of reading within the archives. These moods and feelings importantly resist and replace the tacit and assumed chrononormative reading of design historical sources. Indeed, as historians, we might do well to ask: How does the history of (interior) design feel? A queer question to be sure.

Notes

1. Joel Sanders, 'Curtain Wars: Architects, Decorators, and the 20th-Century Domestic Interior', *Harvard Design Magazine* (Winter/Spring 2002): 16.
2. Mark Hinchman, 'Interior Design History: Some Reflections', *Journal of Interior Design* 38, no. 1 (2013): xvii.
3. See, e.g., Hazel Clark and David Brody, 'The Current State of Design History', *Journal of Design History* 22, no. 4 (2009): 303–8; Clive Dilnot, 'The State of Design History, Part I: Mapping the Field', *Design Issues* 1, no. 1 (Spring 1984): 4–23; Clive Dilnot, 'The State of Design History, Part II: Problems and Possibilities', *Design Issues* 1, no. 2 (Autumn 1984): 3–20; Clive Dilnot, 'Some Futures for Design History?' *Journal of Design History* 22, no. 4 (2009): 377–94; Victor Margolin, 'A Decade of Design History in the United States, 1971–87', *Journal of Design History* 1, no. 1 (1988): 51–72; Victor Margolin, 'Design History or Design Studies: Subject Matter and Methods', *Design Issues* II, no. 1, (Spring 1995): 4–15.
4. José Esteban Muñoz, *Cruising Utopia: The Then and There of Queer Futurity* (New York: New York University Press, 2009), 7.
5. Muñoz, *Cruising Utopia*, 7.
6. Sally-Anne Huxtable, 'Bachelors of a Different Sort: Queer Aesthetics, Material Culture and the Modern Interior in Britain Review', *Interiors*, 6, no. 2 (2015): 205.
7. See John Potvin, *Bachelors of a Different Sort: Queer Aesthetics, Material Culture and the Modern Interior in Britain* (Manchester and New York: Manchester University Press, 2014).
8. Elizabeth Freeman, *Time Binds: Queer Temporalities, Queer Histories* (Durham and London: Duke University Press, 2010), 3.
9. Freeman, *Time Binds*, 4.
10. Peggy Phelan, *Unmarked: The Politics of Performance* (New York and London: Routledge, 1996), 6.
11. Ann Cvetkovich, *An Archive of Feelings; Trauma, Sexuality, and Lesbian Public Cultures* (Durham and London: Duke University Press, 2003), 8.

12. Walter Benjamin, 'Paris: Capital of the Nineteenth Century', in Benjamin, *The Arcades Project* (Cambridge, MA, and London: The Belknap Press of Harvard University Press, 1999), 19–20.

13. Walter Benjamin, 'Theses on the Philosophy of History', in *Illuminations* (New York: Schocken, 1969), 255.

14. See Charles Rice, *The Emergence of the Interior* (London and New York: Routledge, 2007) and Beatriz Colomina, *Privacy and Publicity: Modern Architecture as Mass Media* (Cambridge: Cambridge University Press, 1994).

15. José Esteban Muñoz, 'Ephemera as Evidence: Introductory Notes to Queer Acts', *Women and Performance: A Journal of Feminist Theory* 8, no. 2 (1996): 6.

16. Ann Cvetkovich, 'In the Archives of Lesbian Feeling: Documentary and Popular Culture', *Camera Obscura* 49, no. 17 (2002): 110.

17. Candace Wheeler, 'Interior Decoration as a Profession for Women', *The Decorator and Furnisher* 26, no. 3 (1895): 88.

18. Jacob von Falke, *Art in the House: Historical, Critical, and Aesthetical Studies on the Decoration and Furnishing of the Dwelling* (Boston, MA: Prang, 1879), 315.

19. Elsie De Wolfe, *The House of Good Taste* (New York: Century, 1913), 5.

20. Frank Alvah Parsons, *Interior Design: Its Principles and Practice* (New York: Doubleday, Page, 1915), vii.

21. 'How Can I Become a Decorator?', *The Upholsterer and Interior Decorator* 71, no. 1 (1923): 97–8.

22. David M. Halperin, 'How to Do the History of Male Homosexuality', *GLQ: The Journal of Lesbian and Gay Studies* 6, no. 1 (2000): 92.

23. Stephen Joshua Vider, *No Place Like Home: A Cultural History of Gay Domesticity, 1948–1982*, PhD dissertation (Cambridge, MA: Harvard University, 2013), 29–30.

24. Dorothy Rothschild, 'Interior Desecration', *Vogue* (USA) 49, no. 8 (1917): 54.

25. Max Nordau, *Degeneration* (New York: D. Appleton, 1905), 11.

26. Rothschild, 'Interior Desecration', 54.

27. Mrs H. R. Haweis, *The Art of Decoration* (London: Chatto & Windus, 1881), 17.

28. Wheeler, 'Interior Decoration as a Profession for Women', 88. Emphasis mine.

29. Potvin, *Bachelors of a Different Sort*, 286–9.

30. Muñoz, *Cruising Utopia*, 10.

31. Gray Eileen and Jean Badovici, 'From Eclecticism to Doubt', in Constance Constant and Wilfried Wang (eds), *Eileen Gray: An Architect for all Senses* (Cambridge: Harvard University Graduate School of Design, 1996), 69.

Section 3
Days, Hours, Seconds

In this section, we turn our attention to the increasing pace of modern life and its consequences for our understanding of design. As Hartmut Rosa notes, there is a general consensus that time is speeding up: 'Fast food, speed-dating, power-naps and drive through funerals seem to testify our resolve to speed-up the pace of everyday actions, computers compute at ever higher speeds, transport and communication need only a fraction of the time they took a century ago,'[1] Logically we know that time is not passing more quickly; what is it, then, that causes us to perceive this to be the case? As historians, how might we interrogate this sense of the accelerated pace of life as an historical phenomenon, through an enquiry into the 'designed' nature of our temporal experiences? Speed implies not only rapidity but also ephemerality: How might we address design which exhibits the opposite characteristics, namely slowness and longevity?

Hartmut Rosa makes a distinction between two aspects of the increasing pace of modern life. On the one hand, there is the fact of technological acceleration, meaning we are now able to physically move more quickly from place to place: journeys that once took days or weeks may be completed in hours. Space seems to contract as a result, and here we are reminded again of Schivelbusch and his argument about the introduction of 'railway time' in the nineteenth century.[2] At the same time, we are experiencing an increasing pace of social change: people move jobs more frequently, there is less stability in social institutions, there is an increasing divorce rate and so on. To this we might add the dimension of accelerated obsolescence of the technological devices that are now part of our everyday lives. We now have a limited expectation of the lifespan of our mobile phones and computers, and we assume that at some point soon the technology with which we have become familiar will become outdated. Further, these digital devices contribute to another aspect of the perceived pace of modern life. As Judy Wajcman notes, actual working hours have not increased for many people, but the sense of being 'always on', always connected results in a 'time pressure paradox' whereby people feel more overworked, stressed and lacking in leisure time.[3]

David Lawrence's chapter in this section develops the theme of speed, addressing the ways in which the expansion of the underground railway network in London changed city dwellers' experience of time and space. The extension of London's underground lines to the suburbs in the 1930s made possible a new kind of working day for commuters; the increased speed of travel made it possible to live much further from the workplace. Harry Beck's tube map has famously been discussed as a contributing factor in the way in which the London Underground system presents a deceptive relationship between time and space: suburban stations are presented on the map as equally spaced, obscuring the fact that journey times between them are significantly longer than those in the centre of the city. Here Lawrence uses the notions of time and speed to construct an analysis of the whole of the London Underground system. He argues that it is a vast and complex organism in which industrial, graphic and information design systems come together to form one fully designed and – crucially – highly time-regulated experience. For passengers, according to Lawrence, the speed of a journey is only one element, the other being a sense of certainty and predictability

The association of architecture with durability and permanence was discussed by Seher Erdoğan Ford in Chapter 1. Claire McAndrew addresses a similar idea from a different angle, exploring the 1960s neo-futurist plans for the Plug-In City and the Fun Palace, in Chapter 10. Both of these schemes were based on the radical suggestion that cities need not be permanent and that architecture might change and adapt according to users' needs. The plans raise questions about ephemerality and disposability: all buildings are modifiable to some extent, but the schemes proposed here suggest a much greater rate of change. The Fun Palace and the Plug-In City were both conceived as projects with fundamentally socially improving goals in mind. But now that we are living in the digital age, what new kinds of temporality, and thus new kinds of subjectivity, are implied by apps or social media or big data? How might we develop a more cyclical conception of resources, economy and time in relation to design?

Stephen Hayward's chapter considers the ways in which contemporary designers are incorporating ideas of temporality into their work, and once again raises questions about designers' responsibility to imagine a better future. *The Clock of the Long Now* by Stewart Brand and others, for example, is intended as a catalyst for change in the present. The Long Now Clock– a solar-driven clock in the desert of New Mexico – is also a response to the accelerated pace of change in the present: this is a clock that ticks only once a year, and its hands move only once every one hundred years.[4] Rather like the Fun Palace and the Plug-In City, the Long Now Clock exists more as a prototype or provocation rather than a fully realized scheme. Yet the invitation to imagine the world 10,000 years into the future prompts us to recall a similar recalibration of mental time described in Huxtable's chapter, though in this instance the imagined time stretches 'ahead' of us rather than 'behind' us.

As Simon Sadler has noted, *The Clock of the Long Now* developed from Brand's conviction that the designer or architect should pay attention to the frequently overlooked dimension of time:

It is an intriguing commission to measure time, record culture, and preserve dying languages for a 'long now' of ten thousand years; but the clock is obviously a poetic device foremost, a memento of finitude (our lives) and seeming infinitude (the duration of the world), and thereby of our collective and individual responsibility in managing the world.[5]

Stewart Brand was also responsible for the design and production of the *Whole Earth Catalog*, famously one of the first publications to present an image of the whole globe, seen from space, on its cover, 'picturing design's raw material at a new and completely meta level'.[6] The image was intended as a kind of unifying metaphor, but can also be read as a visual representation of multiple temporalities, in the sense that at any one instance (the instance captured by the camera) it is both night and day somewhere in the world.

The *Whole Earth Catalog* emerged from 1960s' counterculture and was built on an interest in evolutionary and cybernetic systems that encouraged an approach to design which foregrounded a sense of long-term responsibility. Brand's other publications, such as *How Buildings Learn*, offer an alternative view of temporality for designers and architects, emphasizing duration rather than finitude.[7] Implicit in much of the discussion about 'fast' or 'slow' design is an underlying moral dimension, since 'slow' is associated with sustainability, mindfulness and environmental concerns. This is an issue of increasing interest to design historians: Michelle Labrague, for example, has discussed the clothing company Patagonia using the notion of 'slow design' to unpack the brand's approach to the production and consumption of sportswear clothing. There is an ethical dimension to this, she argues, since 'slow practitioners are questioning the values of a consumerist society and redefining them through a negotiation of the political-cultural clock of slow with commercial time'.[8] The idea that time and craft have a moral as well as an economic value is of course nothing new; this was after all the underlying principle of the Arts and Crafts movement. Niels Peter Skou develops these ideas further in Chapter 11 in his discussion of recent developments within the 'slow design' movement. Skou discusses the work of a number of contemporary designers whose work seeks to make time visible, and whose work enables consumers to purchase time symbolically 'by proxy'.

Discussion of 'slow design' is in a sense a reaction to the perceived larger forces of the 'network time' now seen to be associated with the hypermodern age. Our new experience of 'network time' means that railway time and clock time are no longer adequate metaphors to describe the pace of life. As Robert Hassan argues, if modernity was characterized by the regularization of time through railway timetables and Fordist production processes, we are now living within the ever-present state of simultaneity implied by the notion of 'network time':

Network time constitutes a new and powerful temporality that is beginning to displace, neutralize, sublimate and otherwise upset other temporal relationships in our work, home and leisure environments.[9]

This is significant, according to Hassan, because,

unlike the clock, the network is unpredictable, volatile and chaotic; but it has an inner logic (that of commerce and instrumentality) that we adapt ourselves to and have difficulty in exercising control over. Moreover, the 'shared experiences' through the 'shared temporality' of the clock, however manipulative and exploitative these may have been, did contain the spaces and the 'time' for reflection, organization and resistance in ways the network leaves no time and no space for.[10]

Toke Riis Ebbessen explores these ideas in his discussion of the design of the Amazon Kindle, an e-book reader that promises to remove the 'tiresome delay' associated with actually purchasing a physical book. Network time implies an expectation of instant gratification, exemplified by the 'order it now, get it delivered tonight' culture in which we increasingly live. Once again, we address the issues raised by digital connectivity and the compression of time into ever-smaller units. Yet, as Ebbessen argues, the design of the e-reader itself is less future-focused than might be imagined: as a designed object, the Kindle retains some of the characteristics of the experience of reading a 'real' book. In a sense, the digital book is an example of non-synchronicity, looking simultaneously to the past and to the future but existing only in tenuous form in the present. Thus time remains a fascinating lens through which design historians can consider the design of objects and their relationship to their users, for the present and the future.

Notes

1. Hartmut Rosa, *Alienation and Acceleration: Towards a Critical Theory of Late-Modern Temporality* (Malmo, Sweden: NSU Press, 2010), 15.
2. Wolfgang Schivelbusch, *The Railway Journey: The Industrialization of Time and Space in the Nineteenth Century* (Oakland: University of California Press, 2014).
3. Wajcman, *Pressed for Time: The Acceleration of Life in Digital Capitalism*, (Chicago: University of Chicago, 2015), 5.
4. Stewart Brand, *The Clock of the Long Now: Time and Responsibility* (New York: Basic Books, 1999).
5. Simon Sadler, 'An Architecture of the Whole', *Journal of Architectural Education* 61, no. 4 (2008): 115.
6. Ibid., 123.
7. Stewart Brand, *How Buildings Learn* (London: Viking, 1994).

8. Michelle Labrague, 'Patagonia: A Case Study in the Historical Development of Slow Thinking', *Journal of Design History* 30, no. 2 (2017): 188, doi:10.1093/jdh/epw050.

9. Robert Hassan, 'Network Time and the New Knowledge Epoch', *Time & Society* 12, no. 2–3 (2003): 226–41. doi:10.1177/0961463X030122004.

10. Ibid., 236.

9 Tube Time: How the Subterranean City Got Faster by Design

DR DAVID LAWRENCE

Introduction

This chapter is about time, enlightenment, buildings, art and design, much of it deliberately invisible to serve the quotidian spaces of the underground railway-subway system. It examines the evolution of the transport network as a sophisticated organism, at once mechanical monster and 'soft machine', to consider how its architectural, industrial, graphic, spatial and information designers have sought solutions for keeping pace with our urge to make the city move ever faster: to save time (Figure 9.1).

If you take a Rolex Oyster Perpetual wristwatch – or any mechanical timepiece – apart, you will have a handful of wheels and springs, but you won't understand anything about the nature of time.[1] Dismantling the exquisite Braun DN 42 functional digital clock (Dieter Rams/Dietrich Lubs, 1975) leaves a handful of circuit boards and injection moulded casing, but no intimation of entropy or eternity. Through the twentieth century, and into the twenty-first, the trains beneath our feet have carried us at speed across the metropolis – and I am writing this in London – forming parts of a giant mechanical, digital, human organism comprising many thousands of time machines. Many of London Underground's machines are some form of clock, measuring units of what we conveniently call time: counting down the time until the next event, detecting the event, announcing it, recording the delay of the 'lost' time.[2] Given the status of the Underground as a highly regulated corporate phenomenon, this chapter also notes relevant observations by Michel de Certeau and Wolfgang Schivelbusch to offer a philosophical commentary on the subject.[3]

The railway builders – of which the most progressive was a combination of several undertakings known as the 'Underground group' – were speculative ventures. Their aim was to fill the space below London with moving transit systems, their business to turn time and distance into profit: speed equals money. They used design endeavours in the fields of architectural, interior, information and product design, to accelerate London travel. Here, I will discuss signs, symbols, signals, maps and meaning – and in particular the ways in which we are brought into the environment of the Underground, and then the means by which design is used for us to automatically follow a path through it 'by means of a whole panoply of codes, ordered ways of proceeding and

Figure 9.1 Tower Hill Underground station, District and Circle lines, 1969. Station woman Miss P Eccleshall speaks into a microphone to make a station announcement. Photograph by Dr H. Zinram. London Transport Museum reference 1998/86171 © London Transport Museum.

constraints'.[4] Taken together, it is about design, speed and time – and a bit of magic deep in the machine. As the city busily goes on around us, try to imagine yourselves down there in the subterranean spaces of the tube. Imagine the mobile devices, mp3 players, buskers, crowds, clutches of shopping bags and the potential for finding, and indeed forgetting, the right stop for the interchange you need to get where you are going 'on time'. Then, beyond the bewilderment of urban transit, become aware too of the cabinets, cables, pipes and computers which make everything 'tick'.

Flow: Architecture and interior design for speed

Several private companies operated the first subterranean railway lines. These enterprises transformed the art of mining and tunnelling into one of precision plumbing: joining together prefabricated segments of cast iron to line headings through the Thames Basin, navigated only by geometry and geology far below any landmark. In 1890, architecture had not caught up with the mechanization of movement; underground station design comprised elements borrowed from classical languages: old features manipulated to meet new needs. The results were at best inelegant. Thomas Phillips Figgis (1858–1948) gave the pioneering deep-tube electric City and South London Railway busy brick-and-stone structures with cupolas to distinguish them from shops and enclose the elevator motors. By 1906, however, Leslie Green (1875–1908) had created a uniform architectural language in deep red glazed faience made by Burmantofts, the same Leeds-based pottery which was producing slender ceramic vases for the most progressive Arts and Crafts homes.

Green regarded the interior arrangement of vestibules, landings and horizontal and vertical passageways of his stations as a seamless travel experience. His holistic approach to railway architecture and interiors, signs and furnishings would become, in Michel de Certeau's words, the

> production of [the Underground's] own space, rational organisation [repressing] all the physical, mental and political pollutions that would compromise it; the substitution of a nowhen, or of a synchronic system; the creation of a universal and anonymous subject . . . a way of conceiving and constructing space on the basis of a finite number of stable, isolatable, and interconnected properties.[5]

It was also exemplary proto-corporate design. For the chthonic voids between street and platform, Green devised patterns of coloured tiles to reduce the oppressive sense of the tunnels, to brighten spaces that were difficult to illuminate because of the circular cross-section, and to give each station a unique colour scheme that would make it familiar to regular travellers. He chose hues from across the palette favoured by the Arts and Crafts movement, from mauve to turquoise, blue to amber to sang de boeuf (deep crimson) (see Figure 9.2).[6]

Leslie Green's tile patterns were so successful that the Underground replicated them when some stations were modernized in the 1990s. When Charles Holden (1875–1960) was charged with extending the Central, Northern and Piccadilly lines during the 1930s, he preferred to render the station depths in a uniform broken white, pursuing an idea that anonymity, overwritten by a precisely controlled hierarchy of signs, would unify the system. Misha Black maintained this strictly minimal approach, selecting pale grey for the Victoria line (1968–1969), and burnt orange for the Jubilee line (1979). Only with the refurbishment of Tottenham Court Road did the Underground break away from visual monotony, commissioning Eduardo Paolozzi (1924–2005) to design extensive areas of mosaic tiling as vitreous storyboards of time, history and movement seen and experienced in the precincts of Soho and Bloomsbury.[7]

Signs and graphics: Persuasive information

Harry Wharton Ford (1875–1947) cannot claim any architectural or spatial innovation – his Underground railway work was in the shadow of Leslie Green's – but he made a difference to the designed environment of the tube which has had an impact unimaginable in 1906. While Green's station tiling patterns caught the eye, when seen at speed they gave, at best, a colourful blur. The Underground was international in ambition: it needed to identify its stations effectively below ground for travellers

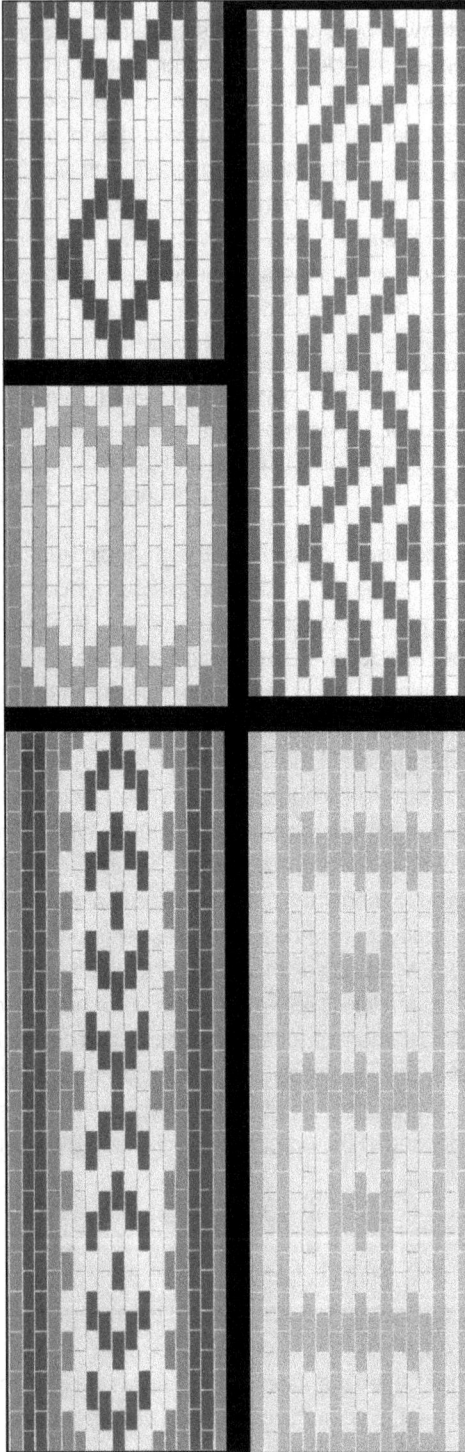

Figure 9.2 Renderings of geometric tile patterns devised by Leslie Green for tunnel stations on the Great Northern, Piccadilly and Brompton, Charing Cross, Euston and Hampstead, and Baker Street and Waterloo railways, 1905. Image © David Lawrence, 2015.

already on the trains. Why? Because much of the Underground's business was in encouraging passengers to travel further – the longer the journey, the higher the fare paid. With a dense network of railways, a good way to promote convenience and increase revenue was to facilitate interchange between lines. This was playing with the notion of convenience, promising at once quick journey times and inviting passengers to make longer journeys.

To make a connection, travellers needed to know where they were, and so emerged the need for fast recognition of the place name. Ford and his colleagues, who by 1906 included Frank Pick (1878–1941), combined typography, colour and shape to create a confident visual device they called a 'target' or 'bullseye'. These discs of scarlet vitreous enamel on steel, crossed by a blue bar whose style was copied from the Paris Métropolitain, were deployed on most stations on the Underground in a few years. Letter designer Edward Johnston refined the symbol during 1916–1920, replacing the disc with a ring and adding his specially designed Underground Railway Alphabet.[8] By 1938, the Underground had evolved a total graphic design idiom, all focused on the conveyance of information unambiguously, in rapid time, to travellers.

Each passenger decision was pre-empted and timed and a visual communication was provided to determine the possible next movement. By these means the Underground group and its successor, London Transport, created a high-speed typography: standard sign types and formats, and a colour scheme within the signs and printed materials, communicating with travellers throughout the station journey from street to train, and back again. This suite of information tools – legible and predictable – has remained at the core of the Underground's management of itself and its public ever since, however complex or unusual the spaces we traverse. The 'bullseye' was ubiquitous across London's transport activities, a distinctive brand mark in every two- and three-dimensional context.[9] In our own time, the 'bullseye' – renamed the 'roundel' – can be seen in transport settings around the world, and has come to be a near-instant synecdoche for London, cities, urbanism and often anything which considers itself to be an 'underground' alternative to popular culture.[10]

Hagiographies of Henry C. Beck (1902–1974) – or 'Harry', as this retiring, spurned, inventor is now popularly known – have set out in detail the great chart of his life as cartographer to the London Underground.[11] We don't need to do this again here; it is enough to know that H. C. Beck's project was to arrange the railway lines of the Underground system as a schematic of connections between one location and another. Its design was influenced by electrical circuit diagrams and by the work of George Dow for the London and North Eastern Railway.[12] Being a diagram rather than a map – for many years it was called the Diagram of Lines – the schematic enabled Beck to achieve the apparent contraction and expansion of distance and duration. Wolfgang Schivelbusch has called this point-to-point abstraction the 'annihilation of space and time'.[13] By moving the London Underground system away from any topographical truth, Beck's diagram created a 'new, reduced geography', without physically changing anything.[14]

Beck's network of coloured links between places of work and interest was committed by letterpress printing machines to small rectangles of card, neatly folded into three panels for every pocket and bag.[15] The map is so smart that it has accommodated numerous additions to the system since 1933, and as you read this there is a draft showing Crossrail 1 (the Elizabeth Line), Crossrail 2 (Hackney–Chelsea) and vectors for routes which we cannot yet conceive. Still circulated in their millions, the descendants of Beck's first map continue to be issued free today, at every Underground and Overground station. To hold one and imaginatively ponder from point to point, suburb to centre and out again across the compass, is as close as we may get as travellers in London to Marcel Proust's moments with the madeleine cake: coincident with all those journeys we have made, and may yet make, through time underground. Alongside the overarching and seductive geometry of the line diagram, Underground publicity has led a stylish choreography of travel where time becomes an elastic concept. Through posters across the transport environment, citizens were enticed into town to shop, watch sports, dance and see movies; they were called out of town to walk, picnic, visit fairgrounds and shows, boat on rivers and lakes; they were advised on when, or when not, to travel. By Underground, and associated road services, Londoners could enjoy urban transits of lightning speed between pursuits of languid duration, packing into a long day work and leisure, public and private pleasures.

Regulation: Machinery and technology

Now let's move back to the interior for a closer look at the equipment of time management in both the Underground's open and undisclosed areas, and in the virtual space of communications. With plate glass and bronze, Charles Holden achieved – for him and for contemporary England – a particularly advanced form of modernity in the kiosks he designed to enclose the ticket-issuing equipment and its operators. Officially termed 'passimeters' and based on less elegant international examples, these were polygonal units fabricated from plate glass – tiny crystal pavilions as crisp as any modernist dream – located directly in the flow of passengers through ticket halls. Passimeters housed ticket-issuing machines (Figure 9.3). Many were supplied by a British-based division of the American Westinghouse Company, who would later claim the 'first all-electric kitchen range', the 'first factory-built radio receivers for home use', washing machines, refrigerators and the cameras which recorded the first humans on the moon.[16] In this way, Underground railway staff obtained the privilege of 'finger-tip control' long before the general public. Actuating keys connected to relays and levers, they became the authors of impulses that printed tickets faster than their eyes could register.

Long before domestic settings could boast of electrical devices, inventors were crafting labour-saving, time-saving mechanisms for the urban railway. Increasingly, numerous arrays of equipment, communicating with each other through copper wires and pneumatic pipes, appeared as a population of anonymous boxes in the spaces

Figure 9.3 Passimeter ticket offices designed by architect Charles Holden, in the collection of the London Transport Museum. Image by David Lawrence, 2015.

of the tube. As much as the Apple Watch is an accessory connecting the human organism to innumerable functions, so the equipment packed into cases and pipes across the Underground linked interfaces with people to enable faster movement. The Underground railway maintained its own signal engineering department to coordinate developments in electric, and then electronic, control of the network. Much of this work was led by the pioneering Robert Dell (1900–1992), engineer to the Underground and author of many patents and inventions for the mechanics and electronics used to speed up the tube and enable it to keep time – a completely 'standardized time'.[17] Dell is unknown to many design historians because his work was deliberately invisible to the public. Industrial innovation must take some form, however: electronic systems require input and output interfaces for it to work with humans and other equipment.

It is Robert Dell who, with his colleagues Tom Challis and Stanley Higgins during 1957–1960, developed an idea already in use in Chicago, USA, to create electro-mechanical 'brains' named Programme Machines (Figure 9.4). Signalling centres housed many examples of these sequencers used to ensure that trains passed efficiently and safely across the network. In essence, the device stores information in holes punched through a Melinex plastic belt that passes over a series of detector fingers – like a self-playing 'pianola' roll – to generate electrical impulses. One type of machine stored the instructions for operation of signalling equipment; the second contained the timetable of trains. Both worked together and were linked to the live

Figure 9.4 A Programme Machine for the automatic routeing of train services, in the collection of the London Transport Museum. Image by David Lawrence, 2015.

movement of vehicles, unrolling by increment over the day and rerolling for the next use. At the other end of the cables energized with data by the Programme Machines, could be found elegant signal units fashioned as smooth aluminium boxes, with radius corners and coloured lamps (red and green or amber and green). Signals regulated the trains; Dell's work regulated people too. His 1955 'Follow the Lights' system was a visual shorthand distilled beyond the typographical information, which featured small coloured and illuminated signs mounted overhead at major Underground stations, to merge and separate streams of moving people. Robert Dell knew that data could be compressed in time too; he subsequently applied to tickets an early form of barcode, and magnetic coatings that could machine-make and machine-read information, placing into passengers' hands unseen data about the origin and destination of their travel. On the platforms themselves, other gadgets completed the Underground's mastery of time. The Platform Hustler was a relay unit which noted the arrival of the train, allowing thirty seconds to elapse before sounding a siren whose clamour impelled the railway workers to fill the vehicles and clear the platforms immediately using live and pre-recorded verbal instructions. Amplified sound (see Figure 9.1) thus joined the apparatuses of advancing speed; with the opening of the Victoria line in 1968, it would be augmented by closed-circuit television.

By the 1970s, London Transport had a real-time subgroup of the Railway Information Working Party to examine ways of 'saving' time. Its published aim was 'to deliver real-time information [to passengers] before leaving home, at the flick of a switch'.[18]

The subgroup was aware that speed was not enough – the passenger's desire to move faster had emotional implications too. Communications needed to be managed and measured, so that messaging promoted reassurance rather than anxiety. This brings us to the outer reaches of a discussion around design for speed: the editing of language itself to engender continuity of travel experience, even when stasis due to human or machine delay might be the reality. Digital realms take this forward for us as the Transport for London journey planner and the Oyster card, whose online presence records an autonomous account of our trajectories across the city.

Terminus

In this chapter, we have considered a very particular example of design working as the hinge between a place of departure and one of arrival. We have seen how the Underground railway builders used design to create spaces beneath the city subject to extreme regulation, and how they came to be adept at practising ways and methods to 'save' time and to 'make' time. The work of Michel de Certeau and Wolfgang Schivelbusch has shown how controlled environments are not to be taken for granted; our freedom must be sublimated as we benefit from this high level of design for speed. Much of this material is a fascinating but overlooked territory of twentieth-century culture, which invites further design-historical-material research.

Seeking ways to reduce the journey time enabled by the Underground highlighted a special third state of being too: those moments called 'dwell time' when a machine or a person is paused between actions. 'Dwell time' is essential for the safe passage of trains following one another. We call it waiting: those caesurae which seem to us too long, however brief and essential they are. We do not want to dwell below ground longer that we must. Idling for a moment, however, let's end with a story from the old Circle line – when trains really did run clockwise and anticlockwise, timetabled carefully to allow the slipping in and out of other routes in their path. It is possible to slide in the course of tube time too: Michel de Certeau alludes to the 'little space[s] of irrationality' that we can locate within the 'production of an order, a closed and autonomous insularity'.[19] I've chosen this piece to suggest that beyond the signs, lights, digitized voices and passenger flows, both statistical and physical, we can still be carried away into the reverie which is a by-product of the order that is the Underground. This is Iris Murdoch, from *Bruno's Dream*:

> It all happened very quickly. They met on an underground train. On the Inner Circle . . . .. Danby surreptitiously passed his station. Gwen surreptitiously passed hers. When they had been all the way round the circle they had to admit to each other that something had happened.[20]

We have seen how modernity in design has made us believe that we can live, and be moved, ever faster. Thankfully perhaps, despite all the efforts of designers to iron out delays and speed up our environments, on the Underground, at least, time can still stand still.

For their contributions to this work, David Lawrence would like to thank: Mike Brown MVO, Zoë Hendon, Allan Hoare, Lyanne Holcombe, London Transport Museum, Anne Massey, Simon Murphy, Sam Mullins, Paddy O'Shea, Doug Rose, Linda Thomson and Caroline Warhurst.

Notes

1. From an eavesdropped conversation on London Underground's Piccadilly line, travelling to Heathrow Terminal 4 station, 10 September 2017.
2. For this chapter I will refer to the underground railway network of London simply as the 'Underground'. Over time, it has been variously the 'Underground group', London Passenger Transport Board, London Transport and Transport for London. In its present form it also comprises the London Overground system and will soon also feature Crossrail 1, a long-distance railway which will serve existing Underground stations and new interchanges of a scale unprecedented in London.
3. Michel de Certeau (trans. Steven Rendall), *The Practice of Everyday Life* (Berkeley: University of California Press, [1984] 1988); Wolfgang Schivelbusch, *The Railway Journey: The Industrialization of Time and Space in the Nineteenth Century* (Oakland: University of California Press, 2014).
4. Certeau, *The Practice of Everyday Life*, 115.
5. Ibid., 94.
6. Doug Rose, *Tiles of the Unexpected: A Study of Six Miles of Geometric Tile Patterns on the London Underground* (Harrow Weald: Capital Transport Publishing, 2007).
7. Richard Cork (ed.) and Eduardo Paolozzi, *Eduardo Paolozzi Underground* (London: Royal Academy of Arts and Weidenfeld and Nicolson, 1986).
8. David Lawrence, *A Logo for London* (London: Laurence King, 2013); Justin Howes, *Johnston's Underground Type* (Harrow Weald: Capital Transport, 2000).
9. Lawrence, *A Logo for London*.
10. Ibid.
11. See e.g. Ken Garland, *Mr Beck's Underground Map* (Harrow Weald: Capital Transport, 1994).
12. Andrew Dow, *Telling The Passenger Where to Get Off: George Dow and the Evolution of the Railway Diagrammatic Map* (Harrow Weald: Capital Transport Publishing, 2005); Doug Rose, 'Henry Beck Invented What?' http://www.dougrose.co.uk/index_henry_beck.htm (accessed 28 November 2017).
13. Wolfgang Schivelbusch, *The Railway Journey: Trains and Travel in the 19th Century* (Oxford: Basil Blackwell, 1980), 41.
14. Ibid., 43–4.
15. Garland, *Mr Beck's Underground Map*.
16. See 'Explore Our History to Discover How Westinghouse Has Been at Work in Our World', Westinghouse Electric Corporation, http://westinghouse.com/heritage/ (accessed 19 November 2017).
17. Schivelbusch, *The Railway Journey*, 50.

18. Report of 'Real-Time' subgroup, in *Report of the Railway Information Working Party* (London: London Transport, 1976).
19. Certeau, *The Practice of Everyday Life*, 111.
20. Iris Murdoch, *Bruno's Dream* (Harmondsworth: Penguin Books in association with Chatto & Windus, 1970), 57.

10 Dreams of the Fun Palace and Plug-In City – Architectural Modularism and Cybernetics in the 1960s

DR CLAIRE MCANDREW

Introduction

This chapter considers the neo-futurist visions of two architectural designs from the 1960s, Archigram's Plug-In City[1] designed by Peter Cook in 1964 and the Fun Palace[2] conceived by Cedric Price in the same year. Each was radical in thinking around architectural modularism and, in the case of the Fun Palace, the embrace of cybernetic thought. Their designs speculated on visions that were temporally adaptive and represented an idealistic belief in a better future, with an aspiration to drive flexibility and versatility from a collection of modular units that could be arranged and re-arranged, time and time again. Reversing the assumed stability of architectural form, the Fun Palace and Plug-In City were conceived as systems where human activity could control and modify the spatial form within which it was framed and so on, ad infinitum. Blending modular architecture, technology and society, these two designs sought to provide liberation from modernism.

Reviewing material made accessible through the Archigram Archival Project hosted by the University of Westminster and the Cedric Price Collection held at the Canadian Centre for Architecture, this chapter examines some of the key expressions of neo-futurism captured by these 1960s, designs. Through this commentary, it sheds light on the ways in which time has been conceived of being designed into the architectural fabric of cities, and how, through the examination of critical debates, we might find relevance for design history today and for the design of contemporary living in the digital age.

New possibilities for architecture

Formed in 1960 at the Architecture Association in London, Archigram was formed of six architects and designers: Peter Cook, Warren Chalk, Ron Herron, Dennis Crompton, Michael Webb and David Greene.[3] This avant-garde collective focused their attention on the new possibilities for architecture, creating fictional alternatives around the aesthetic and functionality of cities. Archigram produced nine (and a half!) issues of an experimental publication that featured these visions and went by the same name – *Archi* meaning architecture; and *gram* taking its meaning from the urgency associated with a telegram.

Plug-In City was designed by Peter Cook in 1964 but is considered the outcome of a number of ideas produced in the early years of the collective. These included, for example, Cook's metal housing cabin (also known as Young People's Housing) designed in 1961, which employed a megastructure of concrete within which removable living capsules were inserted, aptly described as 'car body type units on precast guts'.[4] It was also informed by the Nottingham Shopping Centre Project designed in 1962 with David Greene. Shared permanent shop and office buildings as well as expendable mobile shop units serviced via a tunnel system and removed by cranes, sought to resolve the problems of frequent servicing and unit replacement.[5]

The Living City exhibition at the Institute of Contemporary Arts in London which featured Peter Cook's Come-Go Project (also known as the City Within Existing Technology) in 1963 – a speculative proposal for an infrastructure of services, communications and facilities which would allow cities to literally 'come and go' – was also instrumental in the formulation of the Plug-In City concept.[6] Issue 2 of *Living Arts Magazine*, which served as the catalogue to the exhibition, sought to articulate this vitality in a manifesto and a series of written/illustrated viewpoints. Here, Peter Cook expresses a restlessness with the permanence of built form against the ever-quickening pace of city life:

> 'Fashion' is a dirty word, so is the word 'Temporary', so is 'Flashy'. Yet it is the creation of those things that are necessarily fashionable, temporary or flashy that has more to do with the vitality of cities than 'monument-building'. The pulsation of city life is fast, so why not that of its environment? It reflects rise and fall, coming and going . . . change, so why not build for this?[7]

Through the eyes of the collective, architecture was seen as just one *part* of the city. Vivid portrayals in the exhibition and accompanying catalogue playfully referred to the *other parts* (man, survival, crowd, movement and communication) as 'gloop subjects'. Such gloops were conceived as compartments of the giant brain of the computer that contributed to the totality of the living city. Through such works, it became obvious that the studio ought to explore how the city as a whole could be designed and programmed for change.

Self-destroying, self-building

The Plug-In City is arguably not really a city but a constantly evolving and moving megastructure. Modular residential units 'plug-into' a central infrastructure which incorporates transportation, offices, leisure, even bad weather balloons which inflate to protect its inhabitants (Figure 10.1). Featured in *Archigram* issue no. 4 (1964), the aspiration was to drive flexibility and versatility from a collection of modular units that could be arranged and re-arranged time and time again. Its aesthetic imparts its radical time-based ethic: 'The dynamic processes of Plug-In – its ethic – had to be

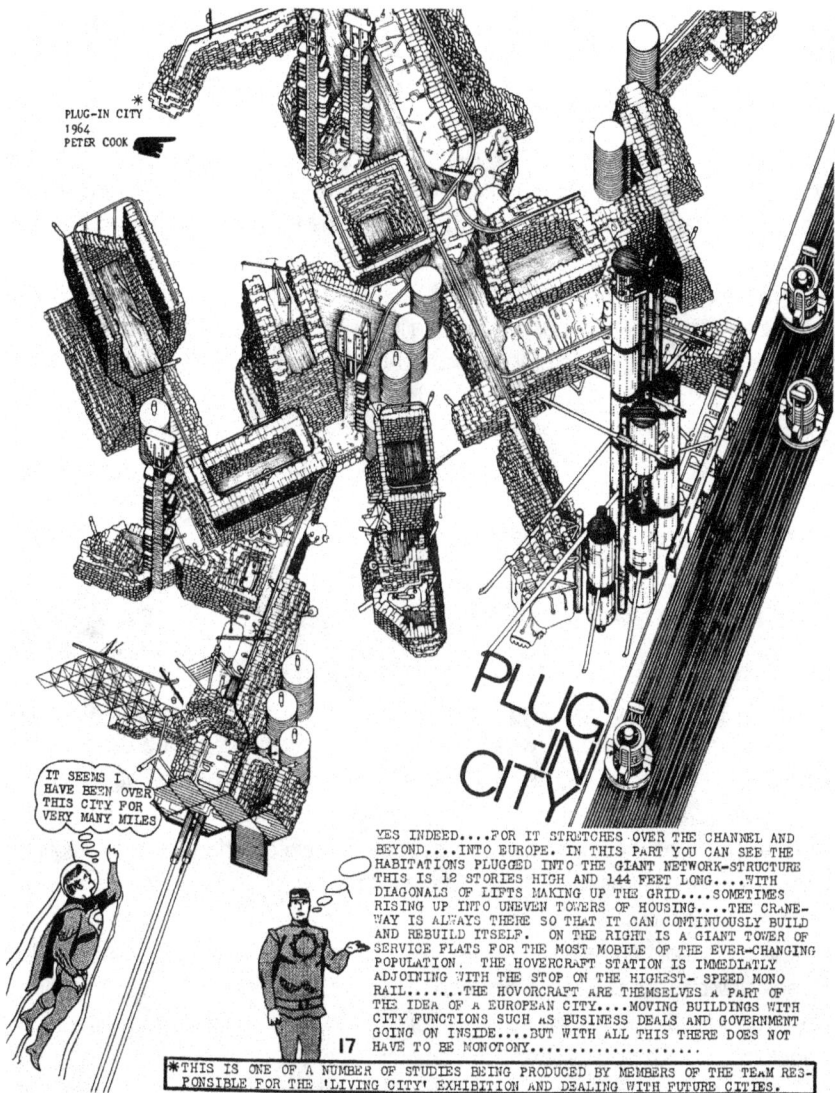

Figure 10.1 Plug-In City axonometric designed by Peter Cook featured in *Archigram* issue no. 4, 1964. Courtesy: The Archigram Archival Project.

made visible, and so became an aesthetic. Plug-In City turned architecture inside-out to make its interior life anterior; expendable apartments were slung happily down the outside of the huge A-frame substructures, rearranged by the cranes sliding back and forth above.[8] A hierarchy of relative permanence is exposed in what were labelled as 'sustenance components', with units planned for obsolescence.[9] The main megastructure was suggested to last forty years, with kitchens, living rooms and bathrooms to be changed every three years.

In an article published in the *Sunday Times* supplement magazine on 20 September 1964, Priscilla Chapman noted: 'On a technical level it is set apart from other plans by its purchase on life as it will be in the future. It grasps the rate at which people and things will change and, in effect, acknowledges throw-away architecture.'[10] Cook's analogy of nourishing the city is not lost on Chapman, with her noting Archigram's basic message that 'the home, the whole city and the frozen pea pack are all the same'.[11] Nor is the restructuring of the relation between people and built form. Describing Plug-In City as a 'self-destroying, self-building system', she notes the inversion of this relationship, that 'it is easily pushed into the shape people want it to be – rather than its pushing people into shape'.[12] It was not just Archigram who had an interest in architectural design and its plasticity. Eccentric and outlandish, this collective certainly pushed this ethic to its limit: 'Archigram injected flexibility with amphetamines and envisaged adaptability on a daily, if not hourly, basis.'[13] Looking back, Mike Webb reflects on how the adaptation of buildings to changes in user needs captured the spirit of the 1960s more generally – again, mirrored in Cedric Price's proposition for the Fun Palace.

'Events in time rather than objects in space'

Reversing the assumed stability of architectural form, the Fun Palace was also conceived as a system of exchange where human activity could control and modify the spatial form within which it was framed. The Fun Palace was the brainchild of Joan Littlewood (theatrical producer), Cedric Price (architect), Gordon Pask (systems consultant) and Frank Newby (structural engineer). The brief was to create a theatre like no other, a space that could transform to host plays, dance performances, wrestling, even political rallies. It was never the intention for it to become a multipurpose venue; the aspiration was far more visionary: to drive flexibility and versatility from a collection of modular units that can be arranged and re-arranged, time and time again. Working with Frank Newby, Cedric Price developed the structural scaffold for the programme. Vertical towers would not only hold vital services, but would be crowned with cranes that would hoist the modules into temporary formations.

The closing statement of the brochure for the Fun Palace (Figure 10.2) reads: 'We are building a short-term plaything in which all of us can realise the possibilities and delights that a 20th century city environment owes us. It must last no longer than we need it.'[14] This disposability parallels the throw-away ethic of Plug-In City. Imagined with process in mind, Stanley Matthews has even gone so far as to describe the Fun Palace as 'events in time rather than objects in space', a statement that could equally be applied to the imaginings of Archigram.[15]

What ultimately distinguished the Fun Palace from the Plug-In City was its embrace of cybernetic thought. As Stanley Matthews describes, Gordon Pask set out the general aim of the cybernetics committee – of which British artist Roy Ascott, whose work spans cybernetics and telematics, was a part – as the development of 'new forms of environment capable of adapting to meet the possibly changeful needs of

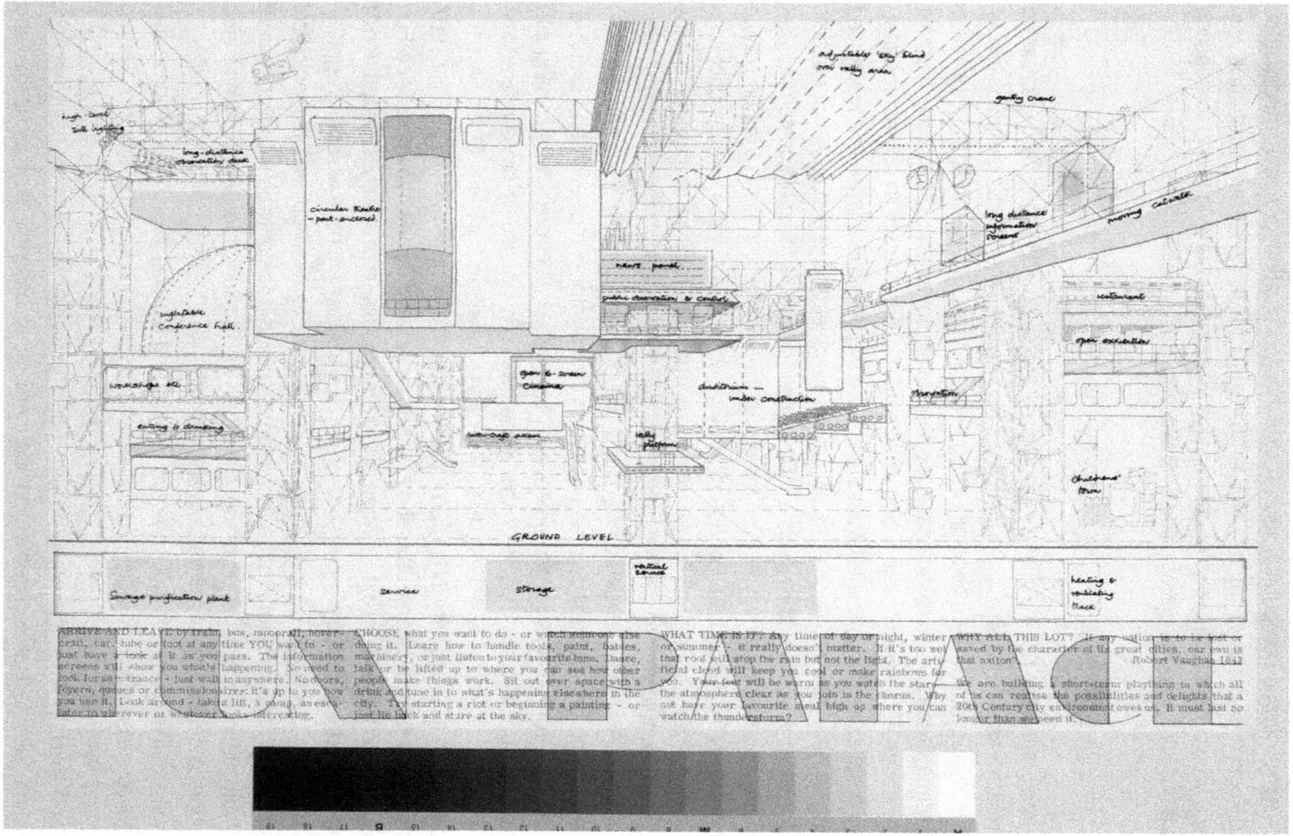

Figure 10.2 Brochure for the Fun Palace Project. Cedric Price (architect) and Joan Littlewood (client), 1964. Courtesy: Canadian Centre for Architecture.

a human population and capable also of encouraging human participation in various activities'.[16] Electronic sensors and response terminals would be instrumental in the collection of information on leisure preferences. The computational power of an IBM 360–30 mainframe computer would provide the specification for spatial modification by detecting clusters of trends. Not simply responsive to human need, the Fun Palace would be anticipatory: understanding patterns of behaviour and forecasting future activities through cybernetic principles and game theory.

Coming to grips with the near future

By *Archigram* issue no. 4 – the very same issue that featured Plug-In City – increasing reference was being made to Cedric Price's Fun Palace. The shortcomings of 1960s' architectural practice were becoming progressively more juxtaposed against their near future imaginaries of an architecture of speed and movement: 'One of the greatest weaknesses of our immediate urban architecture is the inability to contain the fast-moving object as part of the total aesthetic – but the comic imagery has always been strongest here. The representation of movement-objects and movement-containers is consistent with the rest, and not only because "speed" is the main gesture.'[17] That discussions were underway at this time about the viability of locating the Fun Palace along the Lea Valley in East London did not go unmissed.[18] Price was described as the only architect in England translating these ideas into reality and 'coming to grips with the near future'.[19]

Later, in *Archigram* issue no. 7 entitled 'Beyond Architecture' (December 1966), we see seventeen loose sheets and an electronic resistor in a plastic bag indicative, as Dennis Crompton has since noted, of a time when electronics was moving into miniaturization (Figure 10.3).[20] In this issue, we see continued cross-referencing between Price and Cook. First, the 'Time Essay' written by Peter Cook with the sub-heading 'Get in There INTO 1967 You You You It's Up to You'. It reads, 'By 1967 Archigram will have been outbursting for some six years. The Littlewood/Price Fun Palace will be three years old . . . Already there is discussion of a second generation of programmed/expendable/clip-on etc. projects . . . But where have we actually got?'[21] He provides comment on the failure of architecture to keep up with technological progress and an ultimatum to the *Archigram* readership to continue with architecture as mere decoration or to embrace the future and collaborate with programmers, electronics engineers, bio-physicists and so on.

We see this call for change reflected in a second feature, the cut-out which invites its readers to engage in tactile experimentation with the underlying ethos of Plug-In City and the Fun Palace – taking Littlewood's original idea of a 'kit of parts'.[22]

And third, in an article authored by Cedric Price, we see another call to action, this time directed at architects and planners: 'It is essential that architects and planners start exercising their skills in producing proposals and artifacts whose nature, form, performance and expectancy of life will enable activities and actions hitherto unimaginable in both content and frequency.'[23] This is not to say that this is

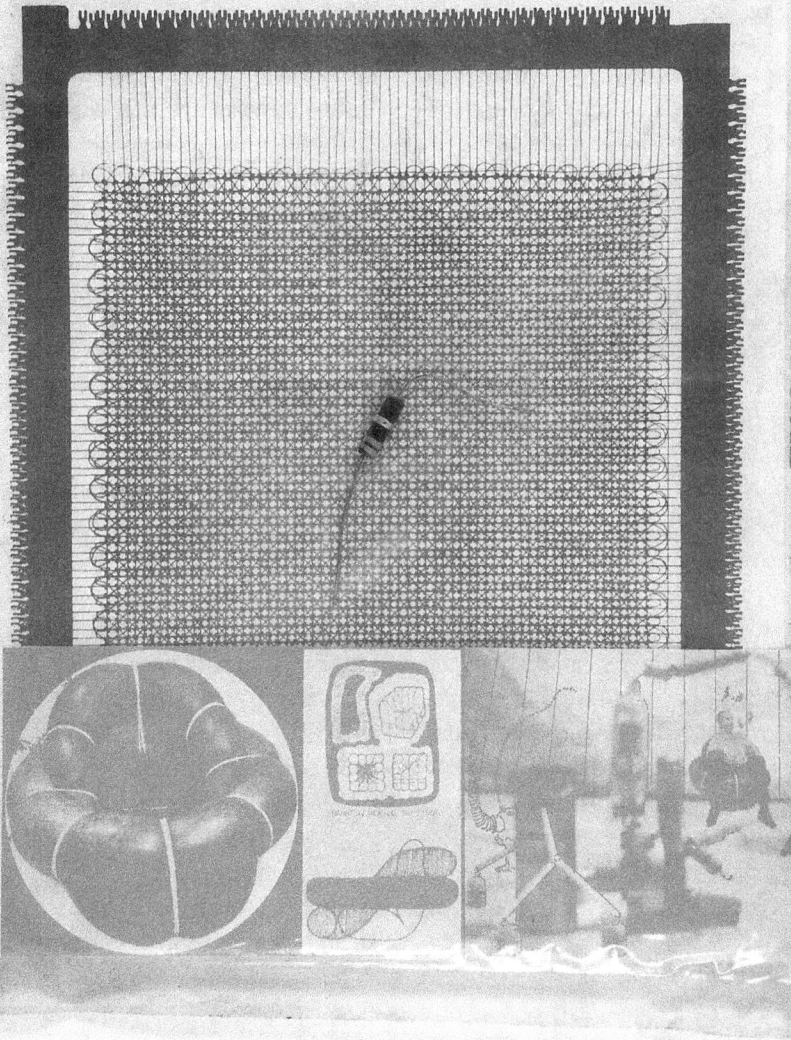

Figure 10.3 Cover of *Archigram* issue no. 7, 1966. Courtesy: The Archigram Archival Project.

a task of ease; it will be one that requires 'conscious design application in calculated uncertainty'.[24] Like Cook, Price shared a dissatisfaction with the lack of change envisaged with buildings and city form, with such assumptions implying human life to be static.

Translating architectural dreams

Purely fantasy during the 1960s, we now find ourselves in an era where people and 'things' are feeding data across the city, shaping our engagement in a dynamically recursive manner. The burgeoning Internet of Things, rise of big data applications and step-changes in building information modelling connecting digital data with designed objects will undoubtedly shift our temporal relationship with cities further still. The design history of the Plug-In City and the Fun Palace can offer direction in this future.

Most arresting about these 1960s designs is their fundamentally social ethos. In an interview with Cedric Price on 13 April 2000, Matthews recounts his declaration that 'The Fun Palace wasn't about technology. It was about people.'[25] The same can of course be argued for Archigram, with its desire to realign the pulsating city with a more flexible architectural form. And yet, there seemed to be an eventual suppression of social framing, and privileging of mathematically informed cybernetic models in the case of the Fun Palace.[26] Even the call for collaboration in 'Beyond Architecture' focused on almost everyone but the social scientists (featuring 'programmers' within this list captures this technological zeitgeist).

The works of French philosopher Henri Bergson, although never directly referenced by Cedric Price, have been cited by Stanley Matthews as a useful lens through which to understand the Fun Palace. He suggests that for Bergson 'reality was not discrete objects and isolated matter but an endless and seamless process of becoming'.[27] Looking towards contemporary social theory might furnish designs of the future with a temporal knowledge of why humans inhabit the world the way they do, how they form, change and develop over time or even disappear. Theodore Schatzki's philosophical account of the constitution and transformation of social life through a meshing of orders (e.g. people, artefacts, things) and practices (e.g. organized activities) over time offers one such direction and brings the benefit of being firmly rooted in what he calls the 'site of the social'.[28]

This type of conversation is all the more urgent now as we start to see the rise of responsive environments, everyday objects imbued with sensors and 'things' that 'speak' to one another, the social applications (and implications) of which remain in their infancy. They are typically defined as 'objects in space' and could arguably do much to borrow from Price's idea of 'events in time'. Put simply, we should not be thinking of the Internet of Things as objects in space, but what they can enable as happenings over time.

The idea of a theory of conversation seemed a natural development from Gordon Pask's work in cybernetics. Originating in the 1970s, it describes how human-to-human, human-to-machine and machine-to-machine interactions can lead to the construction of knowledge. The relevance to today has not gone unnoticed:

> Now, at the beginning of the 21st century, Pask's Conversation Theory seems particularly important because it suggests how, in the growing field of ubiquitous computing, humans, devices and their shared environments might coexist in a mutually constructive relationship. If we think of having conversations with our environments in which we each have to learn from each other, then Pask's early experiments with mechanical and electrochemical systems provide a conceptual framework for building interactive artefacts that deal with the natural dynamic complexity that environments must have without becoming prescriptive, restrictive and autocratic.[29]

Indeterminate architecture, one that endlessly adapts to internal and external influences, is of course, well-versed in relation to the Plug-In City[30] and the Fun Palace.[31] The production of the unknown by society is a radical proposition for a discipline where it is the architects who define and create monuments that endure.

This indeterminate vision was soon to become riddled with philosophical and moral complexity, with Gordon Pask asking the cybernetics committee what was most likely to induce happiness, a question that to all intents and purposes was penned as a beneficial contribution to society. And yet – in the same breath – the neo-futurist aspirations of the Fun Palace started to border on experiments in social control.[32] On the flipside, Philip Beesley and Omar Khan have commented that society could act back and modify the architectural form to suit their desires, suggesting 'The Fun Palace has many shortcomings as a design, but there is an incredible optimism in its projections for collective action that still ring true 55 years later.'[33]

The conscious city does not escape these binds.[34] This is a movement of growing momentum in which built environments are aware and responsive to human needs through data analysis, artificial intelligence and the application of cognitive sciences in design. Such focus on contemporary environments to 'care' invites renewed theoretical consideration, according to Beesley and Khan.[35] In 'Seeking Empathy in the Conscious City' (to be featured in *Designing Cultures of Care*), the ethics of an architectural dialogic in the conscious city are considered, bringing questions of computational neutrality and democratic participation to the fore in the design and curation of 'intelligent architecture'.[36] Such oppositions hark back to the Fun Palace and Plug-In City, but still find relevance in the architectural discourse of the present.

Conclusion

This chapter has considered the visionary dreams of two architectural designs: Archigram's Plug-In City (1964) designed by Peter Cook and the Fun Palace (1961) conceived by Cedric Price. It took as its focus the key expressions of neo-futurism embodied by these mid-century designs. Through this commentary, it has considered the ways in which time has been conceived of being designed into the fabric of 1960s' architecture, pulling the past through to the present, with particular attention paid to how the tropes of architectural modularism and cybernetics might find relevance in contemporary discourse. Contemporary social theory is suggested as a mechanism to furnish designs of the future with a temporal, situated knowledge, and to show that there exists value in thinking about the rising number of 'things' sending data across cities as events in time rather than simply objects in space. Contemplating the recent architectural past in this way might illuminate and inform both present and future thought.

Notes

1. Peter Cook, *Plug-In City Study* (London: Archigram Archival Project, 1964), project no. 60. Although Plug-In City is commonly attributed to Peter Cook, the study comprised a speculative series of proposals with contributions also made by Warren Chalk and Dennis Crompton.
2. Cedric Price, *Brochure for the Fun Palace Project* (Montréal: Canadian Centre for Architecture, 1964), reference no. DR1995:0188:525:001:016.
3. Despite the prominence of Archigram, work of the collective has been relatively absent in written design history. Molly Wright Steenson, *Architectural Intelligence: How Designers and Architects Created the Digital Landscape* (Cambridge, MA: MIT Press, 2017) has, for instance, looked towards the contributions of Cedric Price alongside Christopher Alexander, Nicholas Negroponte and Richard Saul Wurman – four architects who engaged with cybernetics and artificial intelligence among other technologies during the 1960s and 1970s, as pivotal in the creation of a foundation for today's emergent forms of digital interactivity. Archigram's own historiography has retained an independence from such conversations – see e.g. Simon Sadler, *Archigram: Architecture without Architecture* (London: MIT Press, 2005); Peter Cook supported by Warren Chalk, Dennis Crompton, David Greene, Ron Herron and Mike Webb, *Archigram* (New York: Princeton Architectural Press, 1999); Dennis Crompton, *A Guide to Archigram (1961–74)* (New York: Princeton Architectural Press, 2012); Philipp Sturm and Peter Cachola Schmal, *Yesterday's Future: Visionary Designs by Future Systems and Archigram* (Munich: Prestel, 2016); 'A Companion to the Exhibition' at the Deutsche Architekturmuseum, Frankfurt from 14 May to 18 September 2016; and Hadas Steiner, *Beyond Archigram: The Structure of Circulation* (New York and London: Routledge, 2009). This chapter contributes to today's digital landscape, by considering Archigram's Plug-In City and Cedric Price's Fun Palace through the tropes of architectural modularism, cybernetics and in the context of contemporary social theory.
4. Peter Cook, *Metal Houses Project* (London: Archigram Archival Project, 1961), project no. 21.
5. Peter Cook and David Greene, *Nottingham Shopping Centre Project* (London: Archigram Archival Project, 1962), project no. 34.

6. *Living City Exhibition*, exhibition catalogue (London: Institute of Contemporary Arts, 1963).

7. Peter Cook, 'Come-Go: The Key to the Vitality of the City', in Theo Crosby and John Bodley (eds.), *Living Arts* 2, exhibition catalogue (London: Institute of Contemporary Arts and Tillotsons, 1963), 80.

8. Simon Sadler, *Archigram: Architecture without Architecture*. (London: MIT Press, 2005), 18.

9. Peter Cook, *Plug-In City Study: Sustenance Components Simplified, Guide Section 2* (London: Archigram Archival Project, 1964), project no. 60.

10. Priscilla Chapman, 'The Plug-In City', *Sunday Times Supplement*, 20 September 1964, 2.

11. Ibid., 3.

12. Ibid., 3.

13. Mike Webb, 'Boys at Heart', in Peter Cook (ed.), supported by Warren Chalk, Dennis Crompton, David Greene, Ron Herron and Mike Webb, *Archigram* (New York: Princeton Architectural Press, 1999), 2.

14. Cedric Price, *Brochure for the Fun Palace Project*, project no. DR1995:0188:525:001:016.

15. Stanley Matthews, 'The Fun Palace: Cedric Price's Experiment in Architecture and Technology', *Technoetic Arts: A Journal of Speculative Research* 3, no. 2 (2005): 79.

16. Stanley Matthews, 'The Fun Palace as Virtual Architecture: Cedric Price and the Practices of Indeterminacy', *Journal of Architectural Education* 59, no. 3 (2006): 44.

17. Archigram, 'Zoom and Real Architecture', in *Archigram* no. 4 (London: Archigram Archival Project, 1964), project no. 100.4: 18.

18. Although this never transpired.

19. Archigram, 'Zoom and Real Architecture', 18.

20. Dennis Crompton, *Interview with Dennis Crompton* (London: Archigram Archival Project, n.d.), project no. 100.7.

21. Peter Cook, 'Time Essay' (London: Archigram Archival Project, 1966), project no. 100.7: 9.

22. Joan Littlewood, *Joan's Book: Joan Littlewood's Peculiar History as She Tells It* (London: Minerva, 1995), 702.

23. Cedric Price, *CP3* (London: Archigram Archival Project, 1966), project no. 100.7: 13.

24. Ibid., 13.

25. Matthews, 'The Fun Palace: Cedric Price's Experiment in Architecture and Technology', 91.

26. Matthews, 'The Fun Palace as Virtual Architecture: Cedric Price and the Practices of Indeterminacy', 45–6.

27. Ibid., 42.

28. Theodore Schatzki, *The Site of the Social: A Philosophical Account of the Constitution of Social Life and Change* (Pennsylvania: Pennsylvania State University Press, 2002), XI.

29. Usman Haque, 'The Architectural Relevance of Gordon Pask', *AD Architectural Design* 77, no. 4 (July–August 2007): 55.

30. Sadler, *Archigram: Architecture without Architecture*, 16.

31. Matthews, 'The Fun Palace as Virtual Architecture', 39–48.

32. Matthews, 'The Fun Palace: Cedric Price's Experiment in Architecture and Technology', 83.
33. Philip Beesley and Omar Khan, *Responsive Architecture/Performing Instruments* (New York: Architectural League of New York, 2009), 10.
34. Itai Palti and Mosche Bar, 'A Manifesto for Conscious Cities: Should Streets be Sensitive to our Mental Needs?' *The Guardian*, 28 August 2015.
35. Beesley and Khan, '*Responsive Architecture/Performing Instruments*', 5.
36. Claire McAndrew and Itai Palti, 'Seeking Empathy in Conscious Cities', in Laurene Vaughan (ed.), *Designing Cultures of Care* (London: Bloomsbury, 2018).

11 Sign of the Times: Slow Design in the Age of Social Acceleration

DR NIELS PETER SKOU

In 2003, the Dutch ceramics company Royal Tichelaar Makkum introduced a new series of crockery entitled 'Minutes'. The concept was developed by the Dutch design studio Makkink & Bey for the Milan Furniture Fair and the basic idea was that each piece was named after the minutes it had taken to produce. The number of minutes was set by the designer at the beginning of the process and determined what kind of decoration the painter could manage to complete.[1] Furthermore, traces of the production process, like sketches on the underglaze, which normally would have been erased or covered were intentionally left visible in order to create a complex pattern of historical layers of decoration (Figure 11.1).

This collaboration between the otherwise traditional craft-based company and renowned designers like Jurgen Bey and Rianne Makkink, who are normally connected with Droog design and critical design, marked a shift in strategy and the paradox is thus that the shift towards design led to a mediation of the craft process. This mediation was both embedded in the objects themselves through the traces of the process left on them and embodied in the communication around the objects through the naming of the individual pieces and the storytelling of the concept. Whereas it previously would have been considered as a flaw if production marks were left on the finished product, in this case it turned into a virtue, shifting the focus from the product itself to the process of its creation. This shift in focus reflects back on the objects, however, and elevates them from traditional craft products to the sphere of conceptual design art.

This way of conceptualizing the product and staging its production creates a tension between different conceptions of work and time. The popular image of craft processes as creative processes characterized by self-realization and experiences of flow as opposed to industrial work collides with the almost provocatively meticulous quantification of the minutes ascribed to the individual product, which are also used to measure and legitimize its substantially high price. Furthermore, it raises the question of authorship since the products are marketed as works of the designers while the skilled painters doing the actual painting largely remain anonymous, thus positioning the designer as the artist.

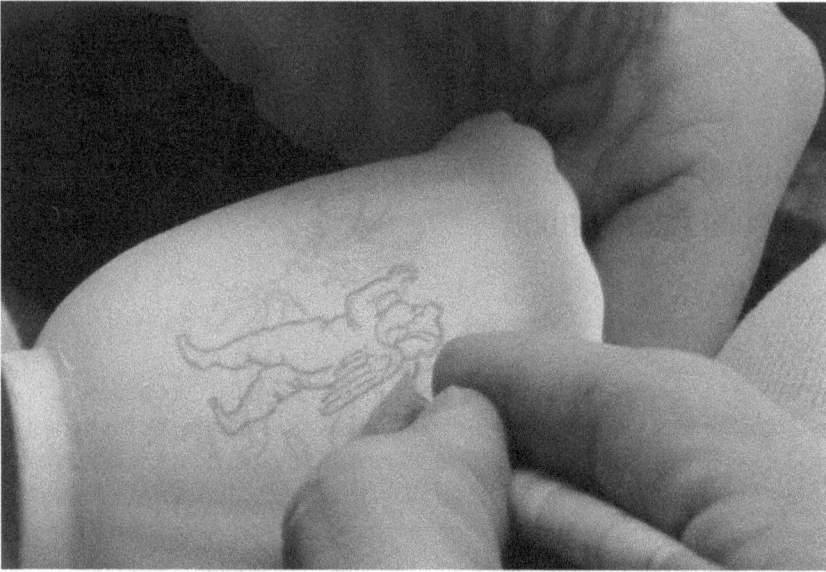

Figure 11.1 Studio Makkink & Bey: 'Minutes service', 2003. © Studio Makkink & Bey, Image by Studio Makkink & Bey.

Even though this case is unusually explicit in the way it conceptually connects design and time, it exemplifies a general interest in time and craft in connection to design which is part of a general cultural trend also visible in movements like maker culture, slow design, emotionally durable design and so on, which largely define themselves as counter-movements to consumerism and late modern accelerated capitalism.[2] This chapter will investigate examples mainly from the field of 'slow furniture' in order to highlight some of the paradoxes and tensions in this trend which we saw sketched out in the introductory example. The general point is to show that even though these movements often refer to historical practices of craftsmanship, they still operate within modern conditions, illustrating a shift in the needs that are met by design from material needs to time as a coveted resource. A general feature is the shift in focus from the material product to temporal processes connected to the material or the production process. What is bought by the consumer is not the product as 'good' in the traditional sense, but the object as a container of time, which calls for the mediation of temporal processes in complex ways. Furthermore, it brings the designer's personality into focus as artist and as embodiment of a 'slow' lifestyle. This symbolic treatment and consumption of time as a limited material resource has been noted by the German sociologist Hartmut Rosa as a significant trait of modern society:

> Perhaps the most pressing and astonishing facet of social acceleration is the spectacular and epidemic 'time-famine' of modern (western) societies. In modernity, social actors increasingly feel that they are running out of time, that they are short on time. It seems as if time was perceived like a raw-material which

is consumed like oil and which is, therefore, getting more and more scarce and expensive.[3]

In this quote, Rosa connects the experience of time as a limited resource with the general cultural dynamic of 'social acceleration', which is a key term in his writings. This frame makes it possible to discuss the cases not only as examples of design strategies but also as symptoms of a cultural demand of time as a scarce resource. Moreover the idea is that the significance of design, which is not treated separately by Rosa, lies in its ability to visualize temporal processes. This chapter will thus focus on selected cases and look at the complex interplay between objects and the communication around them. These examples do not obviously allow for any general conclusions about the nature, value or future of slow design but the theoretical context hopefully represents a framework for discussing their cultural significance beyond their own ideological statements.

Modernity and social acceleration

According to Hartmut Rosa, 'acceleration' must be understood as a process inherent in modernity that spans the material-technological sphere, the social-institutional sphere and the individual experience and pace of life.[4] Technological acceleration encompasses production, transport and communication and leads to a compression of space and distance. Socially the transformation of social relations and modes of action has accelerated. This can be exemplified by the basic categories of family and work, where changes have moved from an intergenerational to an intra-generational level. Finally, on the individual level, we experience the paradox that we are objectively able to do more and more in the same period of time but still experience a growing lack of time. This paradox is rooted in the dynamic that even though technological innovation makes procedures more and more effective, it simultaneously expands the field of opportunities, widening the gap between what could potentially be realized and what it is actually possible to realize.[5]

Even though technology thus plays an important part in social acceleration, Hartmut Rosa does not subscribe to any form of technological determinism. Rather, technological innovation is, in his view, itself a result of other cultural dynamics in modernity. The first is competition as part of capitalist market economy, which calls for both diminishing the time of labour as an expense in production and an increase in the speed of innovation as a competitive parameter. This dynamic is further strengthened by the formation of national states with competing national economies.[6] In this regard, he is aligned with other contemporary diagnostics and critics of the modern state as a 'competitive state'.[7] There is, however, Rosa argues, also a cultural dynamic concerned with secularization, which positions acceleration as the secular counterpart to eternity. If metaphysical concepts of eternity no longer apply, the only alternative is to maximize the experiences and actions contained in a lifetime. The motors of acceleration are thus both social and individual.[8]

Acceleration processes influence all aspects of human existence. Of special interest to design is the way the technological acceleration of production alters the relationship between humans and the physical world of objects. The main consequence is a shift from physical wear to 'moral wear', already observed by Karl Marx, meaning that things are not discarded because they are physically worn or used up but because they have become culturally obsolete due to technology or fashion. Furthermore, things are not reproduced identically but in altered forms, meaning that the material structures of our lifeworld become transitory.[9] In this light, slow design can partly be seen as motivated by a desire to battle this transitoriness and create a higher level of permanence and continuity.

The process of acceleration does not stand alone, though, but is constantly met by processes of deceleration. These encompass the limits set by bodily and natural processes, islands of traditional culture like the Amish people, deceleration as an unintended side effect of acceleration like the traffic jam, conservative and ecological counter-movements and the structural inertia that emerges when acceleration processes undermine the institutions that initiated and governed them in the first place. In the last instance, acceleration turns into the paradoxical notion of 'frenetic standstill' where it becomes a permanent state of affairs devoid of direction and meaning.[10] Even if social acceleration is countered by deceleration processes, they are not in balance. In Rosa's view, the balance is in favour of the acceleration forces and deceleration is mainly residual or reactive.[11]

In Hartmut Rosa's critical conception, acceleration is thus at the same time an inherent dynamic in modernity and a phenomenon that constantly produces new effects which in late modernity threaten to become counterproductive and dysfunctional. Even though Rosa probably presents the most systematic theorization of acceleration, he is by no means the first to discover and describe social acceleration, a fact he acknowledges himself.[12] Read in this light, Georg Simmel's famous essay 'The Metropolis and Mental Life' is all about social acceleration and changes in the experience and conception of time. Simmel describes the psychological character of modern metropolitan life as a product of the acceleration of social and mental processes, where the 'tempo and multiplicity of economical, occupational and social life' in the metropolis is contrasted with the 'slower, more habitual, more smoothly flowing rhythm' of the small town.[13] Moreover, the experience of time is not only accelerated, the complex organization of the city demands a thorough synchronization and calculable exactness of time.[14] In this light, the tension detected in the introductory example between creativity as an organic process and work as an exact time frame externally applied is historically rooted in the two conceptions of time described by Simmel and signifies to a certain uneasiness with the modern rationalization and organization of time.

Slow design and slow furniture

The 'slow' movement has its origin in the concept of 'slow food' which was born in Italy in the 1980s as a reaction to the opening of the first McDonalds restaurant in Rome. It has since spread to other areas like 'slow fashion' and 'slow furniture', where it positions itself against the 'fastness' of modern production cycles and consumption (fast food, fast fashion, mass-produced furniture). From the beginning, 'slow' has thus encompassed the whole field of production, consumption and a general lifestyle and has identified itself as a counter-movement to industrialization and (American) globalization.

The transformation from slow food to 'slow furniture' happened in England where the 'slow furniture' movement was founded by the English journalist Melanie Cable-Alexander, editor of *Country Life*, writing on the maintenance of English manor houses. This reflects the fact that the traditional crafts that the slow movement tries to save and rejuvenate have typically been kept alive by care for historical upper-class buildings or by specialized upper-class niches. In the reappraisal of craft there thus seems to be an alliance between conservatism and counterculture in a common distancing towards modern industrialized material culture. This alliance makes sense, however, if we classify the movements as movements of ideological deceleration.[15] Distributed on the internet by individual designers, slow furniture seems however to have dissociated itself from its conservative roots and to have reached a middle-class audience.

Organic time

Though not strictly defining themselves as part of the slow furniture movement, one of the most radical alternatives to industrial furniture is the practice of 'grown chairs' made through tree shaping. In these cases, trees are manipulated in different ways in their growth process until they assume the shape of a chair and can be 'harvested'. This gives the chair a production time of typically seven years or more. While many similar traditions of tree shaping can be found historically and geographically, like the Japanese bonsai tradition or the tradition of living root bridges of the Khasi tribe in India, it is significant that a number of projects have been presented recently labelled as design projects with the explicit purpose of symbolizing an alternative approach to the manufacturing of objects. In 2012, German designer Werner Aisslinger presented a Chair Farm at the Milan Furniture Fair, and, in England, furniture designer Gavin Munro and his company Full Grown is producing grown furniture on a larger scale. Both designers testify to a utopian vision of 'product plantations'[16] or 'reimagining the way we make objects altogether'.[17] At the University of Stuttgart, a research group in 'Baubotanik' furthermore experiments with transferring the principle to architecture in the German town of Nagold.[18]

In a modern Western context, tree shaping has its origins in United States where the banker and farmer John Krubsack harvested the first grown chair in 1914. The techniques were perfected by the Swedish-American arborist Axel Erlandson who opened a 'circus of trees' on his grounds. Both the aforementioned were farmers and saw their projects partly as hobby projects and partly as an experiment into the extent to which plants could be manipulated. In the late 1970s, tree sculpting was, however, taken up by the ecologically oriented furniture designer and lecturer

Christopher Cattle and inspired artists like the sculptor Richard Reames and the Australian artist/design duo Peter 'Pook' Cook and Bethy Northey.[19]

What is of interest in this context is not the utopian potential in natural growth as a production method but the symbolic role of the conception of 'organic time' in the staging of the projects. Gavin Munro characterizes his furniture as sculptures in four dimensions where time makes up the fourth dimension.[20] Furthermore, age is considered a specific quality of the object: 'There's that same quality that you get with wines and whisky, of age and time, and there's no substitute for that.'[21] This way the object is classified in a certain group of objects that are appreciated for their ageing qualities in contrast to the large groups of objects where ageing is considered as obsolescence or wear.[22] Natural time is, in these cases, considered as an independent constructive force whose quality precisely is that it cannot be completely controlled or replicated by technological production processes.

The notion of organic growth is, however, not just a part of the production process. As a metaphor, it is mirrored in the way the designers describe themselves and their own practice. Peter Cook writes about the development of his designs: 'This design was one of my favourites at that time. We now have a completely different perception for living tree chairs, which incorporates stone or glass into the design of tree chair. It's been seven years since this tree was planted and our designs have been changing and evolving throughout that time.'[23] In this description, not just the tree but also the designs evolve organically. Similarly, an important part of the presentation of Gavin Munro evolves around the fact that as a child he underwent surgery in order to straighten his spine:

> It's where I learnt patience. There were long periods of staying still, plenty of time to observe what was going on and reflect. It was only after doing this project for a few years a friend pointed out that I must know exactly what it's like to be shaped and grafted on a similar time scale.[24]

This quotation both encompasses the notion of patience and the idea of growth as a specific time scale. However, it also points to the element of shaping and manipulation. As mentioned, tree shaping has a long history also in Western culture in connection with, for instance, baroque garden art, where it traditionally has been considered a mode of cultivation. Interestingly enough, the rhetorical opposition between the tree that is bent into shape and the tree that is allowed to grow into its own natural shape is thus central to reformist pedagogy in the tradition of Rousseau, where the bent tree is seen as a symbol of nature being twisted and deformed by an over-cultivated society.[25] In this case, however, the bent tree is considered as a more gentle form of cultivation in comparison to the rest of society.

If we look at Werner Aisslinger's Chair Farm (Figure 11.2), it is also more ambiguous in its statement since the steel frame and the electronic measuring devices connected to the installation make it appear far more futuristic and scientific. There is thus a tension between, on the one side, a romantic idea of reconciliation with nature supported by the often picturesque locations of the design studios/tree farms (not unlike nineteenth-century national romanticist artists establishing their studios in picturesque national landscapes) and, on the other side, tree shaping as an increased level of control and manipulation in relation to nature.

It could be tempting to view these projects in parallel with early modernist utopian projects investigating the potential in new production methods and new materials. The point I have tried to make, however, is that the utopian content might be not so much about materials or production but rather a utopia of being able to perform a radical slowing down of production speed, creating an alignment between the natural time scale and the human time scale, which can be viewed as a utopia of radical deceleration. There is thus a development from the early tree shaping projects that were treated as experimental hobby projects and curiosities done in people's spare

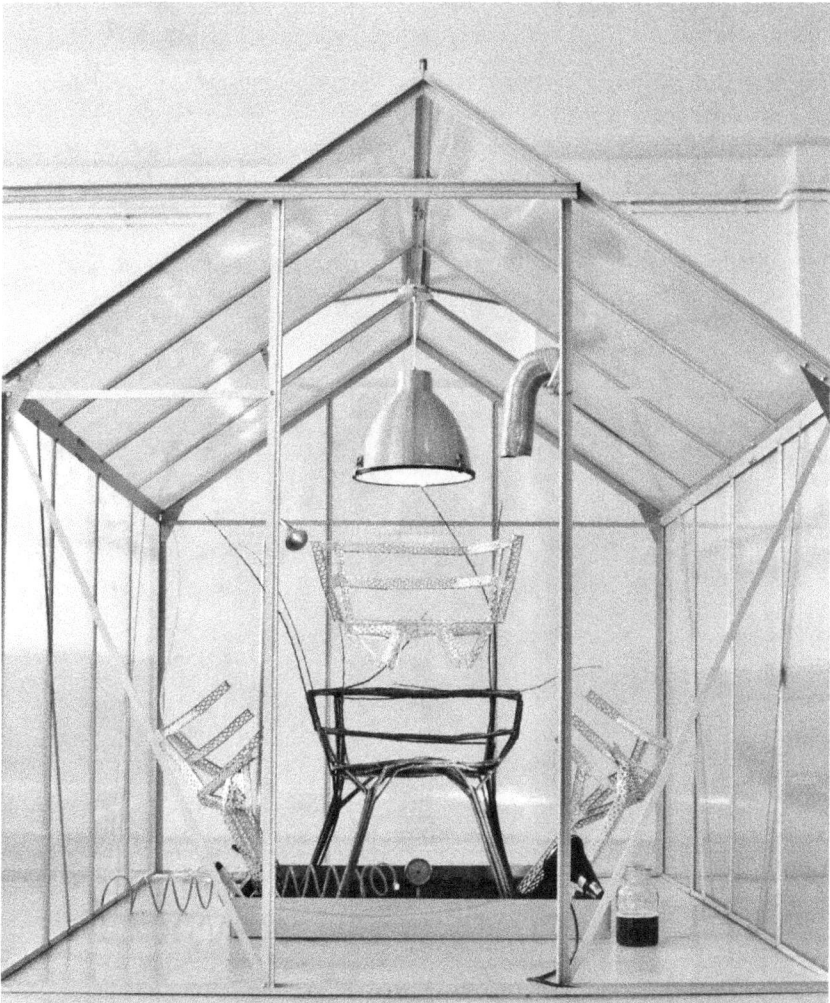

Figure 11.2 Studio Aisslinger: Chair Farm, 2012. © Julian Lechner for Studio Aisslinger.

time to the present projects staged with the symbolic property of representing a utopia for society as such. The symbolic notion of growth is thus present also in more mainstream design like Ronan and Erwan Bouroullec's Vegetal stacking chair made by Vitra or Robby and Francesca Cantarurri's Forest chair made by Fast, where organic growth is treated purely as an aesthetic motif.[26]

Objects and signs

Emphasizing aging as a quality is also emphasizing the way time leaves its mark on objects. The aging of materials or objects is a process where time is materialized while, at the same time, the objects gain a semiotic character of indexical signs in the sense that they can be read as effects of temporal processes. If we turn to a Danish representative of 'slow furniture', the artist and designer Bente Hovendal and her company woodnwonder, this sign quality is explicitly thematized (Figure 11.3):

> The furniture is sturdy and usable while still holding remnants of the original life of the tree within the design.
> Natural shapes stick out from the form, there may be cracks in the surfaces and traces of the use of the chainsaw. Every quirk becomes a part of the design and a wonder within the whole form.[27]

This description underlines how the material and the processing of it are both seen as generative of the form. While being shaped into a functional form, the design is

Figure 11.3 Bente Hovendal: Plank table made of wood with zinc boxes. Both the products and the setting position the furniture as a continuation of the living tree. © woodnwonder/Bente Hovendal. Photo: Geir Haukursson.

also supposed to hold 'remnants of the original tree within the design'. Furthermore, there is a distinction between two forms of marks left on the product. Cracks referring to organic growth and decay, and traces from the chainsaw referring to the processes of work. The image of the furniture as a continuation of the tree is underlined in the mediation where it is placed in a natural landscape (Figure 11.3). This way the tree functions as both concrete material and metaphor and the organic nature of the furniture is communicated both through the surface of the object itself and the media context it is placed in. Design historian Grace Lees-Maffei has distinguished between three ways design and media are connected. Design *as* media, which covers the communicative aspects of the objects; design *in* media, which covers the mediation of design in different media contexts and design *of* media, which covers the design of media platforms.[28] Following this conceptualization, almost all of the examples in this text are characterized by an interplay between the first two aspects.

The designer as mediator

The way cultural meaning is ascribed to slow design is not limited to the objects themselves, however. As described in the introduction, the designer's persona gains importance as mediator and embodiment of cultural values that are transferred to the objects. According to Guy Julier, designers occupy a position as 'cultural intermediaries' involving mediating between avant-garde and popular culture and turning their own professional practice into a lifestyle.[29] We have already seen how Gavin Munro uses his own life story to create a parallel between himself and his products. In the case of furniture designer Christien Starkenburg, a Dutch representative of the slow furniture movement, the notion of slow design as a lifestyle becomes even clearer. While the design itself is labelled as 'timeless', her self-presentation is all about speed and slowness:

> 'I become "slow", when I go fast.'
> Designer Christien Starkenburg believes in a slow lifestyle, which she applies in her work as well as in her life. She is often found on her race bike, whipping past the Friesian countryside. When she cycles, her mind becomes clear, her body becomes one with nature and inspiration is at its peak level. Being mindful and open are important aspects of Christien's slow lifestyle that form the foundation for every SlowWood piece. 'Slow' ensures an attentive and pure process that is in line with her high ecological standards.
> Christien's way of life and design method involve an open mind and the ability to access a sense of wonder. Christien's eyes are always open, looking for beauty in everyday objects. When eyes are open and the mind is slow, beauty is truly found in everything; from a glass vase to a shell on the beach, or from a ribbon on a package to architecture.[30]

This presentation draws heavily on artistic ideas of aesthetic inspiration and the creative process as a 'flow' which connects fast and slow and, in line with current trends, is connected to mindfulness. The point of cycling in this case is not the speed itself but the underlying assumption that it is an activity freed from strategic rational control and purpose. This also calls for a reinterpretation of the classic modernist notion that beauty should be found in everyday objects, freed from preset aesthetic and social object hierarchies. In the modernist context, this was largely politically motivated as a way of liberating aesthetics from social class structure.[31] Here, the notion is individualized as an expression of a specific capability of aesthetic seeing inherent in the designer lifestyle and brought about by slowing down (Figure 11.4).

As Figure 11.4 illustrates, the slow qualities of Starkenburg's furniture are not self-explanatory but are mediated by the designer persona in a staged setting where meditation, cycling and furniture design all function as tokens of a collective lifestyle. This illustrates the point that an essential characteristic of object's meaning is its 'contextual sensitivity'.[32] As several of the examples illustrate, slow design strategies are not necessarily new in themselves; the novelty is largely connected to the context they operate in where they meet a new set of needs. While they draw on historical traditions from, for example, the Arts and Crafts and modernism, they are not about the artistic quality of the objects as such or about meeting social and material needs but rather about answering experienced needs of deceleration.

Slow design as symbolic consumption

Slow design is, in this chapter, treated as a broad frame ranging from highly reflexive design strategies to what must rather be considered as a new frame for presenting and marketing design. Starting from the observation by Hartmut Rosa that due to social acceleration time is increasingly conceptualized and exchanged as a scarce resource, the purpose has been to investigate design as a way of visualizing and materializing time in order to exchange and consume it. This way, slow design is treated more like a symptom than a cure for social acceleration.

This view points simultaneously towards design as a materialization of time and temporalization as a dematerialization of design in the sense that it implicitly or explicitly shifts the focus from the material and functional qualities to the semiotic aspects of the objects. This goes also for the material itself. A common denominator of the examples is that they all work with wood. While there is a long tradition for appreciating wood as material and working with its specific material qualities, these cases highlight how the surface and shape of the wood works as a reservoir of signs either of its own natural growth process or of the work applied to it.

As noted, this sign quality makes it possible to exchange time through the objects. One might even talk about an 'economy of time', which makes slowness and the ability to wait the ultimate luxury. It might, however, also be argued that this way of consuming time is a symbolic consumption 'by proxy', since the consumer may mirror him- or herself in the lifestyle of the designer but is not able to obtain the lifestyle by owning the products. In this sense it is a phenomenon that points to a much larger societal problematic. On its more limited scale it may, however, connect the user with timescales that transgress everyday experience. As Hartmut Rosa puts it,

Figure 11.4 Christien Starkenburg. The furniture is presented as an element in a collection of tokens of a slow lifestyle. © Christien Starkenburg. Photo: Anna de Leeuw.

It remains to be seen whether initiatives like the slow food or the voluntary simplicity movements can spread to such an extent that they actually achieve relevance for society as a whole. [. . .] Nevertheless that does not provide an absolute objection to the effort to establish, as it were, protected spaces in the sense of the aforementioned islands of deceleration that enable other, i.e., slower experiences of time.[33]

Notes

1. http://www.tichelaar.com/projects/minutes-service (accessed January 2018).
2. See e.g. Alastair Fuad-Luke, 'Slow Design,' in M. Erlhoff and T. Marshall (eds), *Design Dictionary: Board of International Research in Design* (Basel: Birkhäuser, 2008) and Jonathan Chapman, *Emotionally Durable Design*, 2nd ed. (London: Routledge 2015), 42–3.
3. Hartmut Rosa, *Alienation and Acceleration: Towards a Critical Theory of Late-Modern Temporality* (Aarhus, Denmark: NSU Press, 2014), 20.
4. Hartmut Rosa, *Social Acceleration: A New Theory of Modernity* (New York: Columbia University Press 2015), 71–80.
5. Rosa, *Alienation and Acceleration*, 31–3.
6. Ibid., 26–8.
7. See e.g. Ove Kaj Pedersen, 'Political Globalization and the Competition State', in Benedikte Brincker (ed.), *Introduction to Political Sociology* (Copenhagen: Hans Reitzel, 2013), 281–98.
8. Rosa, *Social Acceleration*, 193–4.
9. Ibid., 105.
10. Ibid., 80–9.
11. Rosa, *Alienation and Acceleration*, 39.
12. Ibid., 13–14.
13. Georg Simmel: 'The Metropolis and Mental Life', in Richard Sennett (ed.) *Classic Essays on the Culture of Cities* (New York: Prentice-Hall, [1903] 1969), 48.
14. Ibid., 50–1.
15. Cf. Rosa, *Social Acceleration*, 85–7.
16. http://www.aisslinger.de/index.php?option=com_project&view=detail&pid=150&Itemid=1 (accessed January 2018).
17. Sarah Laskow, 'A Forest of Furniture is Growing in England', in *Atlas Obscura* (13 December 2017), https://www.atlasobscura.com/articles/forest-furniture-england-midlands-tree-shaping-chairs-tables (accessed January 2018).
18. https://www.atlasobscura.com/places/platanenkubus (accessed January 2018).
19. Sarah Laskow, 'A Short History of Tree Shaping', in *Atlas Obscura* (13 December 2017), https://www.atlasobscura.com/articles/a-short-history-of-tree-shaping (accessed March 2018).
20. Laskow, 'A Forest of Furniture is Growing in England'.

21. Ibid.

22. Grant McCracken describes in *Culture and Consumption* how patina as symbolic property of the object in modern material culture has been relegated from mass culture to upper-class niches. See Grant McCracken, *Culture and Consumption* (Bloomington: Indiana University Press 1988), 31–43. See also Chapman, *Emotionally Durable Design*, 133–4.

23. http://pooktre.com/photos/living-chair/ (accessed January 2018).

24. https://fullgrown.co.uk/about/ (accessed January 2018).

25. Rousseau starts his pedagogical classic *Emile* by describing how man deforms the child's natural God-given form, using the image of trees in a garden: 'He will have nothing as nature made it, not even man himself, who must learn his paces like a saddle-horse, and be shaped to his master's taste like the trees in his garden.' See Jean-Jacques Rousseau, *Emile, or Education*, trans. Barbara Foxley (1762; London and Toronto: J. M. Dent, 1921), 5.

26. Cf. Rosita Satell, *Født som ikon? Mediernes betydning for nyere møbeldesign*, PhD dissertation, University of Southern Denmark, February 2018, 135–55.

27. http://www.woodnwonder.com/about-woodnwonder/ (accessed January 2018).

28. Grace Lees-Maffei, 'The Production-Consumption-Mediation Paradigm', *Journal of Design History* 22, no. 4 (December 2009): 351.

29. Guy Julier, *The Culture of Design*, 3rd ed. (London: SAGE 2014), 54.

30. https://www.slowwood.nl/2381-2 (accessed January 2018).

31. See e.g. Paul Greenhalgh, 'Introduction', in Greenhalgh (ed.), *Modernism in Design* (London: Reaktion Books, 1990), 1–25.

32. Chapman, *Emotionally Durable Design*, 43–4.

33. Rosa, *Social Acceleration*, 86–7.

12 Fast and Slow: Design and the Experience of Time

DR STEPHEN HAYWARD

An archaeologist of the future might be puzzled by the measurement of time at Schiphol, the international airport for Amsterdam. In most of the public areas, the clocks follow the global vernacular. The flow of time is translated into the segments of a clock face and the rhythms of the airport align with a wider social and economic infrastructure, the 'clock time' that has regulated the conduct of factories, railway stations, schools and so on since the industrial revolution.[1] But in Lounge 2 of the airport there is a surprise. A timekeeper that projects an image of a boiler-suited janitor, painting and then erasing the hands of a clock in a continuous twelve-hour loop. In a setting dedicated to frictionless movement, time becomes poetic, embodied and even, according to the designer Maarten Baas, subversive and authentic, for the Schiphol clock is part of a broader project entitled Real Time.[2] An analogy might be drawn with the humour and spectacle of the Swiss cuckoo clock or, better still, the automaton clock, where the jerkiness of the figures becomes a picturesque tourist landmark. For the 'man in a clock' has been linked to the rebranding of Dutch culture, from tulips and windmills to quirky reinterpretations of everyday life, a reminder that the Netherlands is the home of Droog design.

But that is a rather narrow interpretation, and this chapter opens with a more fundamental aspect of design, history and time; the orientation towards the future. In Part one below we see how the Utopianism of twentieth-century design becomes more speculative in the twenty-first century, and how, in a particular strand of contemporary practice, time is being reimagined. Part two examines a variety of these thought experiments, from The Long Now Clock to 'slow' eating' events and multisensory timepieces. But why is this work important? Underlying the curation of this chapter is what Douglas Rushkoff terms 'present shock', the idea that the present has caught up with future, and that new technology is having a special impact on perception and identity.[3] There are the algorithms that second-guess our future choices and the databases that promise access to all history. Not to mention the disconcerting feeling that the digital life may be outside time, a sort of Dorian Gray existence, suspended in a continuous present.[4] But when did this uncertainty emerge? We begin with an historian's perspective.

Part one: The changing status of the designed future

'Come in 2001 . . . your time is up!'[5] This is the opening line of an article published by Reyner Banham in 1976. It is worth revisiting, not just because it signals the emergence of a 'postmodern' sensibility but it also draws attention to one of the key ways in which design has shaped the understanding of time, how it has given material expression to a common future. Not the destiny of any one person, of course, but a collective ideal based on certain stereotypes. In Banham's terms: a city of towers, with elevated sidewalks, helicopters and a monorail. Banham traces the origins of this trope to the nineteenth-century writings of Jules Verne and H. G. Wells; then onto a phase of visual development, courtesy of the Italian Futurist architect Antonio Sant'Elia, and finally a period of popularization, via the comic books, film sets, science fiction and expos of his youth – the 1930s. Forty years on, Banham felt that this future had 'died of realisation'. Not only was there a perceived link between high-rise living, growing crime and community breakdown but, through over-exposure, the 'monorail future' had become a theme park cliché. The early 1970s seemed like a watershed because a new generation of architects were already exploring alternative, low-density approaches to planning (e.g. Milton Keynes), while the look of the future in mainstream science fiction was turning darker with the gadgetry appearing to have been purloined from an antiquated idea of tomorrow. In this way, Banham foreshadows the noirish retrofuturism of *Bladerunner* (1982), and underlying the aesthetic change was a different conception of time. The future had ceased to be a single destination and had fragmented into various scenarios: Manhattan, the quintessential metropolis, and 'Califuture', the suburban 'autopia'.

We can gauge the present-day standing of the '2001 future' by fast forwarding to a project by a Royal College of Art student, Joseph Popper, from 2012.[6]

Figure 12.1 The One-Way Ticket. Joseph Popper, 2012.

Coming just a few years after President Obama's promise to reinvigorate NASA with funding for deep space exploration, Popper's project The One-Way Ticket could be conceived as *2001: A Space Odyssey* for a new generation.[7] The style of Popper's spacecraft and the accompanying video certainly pay homage to the Apollo missions of the 1960s, but the tone is rather different. In contrast to Kubrick's meticulous attention to detail, Popper's 'future' is charmingly inept. His film shows the astronaut existing on a diet of tinned tuna, while the designer quips how he has delivered zero gravity on a zero budget. We have the disconcerting sense of conflicting realities: the emotional reality of the astronaut who plays Robinson Crusoe in space; the technological reality of the space ship as a life support system and the normally hidden reality of the staging – the painted cardboard, the wobbly camerawork and the props. The dissonance is alarming if we judge Popper's project by the standards of a nineteenth-century realist novel, or an 'out of the box' software programme. But in the context of the avant-garde theatre, or modernist literature and art, from Duchamp onwards, disconcerting narratives and the 'alienation technique' are par for the course. And this brings the status of The One-Way Ticket into focus. The project removes the 'fourth wall' from design revealing, with irony, how engineering ordinarily assumes a narrow conception of the human being, and how our understanding of technology is heavily dependent on learned visual cues or affordances. The One-Way Ticket moves inexorably towards questions like: If a fake spaceship can be emotionally convincing – and a major function of space travel has been to signal soft power – why go to the trouble of building the real thing?

But is it useful to see such work as part of a broader tendency in design and, if so, where does this work belong? This is a question that has pursued Dunne and Raby, a partnership that has most recently identified its outlook as *Speculative Everything: Design, Fiction and Social Dreaming*.[8] Their dilemma arises from the sense in which it is far easier to say what they are *not* doing, than what they *are* doing. Not commercial forecasting or future-proofing, not academic ethnography (their interventions are provocative), not even radical design in the late 1960s and early 1970s sense, for while the team echo the critical tone, the use of scenarios and even, on occasion, the aesthetic of Superstudio, Archizoom and others, their work shuns an explicit political agenda and aims instead for what they call an 'aesthetics of unreality' and 'one million little Utopias'. Paradoxically, it is this ambivalence that enables Dunne and Raby's work to be compared with more 'conventional' communications design. We might say that, in their terms, a successful design fiction is one that achieves an *unambiguous ambiguity*, not unlike the more sophisticated examples of fashion photography and advertising.

A criticism levelled against Dunne and Raby is that the concern with aesthetics overshadows more 'fundamental' issues.[9] Similarly, there is the relativism of the phrase 'one million little Utopias'. A very different stance is presented in Massive Change, an exhibition conceived in 2004 by the Canadian designer Bruce Mau. The accompanying book-cum-manifesto calls for a globalization of the design agenda based on the urgency of world problems: climate change, resource depletion, famine and poverty.[10] From this perspective, the concern with ambiguity and storytelling might seem irresponsible or solipsistic. But is it possible to combine these positions, to see the bigger picture through a poetic lens? The question is inspired by a growing tendency to explain technology in terms of organic metaphors. For instance, Steven Johnson's *Emergence: The Connected Lives of Ants, Brains, Cities and Software* (2001), or John Durham Peters's *The Marvellous Clouds: A Philosophy of Elemental Media* (2015). This fluid or viral image of change seems more compatible with the multidimensional character of contemporary problems. For concrete examples we can look to Ezio Manzini's[11] long-term documentation of 'sustainable everyday' practices in Europe (from 2003), or John Thackara's recent (2015) recommendations on *How to Thrive in the Next Economy*. According to this vision of a sustainable future, the initiative lies in local empowerment, local currencies and local agendas. And herein lies an opportunity for 'social dreaming', to aggregate these community actions into a bigger narrative and so counterbalance more established, teleological accounts, like Moore's Law in respect of computing power or the imperative of gross domestic product.

This possibility sets the scene for Part two of this chapter. To what extent can projects that reconsider the meaning of time be both poetic and prescriptive, affective and effective?

Part two: *The Clock of the Long Now*

My first example is potentially the most imposing thought experiment of all time. A clock as big as a mountain top that is intended to operate accurately for at least 10,000 years, a figure derived from the current age of human civilization.[12] The Long Now Clock is an intriguing combination of heroic engineering, myth making and experience design. As a technical problem, first announced in the early 1990s by the computer designer and sometime fellow of Walt Disney Imagineering, Danny Hillis, there are overtones of John Harrison's eighteenth-century struggle to master longitude or, in the field of computing, Charles Babbage's now iconic Difference Engine from the early Victorian era.

The Long Now Clock has a similarly exacting brief, to operate with the minimum of maintenance and be powered by a combination of the sun's heat, topped-up by occasional manual winding. And as with the historical examples, it is as likely to be important for the debate it inspires as any eventual physical realization for, at its heart, is the idea that an iconic monument or image can act as a catalyst for cultural change. This is an aspect of the project that is especially important to Stewart Brand, the ecologist and president of the Long Now Foundation (established 1996). In the late 1960s, he had lobbied for the publication of the first NASA photographs to show Earth in its entirety and, as cover images for the *Whole Earth Catalog* (1968–1972), they became a trademark for the environmental movement. The images added credence to the idea that from outer space political borders no longer mattered, and that Earth had the vulnerability of a child. The Long Now Project promises a similar change of heart *and* perspective, deep space becoming deep time.

An immediate issue of course, is the credibility of a 'fabricated' icon, given that heritage status tends to be retrospectively awarded, and we have become increasingly wary of 'fake news'. And yet the Long Now Clock has many of the features of an aspiring cathedral of the Anthropocene. To start with, the remote and mountainous location, which turns a visit into a 'pilgrimage' with overtones of the hilltop monasteries of Meteora in central Greece. Then, the immersive nature of the experience. The visitor will ascend through the clock and because of its analogue mechanism – chosen for reliability – there will be the spectacle of the moving parts and chimes, specially programmed by Brian Eno, no less, to strike in unique combinations for 10,000 years.

Even if the Long Now Clock never develops beyond its current status as a scale model, it is doing its job as a physical thought experiment, raising issues of sustainability, responsibility and the meaning of progress in the context of an evolving brief. But there is always the danger of hubris. Can the world really be saved by a giant clock, and can any monument preserve its status for more than a few generations? Remember how the cathedrals of Europe have gone from spiritual centres to tourist destinations in less than a tenth of the proposed lifespan of the 10,000-year clock.

Slow design

If the Long Now Clock is, in reality, more an expression of immediate fears than a message to a far-off future, then we should expect to see echoes of its concerns in other areas of the culture. This is not so much a reminder of the ongoing efforts of national governments to address climate change via protocols and treaties but more emergent, often web-enabled initiatives like 'collaborative consumption' or, most relevant to the topic at hand, the slow food movement.[13]

The mythology of this campaign is well known. In 1986, Carlo Petrini, a Communist political activist, organized a protest against the opening of a new branch of McDonalds in Rome; in 1989, the campaign inspired a manifesto, emphasizing the environmental benefits and cultural worth of regional food, and in the next few decades the message became the focus for local initiatives across the world. More intriguing perhaps is how the media coverage fuelled a cultural meme. By attaching the term *slow* to an ever-increasing range of phenomena, from cities to sex, it has become possible to redesignate an existing practice as *fast* and, by implication, *shallow* and so 'hollow out' a space for an alternative which is, by default, *authentic* and *wholesome*. In 2005, Droog design appropriated the slow label with characteristic playfulness. 'Slow fast food', was a temporary snack bar at its headquarters in Amsterdam.[14]

On the face of it, the design interest in slow living suggests a comparison with European Romanticism and the Arts and Crafts movement. We might even call William Morris an honorary 'slow designer', given his opposition to the pace of industrialization and his enthusiasm for the rural crafts. The difference would be in

Figure 12.2 *Dinner Delight*. Droog 2005.

how contemporary designers have found worth in mass-produced commodities, while paying much more attention to the 'user experience'. In Droog's case, 'slow living' has given rise to projects that combine elements of the theatre, or a game, with a kind of participatory, behavioural research.

In 2004, for example, Droog's presence at the Salone del Mobile, Milan, was entitled *Go Slow*.[15] At first glance, the exhibit was unfashionably didactic, there were notices imploring the visitor to 'decide slow', or 'choose slow', in the manner of a mid-twentieth-century 'good design' exhibition. But the signage was hand-embroidered and so more redolent of the 'Drink Me' label from *Alice in Wonderland*, and this set the tone for the event. For, as an introduction to a different kind of consumerism, *Go Slow* acknowledged the complicity of the modern shopper. For instance, the pop-up 'restaurant' reappraised the food experience through a tongue-in-cheek subversion of norms. Not only were the menu cards hand embroidered but the waiters on table were conspicuously older and, presumably, more patient than the norm. The seating was a jumble of historical types painted an ethereal white, and the food was served in tiny portions in tiny bowls, so that an uncooked vegetable took on the significance of a vintage wine.

The inverted logic of *Go Slow* was echoed in a Droog collaboration with the leading food designer Marije Vogelzang.[16] *Dinner Delight*, as presented in Amsterdam for Christmas 2005 was a playful participatory experiment, for at its heart it examined a hypothesis. What is the relationship between dining and its accoutrements, and how might the experience be improved by making these tools *less* efficient? Vogelzang primed the experiment with a wearable napkin-cum-tablecloth intended to restrict movement and tableware that divided a familiar meal into its constituent parts. In order to enjoy the food in a conventional or new form it was necessary to collaborate, the result recalling a gastronomic version of Twister.

A clock of the emotions

As different ways of challenging the standard perception of time, the Long Now Clock and a pop-up dining experience might seem to occupy opposite ends of the spectrum. The common ground lies in what some commentators are calling the 'performativity' of things: the way that objects carry a cultural memory based on use and association; how they offer up capabilities to the user and how it is possible to mobilize these narratives in the invention of new traditions or rituals like the Long Now Clock, or to parody or 'hack' these codes, as with Droog's involvement with slow.[17]

My third group of case studies, drawn mainly from the exhibition *O'clock: Time Design, Design Time* (Milan Triennale Design Museum, 2011–2012), demonstrates the versatility of the 'appropriation' technique. We have already seen one example: the show contained an earlier version of Maarten Baas's Schiphol airport clock. In a similar vein, Mark Formanek developed the comic potential of a digital clock.[18] Ordinarily such devices operate with an inscrutable efficiency, but what happens if the digits are reimagined as unwieldy planks of wood and a team of builders are filmed scurrying to assemble and disassemble the numbers in real time? *Standard Time* (2007) recalls the Laurel and Hardy film *The Finishing Touch*.[19]

A similarly human-centred treatment of technology was demonstrated in Shadowplay, a clock by breadedEscalope.[20] This was 'user-centred' in the obvious sense that the clock face was an on-screen projection activated by touch. But the hands were deliberately indistinctive, and there were no numerals, so that in terms of the cultural imagination, Shadowplay might be said to have reinvented the poetry of the sundial.

One way of characterizing the 'performative' or ritualistic aspects of these projects is as a liberation from the Western, linear conception of time. Time becomes something that is endlessly repeatable and subject to personalization.[21] This was the inspiration behind Thoron Arnadottir's 'cyclical' timekeeper, the Sasa Clock.[22] The designer translates the African *Kiswahili* word 'sasa' as *what is now*? and finds an answer to this ontological question in a beaded necklace. The Sasa Clock has two modes. When in use as a wall clock, the necklace is looped over a carousel, and the changing positions of the specially coloured beads indicate the circuit of time. Establishing the precise time in a Western sense is difficult; the beads must be counted like an abacus, and the smallest increment is five minutes. But accuracy is not the point for, as with a sundial, time has to be interpreted. The second mode for the Sasa Clock is as a wearable necklace, enabling time to become part of a public persona – as in an ethnic fashion accessory – and more subtly, to offer the tactile feedback of a rosary, where the necklace functions as a sort of meditation device.

In everyday life, the most obvious connection between time and subjectivity are the memories that accrue to specific places and possessions. This is the lesson of design ethnography and it presents a challenge for the designer: To what extent is it possible to elicit emotions?[23] We know that advertising habitually works with stereotypes, and we have already considered some of the more clichéd aspects of the designed future, but is it possible to imagine something less mediated and more personal? This has been a concern of the Design and Emotion Society for nearly twenty years, and it represents the new frontier for the advocates of authenticity in the context of an increasingly discerning, experience-based economy.[24]

In the exhibition *O'clock*, a number of the designers engaged with reminiscence, but the extent to which they captured its finer nuances is debatable. For instance, Michael Sans's *Cuckoo Clock*, a 'crucified' taxidermy specimen, was a controversial addition to an art historical tradition that expresses a universal truth through metaphor – mortality represented as a 'still life', a *memento mori*.[25] Closer in spirit to the concerns of the Design and Emotion Society was a clock exhibited by Martí Guixé entitled Time to Eat.[26] Although this was a prototype intended for a future in which food had become so bland that it was necessary to be reminded when to eat, it did draw on a sound psychological principle – the evocative power of taste and smell, the clock emitting cooking aromas at the relevant times of day. In Western culture this mechanism recalls Marcel Proust's reaction to the madeleine. But there is also a precedent in the horology of China and Southeast Asia. The incense clock, as first developed in the Song dynasty (960–1279), points to a human capacity to 'smell' the time of day.[27] As a design challenge, this would involve training the user to react to aromas, in the way that manufacturers already employ scent to accentuate the 'newness' of clothing and cars, but it does raise a further question – can such nudges ever match the 'authenticity' of an involuntary memory? The marketplace has already presented us with 'distressed' furniture, jeans and so on but are these as personal as, say, an old shopping receipt which has been inadvertently lost, then *providentially* found? For in such cases there is a ready tendency to invoke a supernatural agent, like destiny or fate.

My final example does not seek to mimic a revelation but to enable a discussion in a context which is still emergent. What is the status of the data that underpins our digital lives? Who owns it, what might it look like and is it the stuff of which Proustian memories are made? Silver Lining is a jewellery collection, designed in 2011–2012 by Central St Martins' student, David Blair Ross[28] (Figure 12.3). Like a number of projects from the past decade or so, it seeks to understand the rise of digital culture in terms of physical or analogue metaphors. (An historical precedent might be the hydraulic computer MONIAC [1949], built by the economist Bill Phillips to visualize the different flows within the money supply.) Ross's approach was to convert the GPS coordinates that are unwittingly recorded on an iPhone into a series of three-dimensional temporal 'maps', and to return this data, in brooch or ring form, to its 'rightful' owners. Thus, on an immediate level the project concerns privacy, ownership and the possibility of a wearable digital identity. But it also reimagines the association of jewellery with rarity,

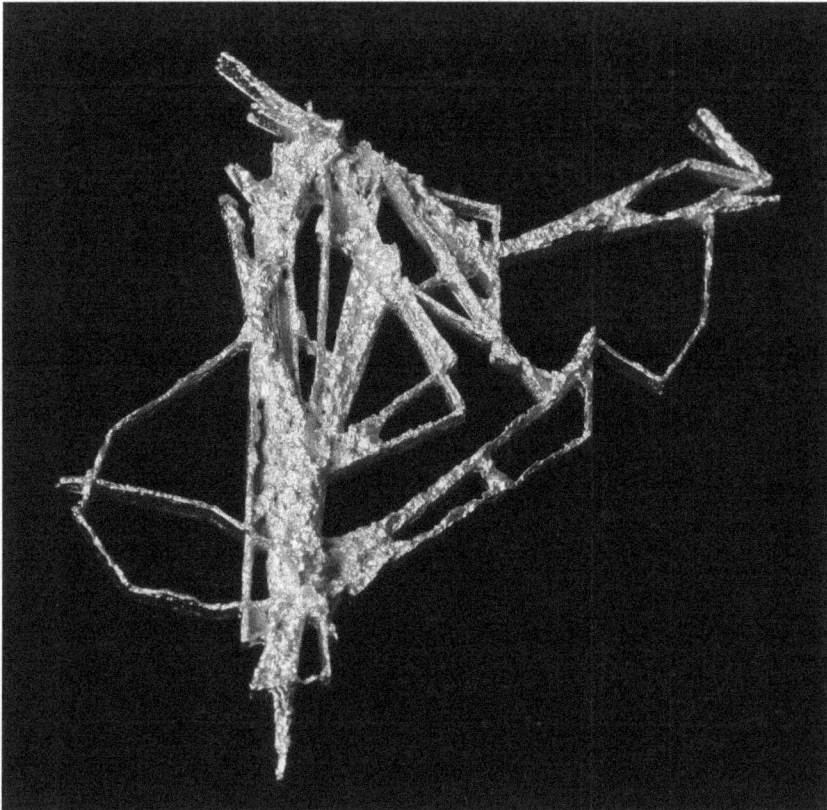

Figure 12.3 Silver Lining. David Blair Ross 2012.

skill and sentiment, for while Silver Lining may have uniqueness, it is an authenticity mediated by an artificial intelligence, a ghost in the machine.

Conclusion

This chapter began by imagining the reactions of an archaeologist of the future to the representation of time at an airport. It was my attempt to defamiliarize the ordinary, in the same way that the projects assembled in this chapter have sought to reimagine the experience of time. I characterized this development as a symptom of 'present shock' or digital time compression, and this prompted a genealogical enquiry. Part one described a shift from the Utopianism of the twentieth century to a more speculative, user-centred perspective, though it is important to stress that a different starting point, in say design for disability, would have yielded a different back story. The airport scenario illustrates the point. As a technological 'apparatus', Schiphol endorses a conventional, functionalist understanding of design, it prioritizes safety, efficiency and, of course, consumerism. The Maarten Baas piece is unusual in being relatively difficult to categorize. The 'man in a clock' could be a promotion for new Dutch design, an icon of slow living or a therapeutic diversion. And without a clear sense of purpose, it might be difficult to appraise. In this chapter I refer to the pursuit of an 'unambiguous ambiguity'. I would add that the Schiphol clock offers guidance on how this design tendency is likely to develop. In finding a sympathetic niche, it represents a bridgehead between the questions currently being explored in design schools and specialized exhibitions, and the public domain.

Notes

1. David S. Landes, *Revolution in Time: Clocks and the Making of the Modern World* (Cambridge, MA: Belknap Press, 2000); Barbara Adam, *Time* (Cambridge, UK: Polity, 2004).
2. Maarten Baas, *Real Time*, http://maartenbaas.com/ (accessed 1 December 2017).
3. Douglas Rushkoff, *Present Shock: When Everything Happens Now* (New York: Current, 2015).
4. Helga Nowotny, *Time: The Modern and Post-modern Experience* (Cambridge, UK: Polity Press; Cambridge, MA: Blackwell Publishers [distributor],1994); Nicholas Carr, *The Shallows: How the Internet Is Changing the Way We Think, Read and Remember* (London: Atlantic Books, 2010); Robert Colville, *The Great Acceleration* (London: Bloomsbury, 2016); Judy Wajcman, *Pressed for Time: The Acceleration of Life in Digital Capitalism* (Chicago: University of Chicago Press, 2015).
5. Peter Reyner Banham, 'Come in 2001', *New Society* (8 January 1976): 62–3.
6. Joseph Popper, *The One-Way Ticket*, http://www.josephpopper.net/works/ (accessed 1 December 2017).

7. Barack Obama, 'Remarks by the President on Space Exploration in the 21st Century' (15 April 2010), https://www.nasa.gov/news/media/trans/obama_ksc_trans.html (accessed 1 December 2017).

8. Anthony Dunne and Fiona Raby, *Speculative Everything: Design, Fiction, and Social Dreaming* (Cambridge, MA: MIT Press, 2013).

9. Cameron Tonkinwise, 'How We Intend to Future: Review of Anthony Dunne and Fiona Raby, *Speculative Everything: Design, Fiction, and Social Dreaming*', *Design Philosophy Papers* 12, no. 2 (2014): 169–87.

10. Bruce Mau, *Massive Change* (London: Phaidon Press, 2004).

11. Ezio Manzini, Sustainable Everyday Project, http://www.sustainable-everyday-project. net/ (accessed 1 December 2017).

12. Stewart Brand, *The Clock of the Long Now: Time and Responsibility* (New York: Basic Books, 1999).

13. Rachel Botsman, *What's Mine Is Yours: The Rise of Collaborative Consumption* (London: Harper Business, 2010); Wendy Parkins and Geoffrey Craig, *Slow Living* (Oxford: Berg, 2006).

14. Droog, *Slow Fast Food*, http://www.droog.com/project/slow-fast-food (accessed 1 December 2017).

15. Droog, *Go Slow*, http://www.droog.com/project/go-slow (accessed 1 December 2017).

16. Droog, *Dinner Delight*, http://www.droog.com/project/droog-dinner-delight-2006 (accessed 1 December 2017).

17. Adriana Ionascu, 'Poetic Design: A Theory of Everyday Practice', PhD dissertation, Loughborough University, 2010; Kristina Niedderer, 'Designing the Performative Object: A Study in Designing Mindful Interaction through Artefacts', PhD dissertation, University of Plymouth, 2004; Gareth Williams, 'Towards a Theory of Performative Design: Writing about Design and Designers since 1990', PhD dissertation, University of Kingston, 2016; Damon Taylor, 'After a Broken Leg: Jurgen Bey's *Do Add* Chair and the Everyday Life of Performative Things', *Design and Culture* 5, no. 3 (2013), 357–74.

18. Mark Formanek, *Standard Time*, http://www.standard-time.com/index_en.php (accessed 1 December 2017).

19. *The Finishing Touch* (1928), [Film], Dir Clyde Bruckman, USA: MGM.

20. breadedEscalope, *Shadowplay*, https://vimeo.com/140771358 (accessed 1 December 2017).

21. Michael G. Flaherty, *A Watched Pot: How We Experience Time* (New York: New York University Press, 1999); Catherine Bell, *Ritual Theory, Ritual Practice* (Oxford: Oxford University Press, 1992).

22. Thoron Arnadottir, *Sasa Clock*, http://thorunndesign.com/sasa/ (accessed 1 December 2017).

23. Sherry Turkle (ed.), *The Inner History of Devices* (Cambridge, MA: MIT Press, 2008).

24. James Gilmore and B. Joseph Pine II, *Authenticity: What Consumers Really Want* (Boston, MA: Harvard Business School Publishing, 2007); Design and Emotion Society, http://www.designandemotion.org/ (accessed 1 December 2017).

25. Michael Sans, *Cuckoo Clock*, available online: http://michaelsans.com/projects02/ cuckooclock/ (accessed 1 December 2017).

26. Designboom, 'O'clock: Time Design, Design Time at Triennale Design Museum, Milan', 2011, https://www.designboom.com/design/oclock-time-design-design-time-at-triennale-design-museum-milan/ (accessed 1 December 2017).

27. Silvio Bedini, 'The Scent of Time', *Transactions of the American Philosophical Society* 53, no. 5 (1963): 1–50.

28. David Blair Ross, *Silver Lining*, https://vimeo.com/44010789 (accessed 1 December 2017).

13 Delivered in Less than Sixty Seconds: Temporal References in the Design and Discourse of Digital Reading Devices

TOKE RIIS EBBESEN

At the event that launched the first Kindle e-book reader in 2007, Amazon founder Jeff Bezos posed the question, 'Can you improve on something as highly evolved and well suited to its task as a book?'[1] (Figure 13.1). Bezos preceded this statement by a tale of the long history of the book, going back to milestones such as antique illustrated codices (paged books) and the invention of the Gutenberg press. As will be argued, the Kindle itself also referred heavily forth and back in time through features embedded in its design.

This chapter considers how time can be studied in the design and discourse on digital reading artefacts, such as the Kindle, and in designed artefacts in general. It asks what role time plays and gives an overview of how intentional temporal representations of time movements can be used to understand designed artefacts.

While earlier interaction and media studies research has opened promising avenues for research into the design and materiality of digital media, in general the role of temporal references in the design of digital book readers in particular has received less attention.[2] Digital artefacts like the Amazon Kindle are frequently posited as futuring objects, that is, as vehicles for a reimagination of the future destiny of the book, from aesthetic, technical and societal perspectives. At the same time, many authors, readers and other stakeholders in the business of the book tend to prefer the 'good old' paper book of the past[3] or at least offer mixed sentiments towards reading books in digital formats.[4] Digital media are often framed in relation to time, for instance using notions such as the immediacy of the present[5] or compression of time and space,[6] and connected to moralizing notions of shallowness, restlessness and even physical diseases such as stress and anxiety.[7] No matter the position, across conflicting or paradoxical viewpoints in the debate on the role of digital reading artefacts, evocations of time, pointing towards the future, past and present, are intentionally used in both their discourse and design. This chapter questions how such intentional representations of various temporalities are employed by the Amazon Kindle as a primary case study, supplemented by various examples. The aim is to suggest an explanation of the role of conflicting temporal references in design and to sketch a basic framework with which to discuss the strategies and

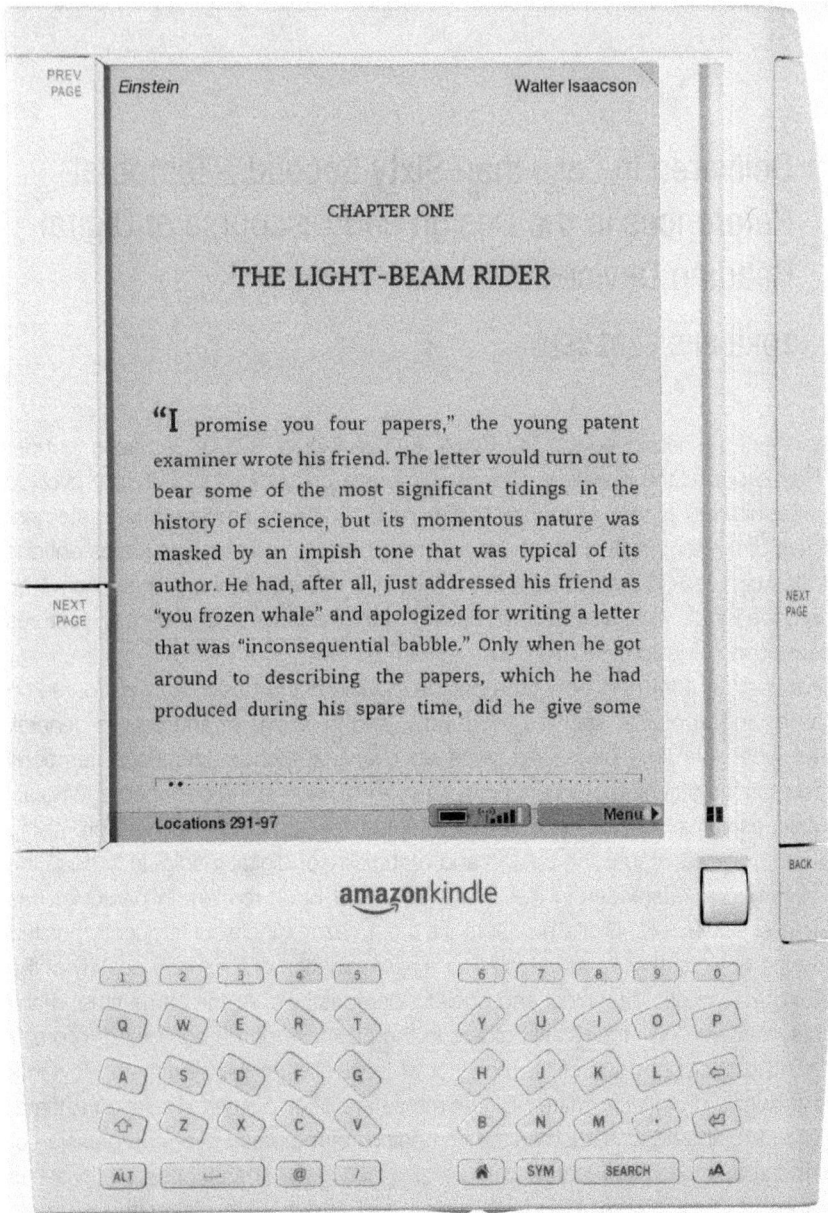

Figure 13.1 The first Amazon Kindle, released in 2007. Press photo courtesy: Amazon. com, Inc.

means through which time is intentionally referenced in the design and discursive mediations. Thus, the chapter suggests a starting point for temporal criticism of design, not only as objects *of* design history, but also as objects *designed* with a history. The broader aspiration is an understanding of how temporal markers are employed to give meaning to the many electronic artefacts of the digital age in which we live.

Questioning temporalities in digital design

Any performative act objectified in an artefact is fundamentally future-oriented, as anthropologist Alfred Gell has argued.[8] While such future-oriented instrumentality may hold true for many artefacts, the explicit conception of futuring, inherent in the discourse of design, is a very modern endeavour, connected with the underlying ideals of progress inherent in the modern development novel from the eighteenth century and in the modernist art and design movements of the twentieth century where the idea of personal and social progress was perceived as a both aesthetic and ethical imperative.[9] While the idea of progress in modernism has been broadly challenged, for example in the postmodernist and network topologies of later theories of Baudrillard or Latour, many designers and producers in practice still adhere to the idea of design as expressing the new, and therefore also their practices of objectifying sociality through artefacts as something with an exclusively positive scent of the future attached to it.[10]

Design historian Tony Fry has argued convincingly that in the light of the obvious breakdown of positive visions of the future, as manifested by the environmental and socioeconomic crises, both design practice and history should engage with the future in a more critical way.[11] Fry has coined this 'defuturing'.[12] In the same vein, the movement of intervention-oriented, critical design, pioneered by Anthony Dunne, aims to transform design into a critical practice rather than just reproducing the aspirations similar to the modernist design movement.[13] However, strictly speaking, the design and technology-critiquing practices promoted by Dunne and others which aim to intervene in the process of making are still mesmerized by the future-oriented temporal regime of modernism. They therefore continue to confuse the ends, a preferred social situation, with the means, the design of artefacts.

More important, the future is not the only temporality inherent in design. Aspects of the past and present must also be considered. Concerning the role of the past in design, Ton Otto argues, 'All processes of design include a vision not only of the future but also of a past that makes the desired future possible.'[14] In other words, design practice and criticism ought not only to be concerned with the critical aspects of design futuring but also with multiple layers of temporality embedded in design and its discourse. Hence, as also Fry admits, practitioners and analysts of design should not only engage with the critical, dystopian aspects design, but should also engage on a deeper level by acknowledging the wider critical aspects of layering of the past, future as well as the now, from which the future is projected and the past is construed, in any design project. In conclusion, a coherent framework for understanding intentional time representation in the design of artefacts, digital or nondigital, needs to encompass present-focused, future-oriented and historical references. However, multiple temporalities may seem to overburden a unified understanding of modern design and, in many artefacts, conflicting temporal markers can be identified.

Non-synchronic time movements

The above-mentioned complexities of time can, it is suggested, be resolved by engaging with a multi-temporal understanding of time, as suggested by historian Helge Jordheim.[15] He contends in his critique of the idea of temporal regimes – which he defines as 'a set of practices prescribed or adopted to regulate the rhythms of a society or other kinds of individual or social rhythms' – that very different time conceptions such as (1) the essentially modern anticipation of the future, or the idea of 'progress', (2) intervening in the present and (3) evoking the past, are often simultaneously represented – in the same period, in singular artefacts and accompanying discourses. They do this, even though they, as Jordheim says, may appear to be 'out of sync' with each other.[16]

These 'non-synchronicities', as Jordheim calls them, make it difficult for observers to 'construct meaningful cause–effect chains or narratives that can be used to plan our actions, or, indeed, anchor our identities as readers'.[17] Hence, designed artefacts may embed 'multiple temporalities', carrying differing time regimes and drawing on different technologies to regulate the sets of practices associated with them.[18] The question is, what is this seemingly paradoxical overlaying of time instrumental in bringing forth?

As Marc Augé reminds the reader in his excellent book of the same name, *oblivion* is central in understanding the role of temporality in human affairs. 'One must know how to forget in order to taste the full flavour of the present, of the moment, and of expectation, but memory itself needs forgetfulness; one must forget the recent past in order to find the ancient past again.'[19] A precondition for understanding something in the mode of a certain temporality is to systematically forget other temporalities. To experience the present, it is necessary to abandon the past and the future. Similarly, one has to forget the present in order to experience something as nostalgic or retro, and focusing on the future requires forgetting the past. Artefacts play an active role as agents of forgetfulness by essentially blurring cultural conflicts through design and accompanying discourse. Hence, artefacts can be understood as 'synchronizers', designed by producers and designers to purposely unite the associated disjointed temporalities at play within the period of production. They synchronize the non-synchronized by arching across temporalities in the way they are designed and mediated. As Jordheim concludes in his work on multi-temporality, 'The reference to the temporalities and timing issues in digital publishing [. . .] is [. . .] by necessity closely linked to the wide spectrum of linguistic and material practices deployed in attempts to deal with the temporal multiplicities and non-synchronicities of global space, for example, by, as Kleinberg suggests, achieving digital "immediacy" or indeed "synchronicity" '.[20]

These temporalities represented in design, with the purpose of synchronizing, can more specifically be understood as 'time movements', as suggested in the framework of Schmitt and Simonson.[21] Adapting their framework, design can synchronize the *past*, the *future* and the *now* using six different strategies: representing as nostalgic, retro, legacy, avant-garde, defuturing, contemporary or classic (see a model of these time movements in Figure 13.2).[22]

Past-looking representations either reproduce former, perceived 'authentic' styles or material elements to invoke interpretations as pure *nostalgia*. If more detached, cynical or ironic elements are present,[23] often referencing 'popular' or culture,[24] nostalgia may instead turn into *retro*. *Legacy* representations also reference the past, not by nostalgia but by using historical reference to further promote advanced objects, which use the latest technology and design, as though they are grounded in a long line of predecessors.

Future-oriented representations invoke the future as either *avant-garde* or *defuturing*, using perceived exotic materials, new typefaces, radical new form or by mixing known styles or elements in non-obvious ways. Sometimes this is accompanied by images and discourse that invoke associations of social and cultural utopias or dystopias, which the product somehow will help to realize.

The now can be represented as either in or out of time. Fashion, media and fast-moving goods are often represented as *contemporary*. They then typically reference the latest technologies and most widespread design trends, patterns, colours or materials at the time of production, representing themselves as products of their time, intervening in their present. Terms such as 'current', 'in vogue' or 'state of the art' are sometimes used but this mode of representation can also be subtler, identified only by the use of the hottest buzzwords and elements of its time. Alternatively, the now may be represented as the *classic*, typically posited as 'timeless' or heaved somehow out of time. The classic is typically connected with deep traditionalist sentiments, and often references simplified styles or elements, which typically appears relatively less adorned, simple and monocoloured.

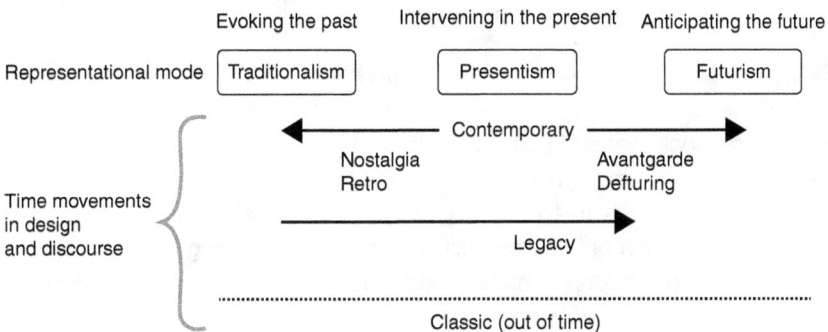

Figure 13.2 A model of representational modes and synchronization through time movements. Adapted by the author from Schmitt & Simonson, 1997: 175.

It is important to note that this mode of analysis is not interested in design as unintentional 'objects of their time', as proposed by Tim Dant.[25] In his treatment of objects of material culture as temporal, he identifies three ways that artefacts can represent their own time of production: as a product of the technologies or materials that made them possible, as pointers to the product-aesthetics or epochal style at the time of launch or as a product of the time in which it they are re-evaluated and appropriated. However, Dant's retroactively identifiable temporal traits of objects are not to be confused with *intentional* representations of design and discourse, deliberately planned to promote certain synchronizations. It is also important to note that in the same artefact these references of time movement can be combined and mixed in various ways to produce novel effects.

Kindling discourse: Time compression and presentism

In the following, the strategies and mechanisms involved in temporal synchronization are exemplified in examining the references of time movements found in the design and mediations of a prominent digital book reader, the Amazon Kindle (Figure 13.1). The Kindle is a particularly interesting case. It is probably the most well-known e-book reader worldwide, something mirrored in the Kindle sales numbers. In 2015, Amazon held a market share of up to 74 per cent of total e-book sales, at least in the United States.[26] While the Kindle may appear as just another bland electronic device, and from a purely technological viewpoint probably was not at the cutting edge at the time of its introduction, I argue that this would overlook the significant complexities of the temporalities unfolding in its design and discourse. Similarly, earlier devices, such as the Rocket Book, had set a historical precedent in their use of temporal references in both design and marketing materials.

As Galey notes, it is important to understand the 'enkindling reciters who precede us in telling the story' about a book.[27] At the aforementioned launch of the Kindle, where Bezos posed the rhetorical question on how to improve on the long evolution of the book, the answer was not a revolution in reading through the design of the Kindle and its technological setup. Instead the accompanying product slogan referenced the *distribution* of books: the Kindle simply promised 'getting a book delivered in less than 60 seconds'.

First, this statement concerns *time compression*. Traditional book ordering and delivery was, before the advent of the Internet, characterized by being a slow business. The book circuit, in which books were still produced, consumed and mediated – from authors pitching ideas to agents to book buyers reading reviews or recommending books to friends – was typically a process spanning years.[28] Whereas the digitization of book production had earlier beginnings with the advent of word processing, desktop publishing and other technological innovations in the early 1980s, the consumption and reading elements of the book business were, by the beginning of the new millennium, still underdeveloped. The early success of the Amazon Internet store had been a true revolution in the distribution of physical books, achieved by making direct ordering from the website and fast delivery by postal services available for regular consumers. Thus, Amazon aimed to do away with 'unnecessary' intermediaries in the book circuit, namely local book stores and book distribution networks. Although in 2007 Amazon had already succeeded in creating an efficient web-based business based on the sale of physical books and had diversified into other areas of consumption such as clothes and electronics, it still took several days before a book ordered on the Amazon website would reach the customer. The introduction of a digital book network, which included mechanisms for producing, authoring, buying, distributing and consuming books in digital form, allowed Amazon to make the tangible, material part of the book circuit that concerned consumers, near instantaneously available and ultra-convenient. Thus, the discourse of time compression set the scene for this more important immaterial design change.

Second, this compression of time constituted Amazon and the Kindle itself as a product representative of the then contemporary, a marker 'of its time', a product of the latest electronic and digital technologies available. As Bezos also mentioned in his speech, 'Every thousand years there's a paradigm shift in reading.'[29] The Kindle was bestowed the revolutionary honour of being something completely new, an altogether new vehicle for reading. Put differently, a still more compressed delivery time elaborated a sense of presentism, a discursive obsession with the contemporary, in contrast to the denouncement of the *longue durée* of the legacy printed book. Thus, time compression and a complete break with the past went hand in hand in the introduction of the device and also in later marketing.

Kindled design: Avant-garde of technology and historicization

While shrinking the time it took to order a book, as well as appearing as a simple and contemporary device, the design of the first Kindle was teeming with references to time movement that tells quite another story (Figure 13.1). As Craig Mod poetically notes, a paper-based book is 'traditionally, an island unto itself. Immutable. A system self-contained. One requiring great efforts to extend beyond the binding.'[30] In contrast, Johanna Drucker and other book historians have argued that digital reading artefacts, optimized for 'conditional documents', like the Kindle, must be considered to be of a more distributed, performative and thus processual and generative character than traditional books, due to their digital nature.[31] However, similar to regular paper-based books, their tangible interfaces and hardware design still offers frontstage surfaces on which temporal references are mapped by designers. Therefore, similar to other artefacts, their design and promotional discourse evoke the past, anticipate the future and intervene in the present through markers of time, representing different temporalities, using traditional, futuristic and contemporary symbolisms. Thus, while contemporary presentism was obviously pertinent in its discourse, the design of the Kindle also carried features meant to represent both the future and the past. They were expressed both in the material configuration of the device and in its constitutive elements.

First, the Kindle might have discursively represented a reading revolution. It might also be an example of a then contemporary electronic device, made possible by cutting-edge levels of electronics miniaturization and screen technology (e-ink). However, several elements of its design appear carefully chosen to signify that the Kindle was preserving the legacy of the paper book, only more advanced.

The overall size of the device, although changed and supplemented in later iterations of the Kindle, such as the Kindle DX or Oasis models, was clearly similar to that of a classic paperback. Although no longer the reading vehicle of just one book, but potentially all the books available for download through the built-in Kindle store, the interface and interactive hardware controls of the Kindle preserved important features of the well-known mass-produced and consumed paper book, although in an abstract, remediated form. Kindle e-book files were basically simplified websites. Packed for offline storage on Kindle devices, books were available as self-contained texts that could be downloaded. Thus, they mimed the isolated collection of sheets in a paper book rather than the networked character of most cyber-texts, like web pages. In addition, these individual books were written by identified authors, had an easily identifiable book title and, most importantly, a book-like interface for reading them. The layout presented to readers reiterated the linear reading sequence, for instance by presenting the reader with numbered 'locations' similar to pages, even though these were in fact generated dynamically on the basis of generated position markers in the book. Finally, elements like page headers with titles, and the physical back/forward buttons simulated the well-known page turning of the printed book. In the terms of Espen Aarseth, the book reading experience of the Kindle was presented as being non-ergodic.[32] That is, they underplayed the multiple interactional possibilities of the digital, implying little more effort for readers than reading a traditional book. These references positioned the Kindle as the culmination of a long line of book evolution. Hence, in marketing discourse, the Kindle was presented with many markers of legacy, carrying the heritage of the printed book into the future.

On a more stylistic level, equally backward-looking references can be discerned in the Kindle itself, although these are of a more recent character than the much longer legacy temporality outlined. For instance, the unique tilted layout of the keyboard buttons of the device may have evoked memories of pocket calculators or digital watches of the late eighties. Thus, these design features that may originally have referenced a futuristic digital world could also be interpreted by readers in a more ironic light – as retro design.

This use of retro markers was, however, not a new design strategy, as this was integral to the very first single-purpose e-reader available on the market, the Nuvomedia Rocket Book. Launched in 1998, the Rocket Book is generally recognized as the first dedicated single-purpose digital e-book reader device available in the general market.[33] Similar to the earlier Nuvomedia Rocket Book, the streamlined retro-futuristic elements of the Kindle and its logo played together with a vision of the future of book reading, probably well-received by the nerdy, reading geeks who were at least among the early audience for such devices. A comparison

Figure 13.3 The first e-book reader, the Nuvomedia Rocket Book. Courtesy: Thor Dekov Buur.

with the Rocket's use of design and linguistic elements is therefore timely. First, was the Rocket Book named 'Rocket' as a retro-futuristic temporal reference, or was this just a random quirky name given by its nerdy, entrepreneurial developers? While this probably resonated well with the sci-fi reading geeks who were the intended audience for the device, such an interpretation is also supported by the mediations of it in marketing.[34] Hence, the Rocket's promotional tagline 'where will you take it', as well as a series of illustrations in brochures showing consumers in so-called unconventional situations clearly referenced a utopian avant-garde future heavily.[35]

On the other hand, it seems apparent that this device was also performing temporal synchronization. Though launched in an era where reading was obviously moving from paper to screen due to the early expansion of personal computers, CD-ROMs and the World Wide Web, the later Kindle design shared many of the book-nostalgic elements of the Rocket, pointing back to familiar physical book features such as browsing through back/forward buttons and books as encapsulated single-purpose artefacts locked in singular files.

With its white or beige rounded plastic casing, the original Kindle would feel at home in a typical seventies sci-fi setting visioning the future through futuristic props, like *Star Wars*. At the same time, the use of the unadorned, geometrically shaped, white plastic case is a typical signifier of classic modernism in design, posing the device as a classic, lifted *out of time*, similar to the soft modernist design of Apple and other earlier computer vendors.[36] This apparent confusion of references may be interpreted as reflecting the cultural tensions the Kindle tried to overcome at the time of its launch. For instance, how to unite the promised time compression with the traditional slow time of immersive deep reading, which consumers still looked for in a book.

In the final analysis, the evolution of the Kindle design can be seen to synchronize opposite temporalities, integrating associations in one distributed and performative front-stage artefact, both associated with the careful, long-form time of reading books and with the immediacy of the emerging globalized digital world, where texts are abundantly and readily available.

Conclusion

The purpose of this chapter has been to sketch a better understanding of temporal references in design and discursive mediations of designed artefacts. An understanding of the mechanisms of temporal representation techniques enables a better understanding of how the condition of multi-temporality is handled through intentional design decisions. I have suggested that artefacts can reference multiple temporalities. Design then works to synchronize social and cultural tensions of both digital production and consumption through different referencing of movements in time in both the design of material features and in mediating discourses. Cases like the Amazon Kindle or Rocket Book show a considerable variation of such temporal design strategies.

I have argued that strategies invoking legacy and retro design and discourse are pertinent in the Kindle. Of course, the Kindle is not representative of all digital book readers, but may, due to its still comparatively vast popularity and brand recognition, echo broader trends, for instance the many other hybrid or 'post-digital' media objects of current popular culture.[37] As Ton Otto writes, 'Visions of the future and past create subject positions or identities.'[38] Hence a possible explanation of why these strategies of evoking the past may appear so powerful may be that they provide consumers with a tangible coherence of narrative, life and identity in an increasingly immaterialized media culture. Restless consumers search for consistency and meaning, as also evidenced in the increasing dominance of identity-providing brands. In other words, although these devices may cause time compression and feelings of unconnected immediacy, as suggested by Hartog and Brown, they may heal these identity wounds through synchronization with the past.[39]

Finally, the purpose of focusing on intentional time references in the design of digital book readers has not been to overlook or forget the cultural and social tensions in which the design of modern book artefacts is embedded, or to deny the role of the content of the reading of texts of literature they facilitate or their true more liquid and networked character. An understanding of the proposed temporal strategies as well as of the illusionary mono-temporal conception of epochal technology opens for more rich design criticism, which may then become a part of further research enquiries into the realms of the social and cultural in a digital age.

Notes

1. Ryan Block, 'Live from the Amazon Kindle Launch Event', 19 November 2007, para. 9:47, https://www.engadget.com/2007/11/19/live-from-the-amazon-kindle-launch-event/.
2. Heekyoung Jung and Erik Stolterman, 'Digital Form and Materiality: Propositions for a New Approach to Interaction Design Research' (New York: ACM Press, 2012), 645, doi:10.1145/2399016.2399115; Mikael Wiberg, 'Methodology for Materiality: Interaction Design Research through a Material Lens', *Personal and Ubiquitous Computing* 18, no. 3 (March 2014): 625–36, doi:10.1007/s00779-013-0686-7.
3. Andrew Perrin, 'Book Reading 2016', Online report, *Pew Research Center* (1 September 2016), http://www.pewinternet.org/2016/09/01/book-reading-2016/.
4. Among many studies, see e.g. William Douglas Woody, David B. Daniel and Crystal A. Baker, 'E-Books or Textbooks: Students Prefer Textbooks', *Computers & Education* 55, no. 3 (November 2010): 945–48, doi:10.1016/j.compedu.2010.04.005; Margaret K. Merga, 'Do Adolescents Prefer Electronic Books to Paper Books?' *Publications* 3, no. 4 (11 November 2015): 237–47, doi:10.3390/publications3040237; Nick Scullin, 'Attitudes towards and Use of Ebooks at the University of Canterbury', 2015, http://researcharchive.vuw.ac.nz/handle/10063/5282; Noa Aharony and Judit Bar-Ilan, 'Students' Academic Reading Preferences: An Exploratory Study', *Journal of Librarianship and Information Science*, 6 July 2016, doi:10.1177/0961000616656044; Naomi S. Baron, Rachelle M. Calixte and Mazneen Havewala, 'The Persistence of Print among University Students: An Exploratory Study', *Telematics and Informatics* (28 November 2016), doi:10.1016/j.tele.2016.11.008.
5. François Hartog (trans. Saskia Brown), *Regimes of Historicity: Presentism and Experiences of Time* (New York: Columbia University Press, 2015); Ethan Kleinberg, 'Introduction: New Metaphysics of Time', *History and Theory* Virtual Issue 1 (August 2012): 2, http://bit.ly/newmetaphysics.
6. Paul Virilio, *Speed and Politics: An Essay on Dromology* (Los Angeles: Semiotext(e), 2006).
7. Nicholas G. Carr, *The Shallows: What the Internet Is Doing to Our Brains* (New York: W. W. Norton, 2010).

8. Alfred Gell, *Art and Agency. An Anthropological Theory* (Oxford: Clarendon Press, 1998), 256.

9. Paul Greenhalgh (ed.), *Modernism in Design* (London: Reaktion Books, 1990), 18.

10. Judy Attfield, *Wild Things: The Material Culture of Everyday Life* (London and New York: Berg, 2000), 12.

11. Discussed most recently at the annual conference for the Design History Society, 2017, under the theme Making and Unmaking the Environment in Oslo. 'Making and Unmaking the Environment', Website for the Design History Society Annual Conference, 7–9 September 2017, University of Oslo, 2017, http://www.makingandunmaking.net/.

12. Tony Fry, *Design Futuring: Sustainability, Ethics, and New Practice* (Oxford and New York: Berg, 2009).

13. Anthony Dunne, *Hertzian Tales* (London: Royal College of Art, 1999).

14. Ton Otto, 'History in and for Design', *Journal of Design History* 29, no. 1 (February 2016): 58, doi:10.1093/jdh/epv044.

15. Helge Jordheim, 'Introduction: Multiple Times and the Work of Synchronization', *History and Theory* 53, no. 4 (December 2014): 513, doi:10.1111/hith.10728.

16. Ibid.

17. Jordheim, 'Introduction'.

18. Ibid., 514.

19. Marc Augé, *Oblivion* (Minneapolis: University of Minnesota Press, 2004), 3.

20. Jordheim, 'Introduction', 518.

21. Bernd Schmitt and Alex Simonson, *Marketing Aesthetics: The Strategic Management of Brands, Identity, and Image* (New York: Free Press, 1997), 172.

22. Ibid., 175.

23. Elizabeth E Guffey, *Retro: The Culture of Revival* (London: Reaktion, 2006).

24. Sarah Baker, *Retro Style: Class, Gender and Design in the Home* (London: Bloomsbury Academic, 2013).

25. Tim Dant, *Material Culture in the Social World* (Philadelphia: Open University Press, 1999), 151.

26. 'October 2015 – Apple, B&N, Kobo, and Google: A Look at the Rest of the Ebook Market', *Author Earnings* (October 2016), http://authorearnings.com/report/october-2015-apple-bn-kobo-and-google-a-look-at-the-rest-of-the-ebook-market/.

27. Alan Galey, 'The Enkindling Reciter: E-Books in the Bibliographical Imagination', *Book History* 15, no. 1 (2012): 241.

28. Robert Darnton, 'What Is the History of Books?' *Daedalus* 111, no. 3 (1 July 1982): 65–83.

29. Block, 'Live from the Amazon Kindle Launch Event', para. 9:41.

30. Craig Mod, 'Post Artifact Books and Publishing', *Craig Mod*, June 2011. http://craigmod.com/journal/post_artifact/.

31. Johanna Drucker, 'Distributed and Conditional Documents: Conceptualizing Bibliographical Alterities', *Matlit* 2, no. 1 (2014): 11–29, doi:10.14195/2182-8830_2-1_1; Johanna Drucker, 'Boundaries to Protocols: Conceptions of the "Book" in a Networked Environment', *Book 2.0* 7, no. 1 (1 April 2017): 67–78, doi:10.1386/btwo.7.1.67_1.

32. Espen J. Aarseth, *Cybertext: Perspectives on Ergodic Literature* (Baltimore: John Hopkins University Press, 1997), 1.

33. According to Marie Lebert, 'EBooks: 1998 – The First Ebook Readers', *Project Gutenberg News* (16 July 2011), http://www.gutenbergnews.org/20110716/ebooks-1998-the-first-ebook-readers/.

34. See Drake Baer, 'The Making of Tesla: Invention, Betrayal, and the Birth of the Roadster', *Business Insider* (14 November 2014), http://www.businessinsider.com/tesla-the-origin-story-2014-10, an otherwise readable story of the early history of Tesla cars.

35. 'Rocket EBook', *Style Communications* (20 November 2016), http://www.stylecomm.com/portfolio.htm.

36. Paul Atkinson, 'Computer Memories: The History of Computer Form', *History and Technology* 15 (1998): 89–120.

37. Florian Cramer, 'What Is "Post-Digital"?' *APRJA | A Peer Review Journal about Post-Digital Research* 3, no. 1 (2014), http://www.aprja.net/?p=1318.

38. Otto, 'History in and for Design', 59.

39. Hartog and Brown, *Regimes of Historicity*.

Select Bibliography

Aarseth, Espen J. *Cybertext: Perspectives on Ergodic Literature*. Baltimore: John Hopkins University Press, 1997.

Adam, Barbara. *Timewatch: The Social Analysis of Time*. Cambridge: Polity Press, 1995.

Adam, Barbara. *Time*. Cambridge: Polity Press, 2004.

Anderson, Benedict. *Imagined Communities: Reflections on the Origin and Spread of Nationalism*. London: Verso, 2016.

Attfield, Judy. *Wild Things: The Material Culture of Everyday Life*. London and New York: Berg, 2000.

Augé, Marc. *Oblivion*. Minneapolis: University of Minnesota Press, 2004.

Bach, Jonathan. 'Consuming Communism Material Cultures of Nostalgia in Former East Germany', in Olivia Angé and David Berliner (eds), *Anthropology and Nostalgia*, New York and Oxford: Berghan, 2014.

Baker, Sarah Elsie. *Retro Style: Class, Gender and Design in the Home*. London: Bloomsbury, 2013.

Banham, Peter Reyner. 'Come in 2001', *New Society* (8 January 1976): 62–3.

Baudrillard, Jean. *Simulacra and Simulation*. Ann Arbor: University of Michigan Press, 2014.

Bedini, Silvio. 'The Scent of Time', *Transactions of the American Philosophical Society* 53, no. 5 (1963): 1–50.

Beesley, Philip, and Omar Khan. *Responsive Architecture/Performing Instruments*. New York: Architectural League of New York, 2009.

Bell, Catherine. *Ritual Theory, Ritual Practice*. Oxford: Oxford University Press, 1992.

Benjamin, Walter. *The Arcades Project*. Cambridge, MA, and London: Belknap Press of Harvard University Press, 1999.

Berdahl, Daphne. *On the Social Life of Postsocialism: Memory, Consumption, Germany*. Bloomington: Indiana University Press, 2010.

Birth, Kevin K. *Objects of Time: How Things Shape Temporality*. New York: Palgrave Macmillan, 2012.

Botsman, Rachel. *What's Mine Is Yours: The Rise of Collaborative Consumption.* London: Harper Business, 2010.

Boyer, Dominic. 'Ostalige and the Politics of the Future in Eatern Germany', *Neoliberal Historicities* 18, no. 2 (2006): 361–81.

Brand, Stewart. *The Clock of the Long Now: Time and Responsibility*. New York: Basic Books, 1999.

Candela, Emily. 'Mid-Century Molecular: The Material Culture of X-ray Crystallographic Visualisation across Post-war British Science and Industrial Design', PhD dissertation, Royal College of Art and the Science Museum, 2016.

Carr, Nicholas. *The Shallows: How the Internet Is Changing the Way We Think, Read and Remember*. London: Atlantic Books, 2010.

Chapman, Jonathan. *Emotionally Durable Design*, 2nd ed. London: Routledge, 2015.

Chapman, Priscilla. 'The Plug-In City', *Sunday Times Supplement*, 20 September 1964.

Chatwin, Bruce. *The Songlines*. London: Pan, 1988.

Colomina, Beatriz. *Privacy and Publicity: Modern Architecture as Mass Media*. Cambridge: Cambridge University Press, 1994.

Colville, Robert. *The Great Acceleration*. London: Bloomsbury, 2016.

Conneller, Chantal. *An Archaeology of Materials: Substantial Transformation in Early Prehistoric Europe*. New York: Routledge, 2011.

Cook, Peter. *Metal Houses Project*. London: Archigram Archival Project, 1961, project no. 21.

Cook, Peter. 'Come-Go: The Key to the Vitality of the City', in Theo Crosby and John Bodley (eds), *Living Arts Magazine* (2 June) (London: Institute of Contemporary Arts and Tillotsons, 1963), 80.

Cook, Peter. *Plug-In City Study: Sustenance Components Simplified, Guide Section 2*. London: Archigram Archival Project, 1964, project no. 60.

Cook, Peter. 'Time Essay'. London: Archigram Archival Project, 1966, project no. 100.7: 9.

Cook, Peter. *Archigram*. New York: Princeton Architectural Press, 1999.

Cook, Peter, and David Greene. *Nottingham Shopping Centre Project*. London: Archigram Archival Project, 1962, project no. 34.

Correia, João Macedo. *As Louças de Barcelos*. Barcelos: Museu Regional de Cerâmica, 1965.

Cramer, Florian. 'What Is "Post-Digital"?' *APRJA | A Peer Review Journal about Post-Digital Research* 3, no. 1 (2014). http://www.aprja.net/?p=1318.

Crooks, D. *Phantom Ride* [video] (2016). https://www.youtube.com/watch?v=4FrOoxz71Zg (accessed 21 January 2018).

Cvetkovich, Ann. 'In the Archives of Lesbian Feeling: Documentary and Popular Culture', *Camera Obscura* 49, no. 17 (2002): 107–47.

Cvetkovich, Ann. *An Archive of Feelings; Trauma, Sexuality, and Lesbian Public Cultures*. Durham and London: Duke University Press, 2003.

Dant, Tim. *Material Culture in the Social World*. Philadelphia: Open University Press, 1999.

Darnton, Robert. 'What Is the History of Books?' *Daedalus* 111, no. 3 (1 July 1982): 65–83.

De Certeau, Michel (trans. Steven Rendall). *The Practice of Everyday Life* (first published 1984). Berkeley: University of California Press, 1988.

Dell'Unto, Nicolo, Giacomo Landeschi, Anne-Marie Leander Touati, Matteo Dellepiane, Marco Callieri, Daniele Ferdani. 'Experiencing Ancient Buildings from a 3D GIS Perspective: A Case Drawn from the Swedish Pompeii Project', *Journal of Archeological Method Theory* 23, no. 73 (2016): 73–94.

Derrida, Jacques, and Eric Prenowitz. 'Archive Fever: A Freudian Impression', *Diacritics* 25, no. 2 (1995): 9–63.

Doordan, Dennis P. *Design History: An Anthology*. Cambridge, MA, and London: MIT Press, 1995.

Dow, Andrew. *Telling The Passenger Where to Get Off: George Dow and the Evolution of the Railway Diagrammatic Map*. Harrow Weald: Capital Transport Publishing, 2005.

Drucker, Johana. 'Distributed and Conditional Documents: Conceptualizing Bibliographical Alterities', *Matlit* 2, no. 1 (2014): 11–29. https://doi.org/10.14195/2182-8830_2-1_1.

Drucker, Johanna. 'Boundaries to Protocols: Conceptions of the 'Book' in a Networked Environment.' *Book 2.0* 7, no. 1 (1 April 2017): 67–78. https://doi.org/10.1386/btwo.7.1.67_1.

Dunne, Anthony. *Hertzian Tales*. London: Royal College of Art, 1999.

Dunne, Anthony, and Fiona Raby. *Speculative Everything. Design, Fiction, and Social Dreaming*. Cambridge, MA: MIT Press, 2013.

Dunne, J. W. *An Experiment with Time*. London: Faber, 1927.

Edgerton, David. *The Shock of the Old: Technology and Global History Since 1900*. London: Profile Books, 2006.

Emmons, Paul. 'Drawn to Scale: The Imaginative Inhabitation of Architectural Drawings', in Marco Frascari, Jonathan Hale, and Bradley Starkey (eds), *From Models to Drawings: Imagination and Representation in Architecture*, 64–78. London: Routledge, 2007.

Evans, Robin. *The Projective Cast: Architecture and Its Three Geometries*. Cambridge, MA: MIT Press, 1995.

Fallan, Kjetil, and Grace Lees-Maffei. *Designing Worlds: National Design Histories in an Age of Globalization*. New York: Berghahn Books, 2016.

Flaherty, Michael G. *A Watched Pot. How We Experience Time*. New York: New York University Press, 1999.

Forgan, Sophie. 'Atoms in Wonderland', *History and Technology* 19, no. 3 (2003): 177–196.

Foster, Meg. 'Online and Plugged In? Public History and Historians in the Digital Age', *Public History Review* 21 (2014): 1–19.

Freeman, Elizabeth. *Time Binds: Queer Temporalities, Queer Histories*. Durham: Duke University Press, 2010.

Fry, Tony. *Design Futuring: Sustainability, Ethics, and New Practice*. Oxford and New York: Berg, 2009.

Fry, Tony, Clive Dilnot and Susan C. Stewart. *Design and the Question of History*. London and New York: Bloomsbury Academic, 2015.

Fuad-Luke, Alastair. 'Slow Design', in M. Erlhoff and T. Marshall (eds), *Design Dictionary. Board of International Research in Design*. Basel: Birkhäuser, 2008.

Galey, Alan. 'The Enkindling Reciter: E-Books in the Bibliographical Imagination', *Book History* 15, no. 1 (2012): 210–47.

Garland, Ken. *Mr Beck's Underground Map*. Harrow Weald: Capital Transport, 1994.

Gell, Alfred. *Art and Agency. An Anthropological Theory*. Oxford: Clarendon Press, 1998.

Gilmore, James, and B. Joseph Pine II. *Authenticity. What Consumers Really Want*. Boston, MA: Harvard Business School Publishing, 2007.

Gimeno-Martínez, Javier. *Design and National Identity*. London and New York: Bloomsbury, 2016.

Grady, I., and D. Fuchs. *The Ghan: Australia's Grand Rail Journey*. London; Sydney and Auckland: New Holland, 2015.

Gray Eileen, and Jean Badovici. 'From Eclecticism to Doubt', in Constance Constant and Wilfried Wang (eds), *Eileen Gray: An Architect for All Senses*, 68–71. Cambridge: Harvard University Graduate School of Design, 1996.

Greenberg, Cara. *Mid-Century Modern*. New York: Thames and Hudson, 1984.

Greenhalgh, Paul. *Modernism in Design*. London: Reaktion Books, 1990.

Griffin, Roger. *The Nature of Fascism*. London and New York: Routledge, 1991.

Griffin, Roger. *Modernism and Fascism: The Sense of a Beginning under Mussolini and Hitler*. Hampshire and New York: Palgrave Macmillan, 2007.

Gschwend, Annemarie Jordan, and Kate Lowe (eds). *The Global City: On the Streets of Renaissance Lisbon*. London: Paul Holberton, 2015.

Guffey, Elizabeth E. *Retro: The Culture of Revival*. London: Reaktion, 2006.

Halperin, David M. 'How to Do the History of Male Homosexuality', *GLQ: The Journal of Lesbian and Gay Studies* 6, no. 1 (2000): 87–123.

Haque, Usman. 'The Architectural Relevance of Gordon Pask', *AD Architectural Design* 77, no. 4 (July–August 2007): 54–61.

Harries, Karsten. 'Building and the Terror of Time', *Perspecta* 19 (1982): 58–69.

Hartog, François, and Saskia Brown. *Regimes of Historicity: Presentism and Experiences of Time*, New York: Columbia University Press, 2015.

Hassan, Robert. 'Network Time and the New Knowledge Epoch', *Time & Society* 12, no. 2–3 (2003): 226–41. doi:10.1177/0961463X030122004.

Hayes, Cathy. *The Easy eBay Business Guide: The Story of One Person's Success and a Step-by-Step Guide to Doing It Yourself*. London: Right Way, 2014.

Hillis, Ken. 'Auctioning the Authentic: eBay, Narrative Effect, and the Superfluity of Memory', in Ken Hillis and Michael Petit (eds), *Everyday eBay: Culture, Collecting, and Desire*, 167–184. London: Routledge, 2006.

Hinchman, Mark. 'Interior Design History: Some Reflections', *Journal of Interior Design* 38, no. 1 (2013): ix-xxi.

Hobsbawm, Eric, and Terence Ranger (eds). *The Invention of Tradition*. Cambridge: Cambridge University Press, 1983.

Hussey, Christopher. 'High and Over, Amersham, Bucks. The Residence of Professor Ashmole', *Country Life* 60 (19 September 1931): 302–7.

Huxtable, Sally-Anne. 'Bachelors of a Different Sort: Queer Aesthetics, Material Culture and the Modern Interior in Britain Review', *Interiors* 6 no. 2 (2015): 202–8.

Ingold, Tim. *Making: Anthropology, Archaeology, Art and Architecture*. London and New York: Routledge, 2013.

Ionascu, Adriana. 'Poetic Design. A Theory of Everyday Practice', PhD dissertation, Loughborough University, 2010.

Jackson, Leslie. *Contemporary: Architecture and Interiors of the 1950s*. London: Phaidon, 1994.

James, Jason. *Preservation and National Belonging in Eastern Germany: Heritage Fetishism and Redeeming Germanness*. Hampshire and New York: Palgrave Macmillan, 2012.

Joedecke, Jürgen. *A History of Modern Architecture*. New York: Frederick A. Praeger, 1959.

Johnson, Steven. *Emergence: The Connected Lives of Ants, Brains, Cities and Software*. New York: Scribner, 2001.

Jones, M. W. *Principles of Roman Architecture*. New Haven, CT: Yale University Press, 2000.

Jones, P. G., A. Kenny and South Australian Museum. *Australia's Muslim Cameleers: Pioneers of the Inland, 1860s–1930s*. Kent Town, S. Aust.: Wakefield Press, 2010.

Jordanova, Ludmilla. *History in Practice*. London: Arnold, 2000.

Jordheim, Helge. 'Introduction: Multiple Times and the Work of Synchronization', *History and Theory* 53, no. 4 (December 2014): 498–518. https://doi.org/10.1111/hith.10728.

Julier, Guy. *The Culture of Design*, 3rd ed. London: SAGE, 2014.

Jung, Heekyoung, and Erik Stolterman. 'Digital Form and Materiality: Propositions for a New Approach to Interaction Design Research', 645. New York: ACM Press, 2012. https://doi.org/10.1145/2399016.2399115.

Kean, Hilda, and Paul Martin (eds). *The Public History Reader*. London: Routledge, 2013.

Kleinberg, Ethan. 'Introduction: New Metaphysics of Time'. *History and Theory*, Virtual Issue 1 (August 2012). http://bit.ly/newmetaphysics.

Labrague, Michelle. 'Patagonia: A Case Study in the Historical Development of Slow Thinking', *Journal of Design History* 30, no. 2 (2017): 175–91. doi:10.1093/jdh/epw050.

Landes, David S. *Revolution in Time: Clocks and the Making of the Modern World*. Cambridge, MA: Belknap Press, 2000.

Lawrence, David. *Underground Architecture*. Harrow Weald: Capital Transport, 1994.

Lawrence, David. *Bright Underground Spaces*. Harrow Weald: Capital Transport, 2008.

Lawrence, David. *A Logo for London*. London: Laurence King, 2013.

Lebert, Marie. 'EBooks: 1998 – The First Ebook Readers', website, Project Gutenberg News, 16 July 2011. http://www.gutenbergnews.org/20110716/ebooks-1998-the-first-ebook-readers/.

Lees-Maffei, Grace. 'The Production – Consumption – Mediation Paradigm', *Journal of Design History* 22, no. 4 (2009): 351–76.

Macedo, Duarte Ribeiro de. 'Discurso I [Sobre a Introdução Das Artes]', in Antonio Lourenço Caminha (ed.), *Obras Ineditas de Duarte Ribeiro de Macedo: Dedicadas ao Muito Alto e Poderoso Senhor Don João VI, Rei dos Reinos Unidos de Portugal, Brazil, e Algarves por António Lourenço Caminha*, 1–144. Lisbon: Impressão Régia, 1817.

Marsh, Madeleine. *Miller's Collecting the 1950s*. London: Miller's, 1997.

Matthews, Stanley. 'The Fun Palace: Cedric Price's Experiment in Architecture and Technology', *Technoetic Arts: A Journal of Speculative Research* 3, no. 2 (2005): 73–91.

Matthews, Stanley. 'The Fun Palace as Virtual Architecture: Cedric Price and the Practices of Indeterminacy', *Journal of Architectural Education* 59, no. 3 (2006).

Mau, Bruce. *Massive Change*. London: Phaidon Press, 2004.

McAndrew, Claire, and Palti Itati. 'Seeking Empathy in Conscious Cities', in Laurene Vaughan (ed.), *Designing Future Cultures of Care*. London: Bloomsbury, forthcoming 2018.

McCracken, Grant. *Culture and Consumption*. Bloomington: Indiana University Press, 1988.

Merga, Margaret K. 'Do Adolescents Prefer Electronic Books to Paper Books?' *Publications* 3, no. 4 (11 November 2015): 237–47. https://doi.org/10.3390/publications3040237.

Miller, Judith. *Miller's 20th Century Design: The Definitive Illustrated Sourcebook*. London: Miller's, 2009.

Mimoso, João Manuel. 'Origem e Evolução do Galo de Barcelos', *Olaria: Estudos Arqueológicos, Históricos e Etnológicos*, no. 4 (2008–2011): 144–61.

Mod, Craig. 'Post Artifact Books and Publishing', *Craig Mod* (June 2011). http://craigmod.com/journal/post_artifact/.

Moran, Joe. 'History, Memory and the Everyday.' *Rethinking History* 8, no. 1 (2004): 51–68. doi:10.1080/13642520410001649723.

Muñoz, José Esteban. 'Ephemera as Evidence: Introductory Notes to Queer Acts', *Women and Performance: A Journal of Feminist Theory* 8, no. 2 (1996): 5–16.

Muñoz, José Esteban. *Cruising Utopia: The Then and There of Queer Futurity*. New York: New York University Press, 2009.

Murdoch, Iris. *Bruno's Dream*, 1969. Harmondsworth: Penguin Books in association with Chatto & Windus, 1970.

Niedderer, Kristina. 'Designing the Performative Object: A Study in Designing Mindful Interaction through Artefacts', PhD dissertation, University of Plymouth, 2004.

Nordau, Max. *Degeneration*. New York: D. Appleton, 1905.

Nowotny, Helga. *Time: The Modern and Post-modern Experience*. Cambridge, UK: Polity Press; Cambridge, MA: Blackwell Publishers [distributor], 1994.

Otto, Ton. 'History In and For Design.' *Journal of Design History* 29, no. 1 (February 2016): 58–70. https://doi.org/10.1093/jdh/epv044.

Parkins, Wendy, and Geoffrey Craig. *Slow Living*. Oxford: Berg, 2006.

Parsons, Frank Alvah. *Interior Design: Its Principles and Practice*. New York: Doubleday, Page, 1915.

Paterson, Mark. 'More-than Visual Approaches to Architecture: Vision, Touch, Technique', *Social & Cultural Geography* 12, no. 3 (May 2011): 263–81.

Pearce, Christopher. *Fifties Source Book: A Visual Guide to the Style of a Decade*. London: Quarto, 1990.

Pedersen, Ove Kaj. 'Political Globalization and the Competition State', in Benedikte Brincker (ed.), *Introduction to Political Sociology*, 281–98. Copenhagen: Hans Reitzel, 2013.

Phelan, Peggy. *Unmarked: The Politics of Performance*. New York and London: Routledge, 1996.

Pill, Colin. 'Let's Get Spherical', *Vintage Explorer* (February–March 2014): 38–40

Potvin, John. *Bachelors of a Different Sort: Queer Aesthetics, Material Culture and the Modern Interior in Britain*. Manchester and New York: Manchester University Press, 2014.

Powers, Alan. *Britain: Modern Architectures in History*. London: Reaktion Books. 2007.

Price, Cedric. *Brochure for the Fun Palace Project*. Montréal: Canadian Centre for Architecture, 1964, reference no. DR1995:0188:525:001:016.

Price, Cedric. *CP3*. London: Archigram Archival Project, 1966, project no.100.7: 13.

Rice, Charles. *The Emergence of the Interior*, London and New York: Routledge, 2007.

Robertson, Howard. 'An Experiment with Time', *Architect and Building News* 123 (3 January 1930): 12–13.

Rosa, Hartmut. *Alienation and Acceleration: Towards a Critical Theory of Late-Modern Temporality*. Aarhus: NSU Press, 2014.

Rosa, Hartmut. *Social Acceleration: A New Theory of Modernity*. New York: Columbia University Press, 2015.

Rothschild, Dorothy. 'Interior Desecration', *Vogue* (USA) 49, no. 8 (1917): 54–5.

Rousseau, Jean-Jacques. *Emile, or Education*, 1762. Trans. Barbara Foxley. London and Toronto: J. M. Dent and Sons, 1921.

Rubin, William (ed.). *'Primitivism' in 20th Century Art: Affinity of the Tribal and the Modern*. New York: Museum of Modern Art, 1984.

Rushkoff, Douglas. *Present Shock: When Everything Happens Now*. New York: Current, 2015.

Sadler, Simon. *Archigram: Architecture Without Architecture*. London: MIT Press, 2005.

Sadler, Simon. 'An Architecture of the Whole', *Journal of Architectural Education* 61, no. 4 (2008): 108–29.

Samuel, Raphael. *Theatres of Memory*. London: Verso, 1994.

Sanders, Joel. 'Curtain Wars: Architects, Decorators, and the 20th-Century Domestic Interior', *Harvard Design Magazine* (Winter/Spring 2002): 14–20.

Saunders, Anna, and Debbie Pinfold. *Remembering and Rethinking the GDR: Multiple Perspectives and Plural Authenticities*. Hampshire: Palgrave Macmillan, 2013.

Schatzki, Theodore. *The Site of the Social: A Philosophical Account of the Constitution of Social Life and Change*. Pennsylvania: Penn State University Press, 2002.

Schivelbusch, Wolfgang. *The Railway Journey: The Industrialization of Time and Space in the Nineteenth Century*. Oakland: University of California Press, 2014.

Schmitt, Bernd, and Alex Simonson. *Marketing Aesthetics: The Strategic Management of Brands, Identity, and Image*. New York: Free Press, 1997.

Scullin, Nick. 'Attitudes towards and Use of Ebooks at the University of Canterbury', 2015. http://researcharchive.vuw.ac.nz/handle/10063/5282.

Sharp, Dennis, and Sally Rendell. *Connell, Ward & Lucas: Modern Architects In England 1929–1939*. London: Frances Lincoln, 2008.

Simmel, Georg. 'The Metropolis and Mental Life', in Richard Sennett (ed.), *Classic Essays on the Culture of Cities*. New Jersey: Prentice-Hall [1903] 1969.

Smith, Marquard. 'Theses on the Philosophy of History: The Work of Research in the Age of Digital Searchability and Distributability', *Journal of Visual Culture* 12, no 3 (2013): 375–403.

Steiner, Hadas. *Beyond Archigram: The Structure of Circulation*. New York and London: Routledge, 2009.

Sterk, G. *The Ghan Memorial* [Sculpture], 1980, Alice Springs Railway Station. http://monumentaustralia.org.au/themes/technology/industry/display/80046-the-ghan-memorial (accessed 21 January 2018).

Sturm, Philipp, and Peter Cachola Schmal. *Yesterday's Future: Visionary Designs by Future Systems and Archigram* (Munich: Prestel, 2016).

Sullivan, Elaine A., and Lisa M. Snyder. 'Digital Karnak: An Experiment in Publication and Peer Review of Interactive, Three-Dimensional Content', *Journal of the Society of Architectural Historians* 76, no. 4 (December 2017), 464–82.

Taylor, Damon. 'After a Broken Leg: Jurgen Bey's *Do Add* Chair and the Everyday Life of Performative Things', *Design and Culture* 5, no. 3 (2013): 357–74.

Thackara, John. *How to Thrive in the Next Economy* London: Thames and Hudson, 2015.

Thompson, E. P. 'Time, Work-Discipline and Industrial Capitalism', *Past & Present* 38 (1967): 56–97.

Till, Jeremy. *Architecture Depends*. Cambridge, MA: MIT Press, 2009.

Todorova, Maria, Augusta Dimou and Stefan Troebst (eds). *Remembering Communism: Private and Public Recollections of Lived Experience in Southeast Europe*. Budapest and New York: Central European University Press, 2014.

Tonkinwise, Cameron. 'How We Intend to Future: Review of Anthony Dunne and Fiona Raby, Speculative Everything: Design, Fiction, and Social Dreaming', *Design Philosophy Papers* 12, no. 2 (2014), 169–87.

Trodd, Zoe. 'Reading eBay: Hidden Stores, Subjective Stories, and a People's History of the Archive', in Ken Hillis and Michael Petit (eds), *Everyday eBay: Culture, Collecting, and Desire*, 77–90. London: Routledge, 2006.

Turkle, Sherry (ed.). *The Inner History of Devices*. Cambridge, MA: MIT Press, 2008.

Vider, Stephen Joshua. *No Place Like Home: A Cultural History of Gay Domesticity, 1948–1982*, PhD dissertation. Cambridge, MA: Harvard University, 2013.

Virilio, Paul. *Speed and Politics: An Essay on Dromology*. Los Angeles: Semiotext(e), 2006.

Vitou, E. 'Gabriel Guévrékian', *Grove Art Online*. Oxford University Press. www.oxfordartonline.com.

von Falke, Jacob. *Art in the House: Historical, Critical, and Aesthetical Studies on the Decoration and Furnishing of the Dwelling*. Boston: Prang, 1879.

Wajcman, Judy. *Pressed for Time: The Acceleration of Life in Digital Capitalism*. Chicago and London: University of Chicago Press, 2015.

White, Michele. *Buy It Now: Lessons from eBay*. Durham: Duke University Press, 2012.

Wiberg, Mikael. 'Methodology for Materiality: Interaction Design Research through a Material Lens', *Personal and Ubiquitous Computing* 18, no. 3 (March 2014): 625–36. https://doi.org/10.1007/s00779-013-0686-7.

Woodham, Jonathan M. 'Designing Design History: From Pevsner to Postmodernism', *Working Papers in Communication Research Archive, Vol 1(1): Digitisation and Knowledge*, 2001. ISSN 1177-3707.

Woody, William Douglas, David B. Daniel and Crystal A. Baker. 'E-Books or Textbooks: Students Prefer Textbooks', *Computers & Education* 55, no. 3 (November 2010): 945–48. https://doi.org/10.1016/j.compedu.2010.04.005.

Wright Steenson, Molly. *Architectural Intelligence: How Designers and Architects Created the Digital Landscape*. Cambridge, MA: MIT Press, 2017.

Zukin, Sharon. *Point of Purchase: How Shopping Changed American Culture*. London: Routledge, 2004.

Index

Page numbers in *italics* refer to figures and page numbers with n refer to notes.